THE Gibson
ELECTRIC
GUITAR
BOOK

THE Gibson ELECTRIC GUITAR BOOK

SEVENTY YEARS OF CLASSIC GUITARS | *WALTER CARTER*

the gibson electric guitar book

BY WALTER CARTER

A BACKBEAT BOOK

First edition 2007

Published by Backbeat Books (an imprint of Hal Leonard Corporation)

19 West 21st Street, New York, NY 10010, USA

www.backbeatbooks.com

Devised and published for Backbeat Books by Outline Press Ltd,

2A Union Court, 20-22 Union Road, London SW4 6JP, England.

www.backbeatuk.com

ISBN 0-87930-895-8

ISBN 978-0-87930-895-7

EDITOR: Pete Chrisp

EDITORIAL DIRECTOR: Tony Bacon

DESIGN: Lisa Tai

ART DIRECTOR: Nigel Osborne

Origination and print by Colorprint (Hong Kong)

07 08 09 10 11 5 4 3 2 1

Photo previous page: Chuck Berry/Gibson ES-350T

contents

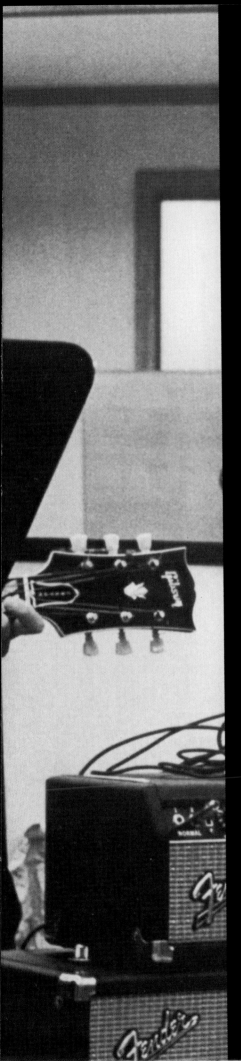

Introduction

Where would music be without **Gibson** electric guitars? What would **Charlie Christian** have used to invent the very concept of an electric jazz guitarist? What would **Scotty Moore** have reached for when Elvis started singing 'That's Alright Mama.'? What would **Chuck Berry** have played to lay the foundation of rock 'n' roll guitar licks? What would **Duane Allman** and **Dickey Betts** have used to create southern rock? What would **B.B. King** have used to bring the Blues to the masses? (And what guitar would be worthy of the name "Lucille"?)

The list of influential guitarists and their **Gibsons** is endless, making it mind-boggling to wonder: What if these players hadn't been playing a **Gibson**? Where would music be? **Gibson** hasn't just made guitars to fill the needs of current players, **Gibson** has often made guitars that are perfect for future guitarists to create new styles of music – music that the makers of the guitars couldn't begin to imagine. From **Gibson's** lone electric guitar in 1935 to the dozens of models offered today, the story of **Gibson** electric guitars is the story of our musical culture.

◁ Trini Lopez/Gibson Trini Lopez Deluxe

GIBSON ELECTRIC GUITARS are embedded in our culture. The body shapes of the Les Paul, Flying V, Explorer, and SG are not only registered trademarks, they are familiar icons for rock 'n' roll music, and they make a serious statement about the artists who play them.

And rock 'n' roll is only the beginning. The jazzman makes a statement when he chooses a Gibson ES–175, the guitar Herb Ellis plays. The L–5CES, that's the guitar Scotty Moore played with Elvis. When a blues player picks up an ES–335, he's playing the kind of guitar Chuck Berry and B.B. King played.

Gibson's role in shaping our music is evident from the very beginnings of the electric guitar in popular music. An image of Charlie Christian, the first man to make a career as an electric guitarist, would not be complete without his Gibson ES–150 or ES–250, with their unmistakable hexagonal-shaped pickup. Today the depth of Gibson's presence in our culture is illustrated in a 2004 television ad showing a little girl honing up on Gibson guitar history as she prepares to go guitar-shopping for her father's Christmas present.

Other companies have produced famous, even iconic guitars, to be sure, but no other company has created more than one or two. Moreover, no other company has produced prestigious models in every style of electric guitar – hollowbody, semi-hollowbody and solidbody – as Gibson.

As happens with any influential person, event, or company, legends have grown around Gibson as awareness of the company's name has extended far beyond the circle of guitar players. Many in the general public might be surprised if told that despite Gibson's influence and success since introducing its first electric in 1935, Gibson did *not* invent the electric guitar and Gibson did *not* invent the solidbody electric guitar (nor did Les Paul). But that only makes the story more interesting, more human, because many of Gibson's innovations came as the company was playing catch-up to other makers or simply trying to survive in an ever-changing market. Like any good story, it has elements of desperation as well as inspiration, of failures as well as success, but there are always "happy endings" when great musicians and great guitars come together.

For any guitar company that started in business before the 1970s, mere survival would be a major accomplishment. For all of Gibson's innovations – Orville Gibson's carved-top acoustic guitars of the 1890s, height-adjustable bridges and adjustable truss-rods in the 1920s, the humbucking pickup in the 1950s – the company's greatest achievement may well be its longevity as a dominant instrument maker. It survived sea changes in musical culture, delineated in the broader historical timeline by World War I, the Depression and World War II – changes that were devastating or even fatal to many fretted instrument makers. It was during one of these periods, when Gibson was in survival mode, that the Gibson electric guitar made its first appearance.

In the early years of the 20th century, Americans were hooked on mandolins, thanks in no small part to the marketing efforts of the Gibson Mandolin-Guitar Co. The company had been formed in 1902 to exploit the innovative mandolin designs of Orville Gibson of Kalamazoo, Michigan. Orville's idea, which he had already applied to guitars and which would eventually carry over to electric guitars, was to carve the top of an instrument into a self-supporting arched shape. He started making instruments with this revolutionary design in 1894 and, by 1902, demand for the "The Gibson" was more than he could handle. Only two of the five original partners of the Gibson company were active in the operation. Sylvo Reams, a musician and local music store owner, ran the company as general manager. Lewis A. Williams, a former mandolin teacher from upstate New York, held the titles of corporate secretary and sales manager, but his functional role could best be described as evangelist. He was a traveling salesman and recruiter of teacher-agents, author of fervent catalog prose, proactive member of the Guild of Banjoists, Mandolinists, and Guitarists, co-inventor of the height-adjustable bridge and, after the death of Sylvo Reams (and Sylvo's brother A.J., who died shortly after succeeding Sylvo), general manager of Gibson. Lewis Williams was an inspiring figure who carried forth the innovative vision of Orville Gibson right up to the threshold of the electric era.

The Gibson company's first dozen years were golden. Williams and his corps of teacher-agents organized amateur mandolin orchestras, which involved women in popular music more than ever before or since, which in turn generated more and more demand for Gibson instruments and produced healthy dividends for Gibsons owners. Then came World War I. Men went off to war, and when they came home, they couldn't turn off the adrenaline. Musicians and audiences alike were no longer satisfied with the sweet, demure sound of semi-classical music played on a mandolin. In a scenario that would be repeated after World War II, when big band music was eclipsed by rock 'n' roll, the post WWI musicians created a more raucous, improvised style called jazz. A mandolin couldn't handle the rhythm chores in a band with trumpet, trombone, and clarinet, but a new type of banjo – the tango or tenor banjo – could. Gibson was in big trouble.

Lewis Williams's solution was to make a better mandolin and revive the mandolin market. To that end, he hired a young mandolin virtuoso named Lloyd Loar. Loar was a graduate of the Oberlin Conservatory and he had a strong interest in the engineering side of all stringed instruments – not just mandolins. With Williams and Loar, the Gibson company had not only the vision, but the burning desire and the means to realize that vision. The company was set to create great new mandolins, banjos, and an instrument few had even dreamed about – an electric guitar.

Loar's new F-5 mandolins, introduced in 1922, are regarded today by most American players as the finest ever made. His banjos were a marked improvement on earlier Gibsons, and they set in motion a serious of innovations that would also culminate in the finest bluegrass banjos ever made. The electric instruments Loar and Williams had planned, unfortunately, were never made. A grainy photo of a minimalist electric bass is all that survives, along with the claim that Loar played an electric viola while he was at Gibson. What does not survive, however, is an explanation of what Loar would have plugged these instruments into. By the time the first electric amplifiers appeared in 1925, Loar and Williams were gone from Gibson.

Loar's mandolins, as good as they were, were not a commercial success, and Gibson's financial condition continued to deteriorate. Williams resigned at the end of 1923. A year later, when the board of directors appointed a non-musician accountant as general manager, Loar resigned. Whether electric instruments were at issue is unknown, but after the failure of Loar's mandolins, and at a time when an amplifier was still more of a concept than a reality, the notion that electrically amplified guitars could save Gibson would have sounded like the ravings of a maniac to Gibson's ownership group. Williams, on his own, introduced the first public address system in Kalamazoo in 1925, and he and Loar eventually got back together to make electric guitars and keyboard instruments under the Vivi-tone brand in the 1930s. In the meantime, Gibson washed its hands of the electric guitar.

Guy Hart, the accountant who was tapped to be Gibson's general manager, got the company back on its feet by concentrating on banjos, but Gibson had barely gotten competitive as a banjo maker in the second half of the 1920s when banjo players began switching to guitar. Gibson's larger guitars, the L-5 and L-4, were as loud or louder than any guitar on the market, but as the size of bands began increasing, guitarists needed even louder instruments. By 1928, the Stromberg-Voisinet company of Chicago (soon to be renamed Kay) took the first step toward filling that need by introducing an electric guitar.

The principle of an electric guitar is very simple – one of the most elementary demonstrations of electricity and magnetism. Wrap a coil of wire around a magnet, then move the magnet. The movement of the magnetic field generates an electric current in the wire. The earliest electric guitar pickups caused the magnet to move by connecting it to the top of the guitar, so that when the strings caused the top to vibrate, the top caused the magnet to move. Unfortunately, the strength of a signal generated by that kind of pickup system was weak, too weak to make an electric guitar anything more than a curiosity.

Guy Hart soon had bigger problems to worry about than an odd-sounding, whisper-quiet electrified guitar. In 1929 the stock market crashed and America plunged into the Great Depression. Then the real trouble started for Gibson. In 1931, the Martin company introduced a bigger and louder flat-top guitar called the dreadnought, along with a line of archtops – a segment of the guitar market in which Gibson had never been challenged. Also in 1931, Epiphone, one of the leading banjo makers, introduced a line of nine new archtop guitars. Gibson was in no position to mount a counter-attack, as Hart had diverted some of the company's production efforts into making wooden toys in an effort to keep Gibson from going under.

In 1932, a company in southern California with the odd name of Ro-Pat-In (soon to be Electro String Instrument) introduced a new approach to a magnetic pickup. The pickup on their Rickenbacker-brand guitars used a pair of horseshoe-shaped magnets to surround the strings (as well as a coil of wire). The vibration of the strings disturbed the magnetic field with a much stronger force than the indirect vibrations of the top of the guitar did in the Stromberg-Voisinet system. A second advantage of this design, one that wouldn't be fully exploited for almost two decades, was that it did not rely on the vibrations of the top of the instrument, and therefore the size, shape and materials of the body were virtually inconsequential. The sound produced by this new kind of pickup was different – it was *not* the sound of an acoustic guitar made louder – and it was slow to catch on with convention-style guitarists, but Hawaiian-style guitarists were in such dire need of the extra volume that they quickly changed the entire style of their music to fit the singing tone and increased sustain that the new instrument produced.

Hawaiian music was popular, to be sure, in the early 1930s, but Gibson's clientele was primarily "Spanish-style" – the term that had come into use to distinguish guitars played in the conventional style from Hawaiian-style guitars, which were played in the player's lap.

> The principle of an electric guitar is very simple – one of the most elementary demonstrations of electricity and magnetism

(The steel bar that Hawaiian-style players used also gave rise to the terms "lap steel," "console steel" for models with legs or a cabinet, and later "pedal steel" for the models with pitch-changing pedals.) In the Spanish guitar market, Rickenbacker offered a decidedly inferior product. While the pickup was powerful, there weren't yet any amps that could exploit that power, and the guitar itself was a cheap archtop that Rickenbacker bought from the Harmony company of Chicago. Halfway across the country in Kalamazoo, Gibson did not heed those first electric sounds from California, but in Rickenbacker's own backyard, the National-Dobro company got the message loud and clear. National-Dobro's resonator guitars had provided a significantly louder acoustic instrument to guitarists in the late 1920s and were now in danger of being passed by in the competition for a louder guitar. The company had been co-founded by George Beauchamp, the man primarily responsible for the development of the horseshoe pickup at Rickenbacker, so it was a personal matter as well as business. National-Dobro introduced the All-Electric model in 1933, and the race was on.

Gibson stayed out of the race initially, concentrating on digging out from the Depression and fighting its competitors in the acoustic market. As bigger and bigger dance bands appeared, guitarists needed bigger guitars. In 1934, Gibson "advanced" the size of its flagship archtop, the L-5, to 17 inches and introduced an even larger model, the 18-inch Super 400. In the flat-top line, the 16-inch Jumbo and subsequent Advanced Jumbo competed head-on with Martin's dreadnoughts. And as a safeguard against another failing economy, Gibson expanded its low-end line, created a budget in-house brand (Kalamazoo), and began building budget-priced guitars to be sold under various distributors' brands.

By 1935 the Electric Spanish guitar was still little more than a novelty, but the electric Hawaiian had made acoustic Hawaiian guitars obsolete. Hawaiians had become a significant part of the guitar market, and Guy Hart decided to develop a Gibson electric Hawaiian. The inventor of Rickenbacker's horseshoe pickup, George Beauchamp, had applied for a patent in 1934 so Hart felt that Gibson had to develop its own design.

Gibson had not had a dedicated R&D department since Lloyd Loar left the company in 1924, so Hart contracted with the Lyon & Healy company of Chicago to develop an amplifier. (Lyon & Healy had once been the largest guitar maker in the United States but had recently sold most of its musical instrument interests to the Tonk Bros. distribution company.) To develop a Gibson pickup, Hart hired a young Hawaiian guitarist and electronics enthusiast named Alvin McBurney, who would soon gain fame as multi-instrumentalist Alvino Rey. Gibson set Rey up in the Lyon & Healy facilities where the amps were being developed. Rey tried out pickup designs on a "breadboard" Hawaiian guitar (which still survives today) that was basically just a rectangular metal frame – yet another early illustration that an electric guitar could be made in virtually any shape imaginable.

After several months of experimentation, Rey took a job with the Horace Heidt Orchestra (he would eventually become famous for his pioneering work on the pedal steel guitar and his "talking guitar" effects) and had to abandon the Gibson project. While Hart had been funding Rey's work, other companies had begun making pickups on the same principle as the Electro/Rickenbacker, despite Beauchamp's patent application (Epiphone's even used the horseshoe magnets). Hart did not want to put any more money into research so, in late 1935, with the patent office still sitting on Beauchamp's application, Hart looked to his staff for help. The employee with the most knowledge of electronics turned out to be Walt Fuller, an amateur radio operator, and Hart told him to just go ahead and copy the Rickenbacker design. Fuller put a steel blade through the middle of a coil of wire so that one end of the blade was situated under the strings of the guitar. The part of the blade under the three highest pitched strings was notched, so that it looked as if there were separate polepieces for those three strings, but they were, in fact, all part of the same piece. At the other end of the blade he attached two rectangular magnets that extended under the top of the guitar. When installed in an archtop guitar, the magnets were so heavy that they had to be secured by three screws through the top. The upper (visible) base of the bobbin (which held the coil of wire) was hexagonal in shape, with pointed ends rather than the rounded ends of virtually all other pickup bobbins of the day (and still today), and it gave the first Gibson electric guitars a distinct, easily recognizable look.

Rickenbacker's original model, the A-22, had been made of one-piece cast aluminum, with a small circular body. It looked like a small skillet with a long handle and was nicknamed the Frying Pan. Following that example, Gibson's first electric was also a one-piece, cast aluminum Hawaiian guitar, but Gibson made it more conventional looking by giving it a guitar-shaped body and overlaying an ebony fingerboard on the neck. In late 1935, Gibson introduced the new guitar as model E-150. "E" stood for electric, of course; "150" was the price for the guitar and the accompanying amplifier (made by Lyon & Healy). If sold separately, the prices broke down to around $100 for the guitar and $50 for the amp. As an indication of how important this new guitar was to Gibson, Hart hired a musician named Julius Bellson, who had been a Gibson teacher-agent since 1922 (when he was 17 years old), to help support and promote it by writing Hawaiian guitar method books. Bellson would work for Gibson for another 35 years, rising to the position of treasurer and publishing the first history of the company in 1973.

Gibson's pickup was competitive with Rickenbacker's, and the E-150 amp, with its ten-inch speaker, was bigger and better than anyone else's. The only problem was the guitar's aluminum body. Gibson's sales force began reporting back to Kalamazoo that dealers didn't think aluminum had the rich, traditional look that musicians associated with a Gibson, so in early 1936, after less than 100 aluminum body E-150s had been produced, Gibson switched to a wood body with a traditional Gibson Sunburst finish.

On February 8, 1936, with Beauchamp's patent still pending, Guy Hart filed a patent application for Gibson's electric guitar. Interestingly, Hart's patent does *not* make a claim on the electric guitar per se, nor on the pickup. Instead, it states that "Instruments of the type ... are well known," which seems to be an attempt to lay the groundwork for a defense against future claims of infringement from Beauchamp. Although Hart's patent describes a hollowbody instrument, the instrument's "walls of substantial thickness whereby said body is deprived of the property of resonance" make it essentially a solidbody electric guitar. The "almost infinite range of tones and volumes" is produced "solely by the vibrations of strings," the patent says. Then it gets to the point: "Accordingly, the necessity for an expensive sounding box is eliminated, the notes being reproduced very faithfully by the electrical pickup." It was only a short step from that statement to the solidbody electric guitar, but it would take 15 years.

Hart's patent was granted on July 13, 1937 (#2,087,106) and assigned to Gibson. Ironically, although George Beauchamp had filed his patent application for the Rickenbacker pickup two years before Hart's application, Beauchamp's wouldn't be granted until a month after Hart's. By that time, so many companies had copied Beauchamp's design, Rickenbacker decided against any legal action.

It took about a year from the introduction of the E-150 for Hart to be convinced that a "Spanish" style model was viable. In keeping with the statement in his patent that an "expensive sounding-box" was unnecessary, Gibson based its first Electric Spanish model on the L-50, a midline archtop model. It had a pearl inlaid logo, rather than the silkscreened logo of Gibson's cheaper models, but with a 16-inch body and dot inlays on an unbound fingerboard, it was obviously not in the same class of professional models such as Gibson's 17-inch L-5 or the 18-inch Super 400. Gibson skimped further on the back of the electric model's body and made it flat rather than arched. The pickup did get a minor cosmetic upgrade – a layer of binding around the edges of the bobbin.

Gibson began shipping the new Electric Spanish model in December 1936 with a retail price of $150 for the guitar and amp set, the same price as the Hawaiian electric set. To distinguish between the two, the Hawaiian became the EH-150 and the Spanish was introduced as the ES-150. The E-150 amp became the EH-150 regardless of which guitar it was sold with. At the same time Gibson began offering conversion pickup units – model E-75 was just the pickup, E-96 included a volume control – that could be installed in the soundhole of a flat-top guitar (later models would attach to the top of an archtop), so that acoustic guitar owners could convert to electric.

As the ES-150 and EH-150 caught on, Gibson began introducing less expensive models. The EH-100 Hawaiian model appeared in 1936 sporting a black body, a white silkscreened logo, a volume control (no tone control) and the same blade pickup but with a rectangular, cream-colored bobbin. The Spanish version, the ES-100, lagged about a year behind, appearing at the end of 1937. It was built on the smaller, 14¾-inch archtop body of Gibson's L-37 or L-30 models, and it, too, had the silkscreened logo and rectangular, cream-colored pickup. A smaller amp, the EH-100 was introduced as a companion to both models. Once again the model number corresponded to the price for the guitar and amp set – $100.

The first prominent guitarist to grasp and exploit the potential of an electric instrument was Eddie Durham (1906–87), a trombonist and arranger as well as a guitarist. With Bennie Moten, Jimmie Lunceford, and other black bandleaders of the late 1920s and early '30s, Durham had always sought greater volume and was an early convert to the resonator guitars that the National company introduced in the late 1920s. On his recordings with those guitars, they are confusingly identified as "amplified" guitars, but there is nevertheless no confusion about his place in history as the first important electric guitarist. His electric guitar is prominent in recordings made with the Kansas City Five (members of Count Basie's band) in 1938, in which he demonstrated the unique capabilities of this new instrument, using sustained chords and fluid solos that an acoustic guitar simply could not execute.

Perhaps even more important in the genesis of the electric guitarist was a trip Durham took to Oklahoma City in 1937, where he made such a strong impression on a young musician named Charlie Christian that Christian stopped playing piano and switched to guitar. It's not known if Durham was playing a Gibson by that time, but when Christian joined the Benny Goodman band in 1939, he was playing a Gibson ES-150.

Goodman was one of the kingpins of the swing era, and as a white man leading an integrated band, he gave Christian far greater exposure to both black and white audiences than he would have had in any other group (virtually all of which were segregated) or even as a solo act. Goodman also let his musicians play in a jazz style that was more advanced than his own personal style, and Christian's blues-bebop set a standard that influenced generations of guitarists to come.

Christian's style established the electric guitar as an instrument with its own voice and personality. Prior to that time, the electric guitar seemed to be unable to compete with large-body acoustics on the acoustic's home turf, which was in big band settings as a rhythm instrument. The bassy sound of the early pickups and the miniscule size of the amplifiers made only the lightest of strums possible. Heavy strumming, the way the big band rhythm guitarists played, overdrove the amps and caused the sound to break up. And even with the amp turned up to the maximum, the earliest electrics were no louder than the large-body acoustics. For single-string lead playing, however, the electric did have the advantage over the acoustic, producing greater sustain and a cutting tone. And that was the style that Durham introduced and Christian exploited.

Christian was immediately recognized as a top-caliber musician. Before 1939 was over, Gibson hosted a guitar clinic at New York Band Instruments, Gibson's Manhattan dealership, and Christian was one of the featured performers. Also demonstrating the Gibson ES-150 was a hotshot guitarist named Les Paul, whose trio was featured on radio with Fred Waring's band. Paul would eventually be Gibson's most successful endorsement artist, often referred to erroneously as the inventor of the electric guitar, but at that time, radio audiences only knew him as an acoustic guitarist, as Waring would not permit him to play electric. The progressive racial attitude of the Goodman band did not carry over to the clinic at New York Band, where Christian performed only with black musicians and Paul only with white players.

Concurrent with Christian's emergence in the Goodman band, Gibson introduced a bigger and better electric guitar, the ES-250. Like the higher-end acoustic archtops, the ES-250 had a 17-inch body and a carved spruce top, but the back was often laminated maple rather than solid. The two-piece maple neck (with a dark center laminate) was also a step above the one-piece mahogany necks of the ES-150 and ES-100. The new model's aesthetics provided strong evidence that Gibson had become a true believer in the electric guitar. The peghead had stairsteps carved into the sides; the tailpiece was an unengraved version of the unit used on Gibson's top archtop, the Super 400; the pickup was bound with three-ply binding; and the fingerboard inlay resembled an open book, a pattern unique to the ES-250.

Charlie Christian moved up to ES-250s – he had a Sunburst and a Natural-finish model. His use of Gibsons alone made Gibson the preferred instrument among electric guitarists. Although his career was cut short by his death in 1942 from tuberculosis, his influence was not. He was so strongly identified with the early Gibson electrics that the bar pickup with the hexagonal bobbin top is still called the "Charlie Christian pickup." Though it is heavy in weight and limited in tone compared to the pickups Gibson developed after World War II, Gibson had to revive it periodically for Charlie Christian disciples.

The notoriety that Charlie Christian, Eddie Durham and the entire world of Hawaiian-style players brought to the electric guitar was not enough to make Guy Hart feel secure. He had become Gibson's general manager in the 1920s in the midst of a devastating shift in musical tastes, as musicians abandoned the mandolin for the tenor banjo. He had pulled Gibson into the upper echelon of banjo makers, but before he could enjoy that success, the guitar began to overshadow the banjo. Hart's experience indicated that the electric guitar would have ten years – 15 at the most – in the spotlight before another instrument would supplant it. It had been introduced in 1932, so by 1940, its time was already half over.

> ## Unfortunately, the electric guitar, as well as the entire musical instrument industry, was put on hold with the bombing of Pearl Harbor

Furthermore, sales of Gibson electrics did not give a clear indication of whether electric guitars would continue to grow or would settle into a position as a "niche" product played only by guitarists in certain genres, such as bebop and Hawaiian. The Spanish models had suffered a slight decline after their initial splash – 530 models shipped in 1937, followed by 462 in 1938 and 407 in 1939 – before topping 500 again in 1940. Hawaiian sales had fallen steadily from 1,375 in 1937 to 780 in 1940 (although Hawaiian sales were bolstered somewhat by Gibson's introduction of budget models under the Kalamazoo brand in 1939).

If the electric guitar were truly here to stay, Hart's experience told him that as soon as other instrument makers recognized the new trend, a flood of innovations would follow. Epiphone, the company that had launched a surprise attack of new acoustic archtop models in 1931, was already proving that. Epi had beaten Gibson out of the blocks with an Electric Spanish model in 1935. Epi had a showroom in downtown Manhattan where company president Epi Stathopoulo himself hosted weekly jam sessions, giving his company a direct connection to influential New York guitarists that Gibson could not match. And, unlike Gibson, which had an amateur radio builder designing pickups, Epi had an electronics lab, pictured in catalogs with a scientist in a lab coat supervising research and development. That man, Herb Sunshine, developed a pickup with six screws for polepieces, giving the player the capablility of fine-tuning the balance of signals from the individual strings. It first appeared on an Epiphone in 1937, on a model comparable to Gibson's ES-150, and then on a better-quality Epiphone in 1939.

With competition already threatening Gibson's success, Hart could not let Gibson rest on the laurels of its first-generation pickup and amps. Gibson immediately appropriated Epiphone's concept of adjustable-height polepieces, and Gibson engineer George Miller filed a patent for a pickup with adjustable polepieces in 1938 (granted in 1939). In 1940, a rectangular, metal-covered pickup with six screw-poles replaced the bar pickup on the ES-100. With the upgraded pickup, the model's name and price were also upgraded to ES-125. On the high end of the electric line that same year, Gibson replaced the ES-250 with the ES-300, a 17-inch archtop with yet another new pickup featuring six adjustable screw-poles. The ES-300 pickup was seven inches long with a tortoiseshell-celluloid cover, rounded at both ends and mounted at an angle so that the polepiece for the bass E-string was near the neck and the polepiece for the high E was near the bridge, in effect making the bass strings bassier and the treble strings brighter. Within a short time, the length of the pickup was scaled down to just over four inches. It was still mounted at an angle but not as severe an angle as the first version. The Hawaiian models, too, were upgraded with the oblong pickup (short version) and the metal-covered pickup. Cosmetically, the ES-300 introduced two new features that would grace many Gibsons to come: double-parallelogram fingerboard inlays and the "crown" or "thistle" pearl-inlaid peghead ornament. Most important, the ES-300 was a commercial success, selling 147 units in 1941, its first full year of production, and contributing to the overall surge in Gibson Electric Spanish sales that year to 718 guitars.

By late 1941, the electric guitar was approaching its first decade of existence and growing in popularity, with Gibson on the leading edge of the movement. Unfortunately, the electric guitar, as well as the entire musical instrument industry, was put on hold with the bombing of Pearl Harbor in Honolulu by the Japanese on December 7, 1941, bringing America into World War II. The U.S. government quickly put restrictions on metal use. For Gibson's acoustic instruments, the critical metal parts were the adjustable truss-rod in the neck and (on archtops) the tailpiece, so Gibson was able to continue production on a limited basis. For electric guitar production, however, metal was required for wires, magnets, screws, jacks, potentiometer housings – virtually the entire system that made a guitar an electric guitar. And amplifiers required all that plus a metal chassis. As Gibson retooled to make parts for military products, the company used up existing supplies of metal guitar parts. When all the electric parts were gone, electric guitar production ceased.

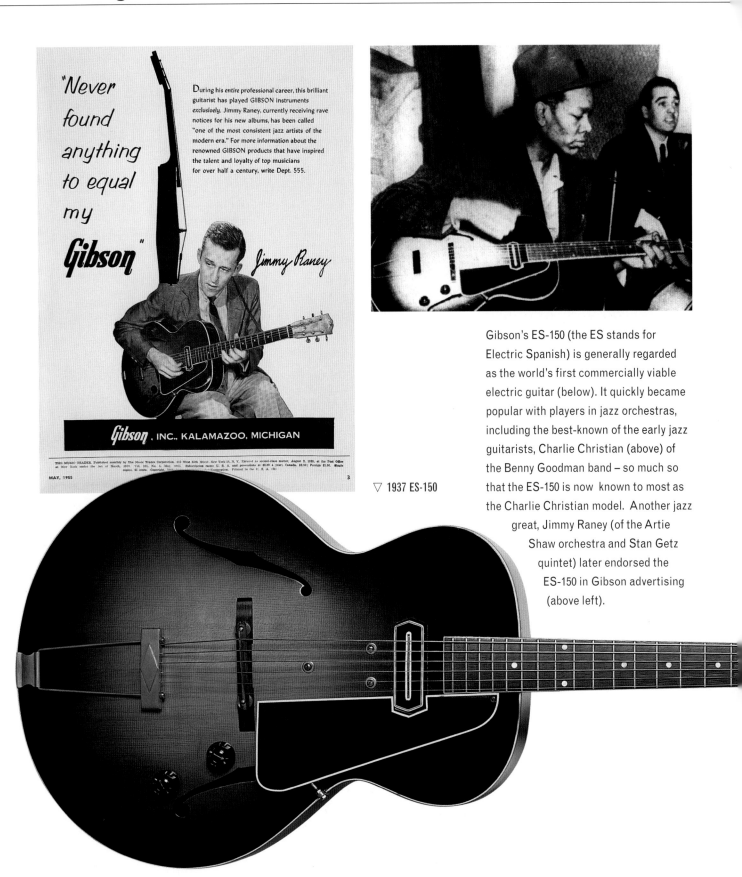

"Never found anything to equal my Gibson" — Jimmy Raney

During his *entire* professional career, this brilliant guitarist has played GIBSON instruments exclusively. Jimmy Raney, currently receiving rave notices for his new albums, has been called "one of the most consistent jazz artists of the modern era." For more information about the renowned GIBSON products that have inspired the talent and loyalty of top musicians for over half a century, write Dept. 555.

Gibson, INC., KALAMAZOO, MICHIGAN

THE MUSIC TRADES. Published monthly by The Music Trades Corporation, 115 West 55th Street, New York 19, N. Y. Entered as second-class matter, August 2, 1935, at the Post Office at New York under the Act of March, 1879. Vol. 103, No. 5, May, 1955. Subscription rates: U. S. A. and possessions at $2.00 a year; Canada, $2.50; Foreign $3.00. Single copies, 25 cents. Copyright, 1955.

MAY, 1955   3

▽ 1937 ES-150

Gibson's ES-150 (the ES stands for Electric Spanish) is generally regarded as the world's first commercially viable electric guitar (below). It quickly became popular with players in jazz orchestras, including the best-known of the early jazz guitarists, Charlie Christian (above) of the Benny Goodman band – so much so that the ES-150 is now known to most as the Charlie Christian model. Another jazz great, Jimmy Raney (of the Artie Shaw orchestra and Stan Getz quintet) later endorsed the ES-150 in Gibson advertising (above left).

Gibson's first electric guitar (right) was originally launched as the E-150 (E for Electric) in 1935 with a cast aluminium body, but after feedback from salesmen that customers didn't think it looked enough like a Gibson, the body was changed to wood with a traditional sunburst finish. By the end of 1936, the name was changed to the EH-150 (for Electric Hawaiian) to differentiate it from the Spanish-neck (standard style) ES model. It was initially available with either six or seven strings but virtually any number of strings was available by custom order. The double-neck EH-150 (far right) has eight strings per neck and two hexagonal "Charlie Christian" pickups. Both of these fine examples are owned by Steve Howe, guitarist with the British progressive rock band, Yes.

◁ 1938 EH-150

▷ 1938 EH-150 double-neck

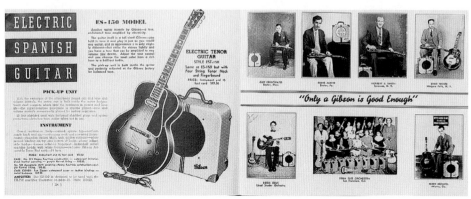

Gibson emerged from World War II a different company – at least in terms of corporate organization. In 1944, 85-year-old John Adams, president of Gibson, Inc., and the last surviving member of the original 1902 partnership, decided to sell the company. The Chicago Musical Instrument Co., which had been founded in 1920 and had quickly become a major distributor, acquired Gibson.

CMI's founder and president, M.H. Berlin had started his career as an errand boy for a Wurlitzer music store and had built CMI with aggressive salesmanship and high expectations. Gibson would change dramatically – and successfully – under CMI's ownership, but as far as guitar buyers of 1945 could see, Gibson simply picked up where it had left off in 1942, with pickup development. All of the prewar pickups – the "Charlie Christian" bar style, the rectangular, metal-covered unit, and the oblong, tortoiseshell ES-300 style – were abandoned. (Surpluses, or possibly custom orders, of the metal-covered style were sold to the Harmony company.) The postwar electric models sported a new pickup under a cover of molded, black plastic. The earliest version had six individual, non-adjustable "slug" polepieces (some example had no visible polepieces at all). The slugs were soon replaced by adjustable screw poles on the Spanish models, while most Hawaiians had non-adjustable poles and no cover. The pickup cover featured triangular "dog ear" extensions on either end, through which a screw secured them to the top of the guitar.

The part number for the new pickup was P-90. The number 90 may have represented a succession of experimental versions, or it may have corresponded to a retail price for the pickup, if Gibson chose to market it as a standalone item. It was never given a trade name, like Epiphone's prewar Truebalance and postwar Tone Spectrum, Gretsch's Dyna-sonic (made by DeArmond) or DeArmond's Rhythm Chief. The Gibson pickup is still famous today simply by its part number, P-90, and, except for the upgrade to adjustable polepieces, there has never been any need for improvement. It was then, as now, as good as it gets for a single-coil pickup.

One subtle but important indication of the superiority of the new pickup was its change in position on the guitar. Prior to World War II, Gibson mounted pickups near the bridge, which accentuated the treble end of the tonal spectrum and reduced the inherent bass-heavy tone of most prewar pickups. The P-90 was much better balanced, as were Gibson's postwar amplifiers (which were now designed and built by Gibson rather than being jobbed out to Lyon & Healy), and the P-90 did not need the treble boost that bridge-position placement provided, so Gibson moved it to the neck position.

The P-90 pickup was just one feature of an overall upgrade to Gibson's postwar electric line – undeniable proof that Guy Hart had not only recognized and accepted the electric guitar as a viable new member of the fretted instrument family, but had also committed Gibson to becoming the leader in developing new and innovative electric guitars. For guitar buyers, this commitment was visually obvious in the physical growth of the ES-125 and ES-150. The new ES-125 was 16 inches wide, over an inch wider than the 14¾-inch prewar version and the same size as the prewar ES-150. The new ES-150 was also an inch larger, having grown to 17 inches wide.

Not so noticeable was a fundamental change in body construction. Where the prewar models were essentially electrified acoustic guitars, made with a solid, carved spruce top and solid (or in some cases laminated) maple back and sides, the postwar models had a body made entirely of three-ply laminated maple. A laminated maple top produces an inferior acoustic sound to a solid spruce top, of course, but, from the beginning, the acoustic sound of the ES-150 had been all but destroyed by the weight and the three mounting screws of the Charlie Christian pickup. The postwar laminated construction indicated that guitar players were increasingly aware that the voice of an electric guitar came, as Guy Hart had stated back in 1936 in his patent application, from the pickup and the amp rather than from the acoustical properties of the guitar body.

The ES-300 also returned after the wartime hiatus, still 17 inches wide. A few early examples were made with a black finish and some had a five-ply maple body, but it soon became standardized with Sunburst or Natural finish and a three-ply body. Its double-parallelogram fingerboard inlays and plate-style tailpiece distinguished it from the less expensive ES-150. It was further distinguished from the lower models in 1947 with the introduction of a cutaway, which had been available on high-end acoustics such as the L-5 and Super 400 since 1939 but not to this point on an electric. The improvement warranted a higher model number, so the cutaway version was dubbed the ES-350. A year later, the ES-350 took another step forward, sporting two P-90 pickups as standard equipment. There was no pickup selector switch, but each pickup had its own volume control. Tone was controlled by a single master control mounted on the cutaway bout.

To the guitar players of the post-World War II years, Gibson's new pickup and larger body sizes made for decidedly improved guitars, and their perception was reflected in a steady increase in sales. In 1948 Gibson shipped over 2,500 Electric Spanish models, more than three times the figure from 1941. Shipping figures also showed that electrics had begun to fall into the same sales pattern as the long-established acoustic lines, with the less expensive models far outselling the high-end models. Prior to World War II, the ES-150 had outsold the cheaper ES-100. In 1948, the ES-125 outsold the ES-150, ES-300, and ES-350 put together. It was a sign that the electric guitar was no longer a novelty and was now an accepted genre of guitar.

Gibson's commitment to electrics was even more obvious in the Hawaiian line, which sported a complete makeover, courtesy of Barnes & Roenecke, a leading product-design company in Chicago. Whose idea it was to job out lap steel designs is unknown (it was more likely M.H. Berlin or someone in the Chicago CMI office than Guy Hart), but the results were impressive. The body shapes were streamlined and featured decorative plastic bridge covers and, in some cases, headstock

As easy as falling off 'The Log'

Introduced in 1940 to replace the ES-250, the ES-300 (below) was distinguished from other Gibson models by its seven-inch long pickup mounted at an angle to improve bass and treble response. This was soon scaled down to four inches and, when production resumed after WWII, replaced with a "dog-eared" P-90. It was one of these later ES-300s that would later become famous in the hands of Danny Cedrone, playing the iconic guitar solo on Bill Haley's 'Rock Around The Clock.' The ES-350 (bottom) was launched in 1947 as a cutaway version of the ES-300 and was further improved in 1948 with two P-90 pickups, each with its own volume control, and a single master tone control mounted on the cutaway bout. Famed for its smooth, mellow tone, the ES-350 became a favourite of jazz greats Barney Kessel and Tal Farlow, both of whom were later to add their names to Gibson artist signature models in the 1960s (see pages 66–67 for more details).

△ 1941 ES-300

△ 1952 ES-350

Dissatisfied with the electric guitars available at the time, jazz guitarist Les Paul (above) began experimenting with a few designs of his own and came up with "The Log" (right). He took a 4x4-inch solid board of pine, fitted it with two home-made electronic pickups, and glued-on the halves of an Epiphone hollowbody guitar. In 1946, Paul took his idea to Gibson and The Log laid the groundwork for what would become the most lucrative artist endorsement agreement in the history of musical instruments.

▷ Les Paul "Log"

covers. Hart was apparently so pleased with them that he named the new models after the design company – the BR-1, BR-3, BR-4, etc. The strength of Hawaiian music was no better illustrated than on the cover of Gibson's first postwar catalog, which featured the exquisite Ultratone (formerly the BR-1), although the monochrome catalog color did not do justice to the Ultratone's cream-and coral color scheme.

Unfortunately, the future of the electric guitar did not lie in the laps of Hawaiian players. Prior to World War II, Gibson Hawaiians outsold Spanish models by more than two to one, and the postwar catalog cover showed that Hart expected the market to continue to be weighted heavily toward the Hawaiians. However, he only had to look back at World War I, when soldiers marched off to the sound of the mandolin and came home to sound of the tenor banjo, to see that Americans would not simply settle back into their prewar habits, particularly when it came to music. To Americans of the pre-World War II years, Hawaii was an exotic land of tropical breezes and lush, romantic music. To postwar America, Hawaii was a military base and the site of the sneak attack that brought America into the war. The calm, soothing sounds of Hawaiian music no longer fit with the general restless atmosphere of postwar years – an atmosphere that would soon give rise to rock 'n' roll music. Teachers and performers of Hawaiian music tried to rebound after the war but, even in Hawaii, the steel guitar fell out of favor except as a tourist attraction. On the mainland it thrived only after it was adopted by country musicians and fitted with pitch-changing pedals. (Gibson had been a pioneer in that field, having offered pedal steels prior to World War II, but the pitch-changing mechanism infringed on a patent and, although Gibson would make pedal steels in the postwar era, none was of professional quality.) While sales of Electric Spanish models boomed in the postwar years, Hawaiians went into a slow, steady decline.

Gibson's apparent success with electric guitars after World War II was matched in the acoustic flat-top line, which featured three new dreadnoughts – the J-45, J-50, and Southerner Jumbo – along with a revamped Super Jumbo 200, all of which endure today as the foundation of Gibson's flat-top line. Despite what appeared to be across-the-board-success, all was not well in the corporate office. Guy Hart had brought Gibson back from near-bankruptcy in 1925, steered Gibson through the Depression and pushed Gibson ahead of the fierce competition on all fronts in the 1930s. And he had done it his own way, answering only to a private group of stockholders who were not actively involved in Gibson's business. Since 1944, however, Gibson had to fit into a larger, multidivisional corporate structure, and Hart had to report to a corporate office. Gibson had to make and sell instruments at a profit, as always, but Gibson was no longer in control of its own success. Technically, Gibson sold instruments to CMI, which in turn sold them to retailers. Gibson was still responsible for developing innovative instruments that guitarists would want to buy, but the company was one step removed from its sales force and dealer base. Furthermore, where Hart had been answering to a retired local judge, now he had to answer to one of the most successful and demanding businessmen in the world of musical instruments. It didn't help matters that, while Gibson was busy making products for the war effort, the metalworkers union organized the Gibson workforce. If Hart was having difficulty controlling costs, dealing with a union only made it harder.

Despite Gibson's appearance of success after World War II, it was not good enough for M.H. Berlin, and he began looking for a solution. Early in 1948, he got a phone call from Bill Gretsch, the gregarious head of the Gretsch musical instrument company. Gretsch was about to have lunch with Ted McCarty, who had just left the Wurlitzer company, McCarty had overseen Wurlitzer's real estate affairs, which included retail stores as well as manufacturing facilities for jukeboxes, organs and other musical instruments (Wurlitzer had been America's largest musical instrument company in the 1920s). McCarty was intending to take a job as assistant treasurer at the Brach candy company. Gretsch thought that, with McCarty's experience on the business side of musical instruments, he could help Berlin assess the problems at Gibson. Berlin asked McCarty to go to Kalamazoo to take a look, and McCarty reported back that Gibson was simply top-heavy in management.

Berlin then asked McCarty to take over Gibson, but McCarty was reluctant to uproot his family from the comfort and culture of his suburban home in Winnetka and to relocate in Kalamazoo, which was, compared to Chicago, a small town in the hinterlands. On the other hand, he was intrigued by the opportunity to use his degree in engineering, which he'd received from Purdue, for the first time in his professional career. The Gibson job fit every facet of his experience and his interests, and he accepted. Although Guy Hart would not be asked to resign until 1950, the Guy Hart era was over at Gibson when McCarty arrived in 1948.

McCarty was not a musician, so he was not locked into a musician's mindset when it came to developing new designs. From the dawn of the electric guitar, Gibson had offered a standalone pickup to convert an acoustic into an electric, but the pickup by itself did not have all the features of an electric guitar – particularly the tone and volume controls. McCarty solved this problem easily and efficiently by incorporating all of the electronics – including the pickup itself – into the pickguard. Introduced in 1948 with one or two pickups, the McCarty pickup, as it came to be known, would fit any Gibson archtop acoustic without requiring any alteration to the top. It was popular enough to be offered with the L-7 as a standard model, called the L-7E and L-7ED (double pickup).

Gibson was not alone among guitar companies in focusing on electric guitars after World War II. National and Epiphone quickly introduced new models with improved electronics. Gretsch had a viable model and would soon have more. Rickenbacker was still a force, although the company only made Hawaiians in the late 1940s. Back in the 1930s, in the face of increasing competition from acoustic

Electric elaboration

Introduced in 1949, the ES-5 was designed to blow the competition into the weeds and is still one of the most elaborate electric guitar Gibson has ever produced. It featured no fewer than three P-90 pickups, gold-plated hardware, a maple body and rosewood fingerboard with large pearl inlay blocks, and was dripping with binding on every edge. Gibson ended production of the ES-5 in 1955 and relaunched it as the ES-5 Switchmaster, featuring a four-way pickup selector.

▽ 1952 ES-5

Artists Proclaim the
NEW Gibson ES-5
"Out of this World"

The famous Gibson L-5 now has an electronic version in the new ES-5 Electric Spanish Guitar. All the notable features of the L-5 are retained, plus the finest Gibson electronic amplification. Artists everywhere are enthusiastic over the three separately controlled, adjustable magnetic pickups. All who have heard the full rich tone reproduction proclaim the ES-5 "out of this world!"

GIBSON, Inc., KALAMAZOO, MICHIGAN

The ES-175 introduced the world to the Florentine pointed cutaway shape in 1949. It soon became a "workhorse" guitar among professionals and has remained a favorite in the jazz world ever since. Early endorsees included Kenny Burrell (right) and Herb Ellis (below), who was later to add his name to an ES-165 artist signature model. Later exponents have included jazzman Pat Metheny and prog rocker Steve Howe of Yes, whose personal 1964 ES-175D inspired a Gibson artist signature model in 2001. The pointed cutaway was also featured on a three-quarter size electric archtop, the ES-140 (below right)

◁ 1953 ES-175

guitar makers, Gibson had surged ahead by creating "over-the-top" models in an effort to proclaim, once and for all, that Gibson was the premier guitarmaker. In 1934, it was the Super 400 archtop. In 1938 it was the Super Jumbo (soon to be J-200) flat-top. In 1949, Gibson created the ES-5 with the intent of leaving the electric competition in the dust. The numeral 5 in the model name was a departure for a Gibson electric, and it signaled something special to the guitar world. It corresponded to the L-5 acoustic archtop, which had been not only the top model in the entire Gibson guitar line when it was introduced in 1922, it was historically important for being the first Gibson with f-holes. Although the Super 400 of 1934 was bigger and fancier than the L-5, the L-5 was still the model preferred by many professional guitarists. The ES-5, by its very name, served notice that Gibson was putting its reputation on the line in the electric market.

The ES-5 lived up to its billing. The body was 17 inches wide, the same as the L-5, with a rounded cutaway. There was binding everywhere – three-ply on the body, single-ply on the f-holes and peghead, five-ply on the fingerboard. The rosewood fingerboard came to a point, the inlays were large pearl blocks, and the hardware was gold-plated. The L-5 did have a fancier tailpiece and tuners, but the ES-5 was close enough. Only a year earlier, Gibson had put two pickups on an electric guitar. With the ES-5, Gibson took the next step and made the ES-5 the first – and still the only – Gibson hollowbody electric with three pickups. The control system was simple but effective, with an individual volume control for each pickup, plus a master tone control mounted on the cutaway bout. At $375 for Sunburst and $390 for Natural, the ES-5 was priced the same as the non-cutaway L-5 acoustic.

In the shadow of the ES-5, Gibson also introduced a smaller, less expensive model in 1949 that, as typically happens in Gibson history, proved to be the better-selling model. The ES-175 featured a 16-inch body and only one P-90 pickup, but it was distinguished from all other Gibsons, and from all other guitars by any maker, by its Florentine pointed cutaway bout. It wasn't a fancy guitar but it didn't carry any hint of cheapness either. It sported the double-parallelogram inlay that was becoming the signature of Gibson's midline acoustic archtop models. It offered the perfect match of good quality at a good price ($175) and it became a "workhorse" guitar among professional musicians. Moreover, it went on to become one of Gibson's best-selling hollowbody electrics of the 1950s – second only to the ES-125.

While the ES-5 may have matched the L-5 in appearance, it still had the laminated maple body that was standard fare for Gibson's postwar electrics. In 1951, Gibson truly brought the electric guitar up to the status of its legendary acoustic archtops with electric versions of the cutaway L-5 and Super 400 models. Both were uncompromised – no laminations, no skimping on ornamentation – although cutting holes in the top of a guitar and installing pickups qualified severely compromises its acoustic qualities. In the postwar years, Gibson's model names for Hawaiians no longer used the EH (Electric Hawaiian) designation, and there was little likelihood of confusing an L-5 or Super 400 with a Hawaiian guitar. Nevertheless, the Electric Spanish nomenclature had become so firmly established that Gibson included it in the names of the new models – L-5CES and Super 400CES (CES for Cutaway Electric Spanish).

With the addition of the L-5CES and Super 400CES, Ted McCarty had a seemingly unbeatable lineup of electric guitars, with prestigious high-end guitars (including the ES-5), a successful midline model for the working musician (the ES-175) and a popular entry level model (the ES-125). ES sales were rising fast enough to offset the waning interest in Hawaiian music, but McCarty felt anything but secure. A serious threat to Gibson's hard-won dominance of the electric guitar market was rising in the west, in the form of a solidbody electric guitar that an upstart California company named Fender had started making in 1950.

The solidbody electric guitar was not a new idea. All electric Hawaiian guitars were effectively solidbodies, with no significant acoustic sound. Among major makers, Rickenbacker had offered a Spanish version of its Bakelite-body Hawaiian guitar by the end of 1937, and Slingerland (the Chicago company best known for drums) had offered a Spanish version of its solid woodbody Hawaiian by 1937 or '38. Even Gibson had made one in 1938 – it was a custom-ordered, double-neck Hawaiian with an eight-string Hawaiian neck and a six-string Spanish neck, but it qualified nevertheless as Gibson's first electric solidbody Spanish guitar. Individuals, too, including W.O. Appleton of Chanute, Kansas, Paul Bigsby of Downey, California, and even Leo Fender had made viable solidbody electric guitars before 1950. Probably the best known solidbody of the 1940s was a 4 x 4 piece of pine with detachable side pieces from a conventional archtop, made and played by a hotshot former radio star named Les Paul.

Gibson, along with all the other established guitar makers, had never taken the solidbody electric guitar seriously. Although Les Paul was one of the most talented guitarists in the business, as well as a fervent evangelist for the solidbody guitar, when he detached the side wings of "The Log" (his nickname for his guitar) to show audiences that the sides weren't necessary, the solidbody electric guitar was suddenly reduced to novelty status. Paul Bigsby made a solidbody for country & western virtuoso Merle Travis, but Travis never made it his main guitar, preferring to stick with large-body archtops.

If Les Paul and Merle Travis couldn't sell the idea of an electric solidbody, Leo Fender didn't stand a chance. He had been a radio repairman who had gained a small degree of success in the late 1940s making lap steels. Hewn out of a single piece of wood, with painted on fret markers and a crinkled finish from being baked in the kitchen oven in Fender's home, they were plain and crude compared to Gibson's elegant Barnes & Roenecke designs. Fender's first Spanish model, the Esquire, was no different in that respect. The body was a slab of wood that anyone with a band saw could make; the maple neck was attached to the body with four screws, and it didn't have a separate fingerboard – the frets were installed directly

Return of the archtop

△ 1953 Super 400CES

The great Joe Pass (top) began playing an ES-175 in the mid 1960s when he was given one as a birthday present by a fan who had seen him play a borrowed Fender Jazzmaster and decided he deserved a more appropriate instrument. In 1951, Gibson elevated the electric guitar to the status of its legendary acoustic archtops with the introduction of the L-5CES (above right) and Super 400CES (above left). Unlike the laminated-bodied ES-5 and ES-175, these two high-end models featured carved spruce tops and solid maple backs and sides.

Wes Montgomery (below) didn't take up guitar until the relatively late age of 19, but soon developed a talent for learning solos by ear – especially those of his idol, Charlie Christian. This ability was enough to earn him his first job with Lionel Hampton's band. He began playing an ES-175 but later graduated to the L-5CES (right), the Cutaway Electric Spanish version of Gibson's venerable acoustic archtop. Gibson later made custom models for Montgomery with only a single pickup in the neck position, identifiable in this photo by its two control knobs. In 1993, this design was also adopted for a Wes Montgomery artist signature model.

◁ 1951 L-5CES

into the neck piece. It was such a rudimentary design compared to a traditional carved-top f-hole guitar that people at Gibson derisively referred to it as the "plank" guitar. And to many ears, it sounded as bad as it looked. Its single-coil pickup, mounted close to the bridge, produced a piercing tone with little of the rich, powerful personality of a Gibson electric.

The Fenders got off to a rocky start. The two-pickup version was initially named Broadcaster, but that infringed on a Gretsch drum model, so the guitar was produced no name at all for a few months before becoming the Telecaster in early 1951. As it turned out, country & western guitarists in southern California found the piercing sound of the new Fenders (helped along in no small part by Fender's excellent amplifiers) to be exactly what they needed to be heard in a dance hall or outdoor show. As Fender gained a foothold in the electric guitar market, the laughter quickly stopped in Kalamazoo.

The sense of urgency that musical instrument makers felt in the 1950s can hardly be appreciated today, when few people have lived long enough to remember a time when the electric guitar and rock & roll music were not dominating forces in popular culture. Observers of the instrument business through the first half of the century, however, would have seen that no instrument had ever had any staying power – not the minstrel banjo of the late 1800s, not the mandolin of the pre-World War I years, not the tenor banjo of the 1920s. The electric hollowbody guitar had come into its own in the mid 1930s, and 15 years had now passed. In this historic cycle of changes in musical tastes, the solidbody guitar appeared to be arriving right on time, ready to push the hollowbody electric into oblivion.

Ted McCarty took Fender's solidbody electric guitar as such a serious threat to Gibson that it called for radical action. A new, innovative, unique Gibson model was not enough. Gibson needed an artist's endorsement to seize the market from Fender. However, Gibson had always steered away from putting an artist's name on a guitar, with two noteworthy exceptions. In the late 1920s, with the guitar gaining popularity over the tenor banjo, and with Gibson trying to break into the flat-top guitar market, Gibson enlisted Nick Lucas to create a signature model. Lucas had made the first "hot guitar" solo record in 1922 and by the time Gibson approached him he was one of the most popular "crooners" in America. Gibson's second artist, Roy Smeck, had a pedigree equal to Lucas's. A multi-instrumentalist nicknamed "The Wizard of the Strings," Smeck appeared in an experimental sound film in 1923, then in a short Vitaphone film (with sound) in 1926 – in effect the first music video – and he had designed a series of Vita-ukes for the Harmony company. Gibson signed up Smeck in 1934 to endorse a pair of acoustic Hawaiian models.

That was it – only two artists with their own Gibson models in the company's 50-year history. The effect was moderate in the case of Lucas, whose model was an excellent guitar but was soon overshadowed by bigger and – in the perception of guitar buyers – better models. And Smeck's influence was negligible, as acoustic

Hawaiian guitars were already passé by the time his models were introduced. The third artist would be Les Paul, and the third time would be the charm for Gibson.

Les Paul had been a Gibson man through most of his career. In his early professional work with singer Sunny Joe Wolverton, he played an L-5 acoustic. He was pictured in Gibson catalogs in the late 1930s as Rhubard Red, a country act on Chicago radio station WLS, playing a Super 400. Fronting the Les Paul Trio as a featured act in bandleader Fred Waring's show, he played an L-7 acoustic, but outside of the band, he played electric guitars. By the 1940s, Les was a firm believer in the superiority of the solidbody electric guitar, and thanks to The Log, he was the leading proponent of the solidbody. He recalls approaching Gibson in 1945 or '46 about making a solidbody. This would have coincided with CMI's acquisition of Gibson, and given Paul's background in Chicago, he probably approached M.H. Berlin. It was Berlin – not Ted McCarty or anyone else in Kalamazoo – who Les would credit (along with himself, of course) with the development of the Gibson Les Paul guitar.

There are two versions of the Gibson Les Paul. In Les Paul's version, he worked out the details of his signature model with M.H. Berlin. Paul preferred a flat top on the guitar, but Berlin, being a violin collector, thought the new model should have an arched top like that of a violin. Paul wanted a solid maple body. As a showman, Paul wanted the finish to exude a degree of style and success that would make Fender's whitewashed "blond" finish look cheap, so he chose gold for the top finish. Paul had developed a new version of the standard archtop-style "trapeze" tailpiece that used the string-anchoring crosspiece as a bridge, and this new "combination" bridge/tailpiece would debut on his new Gibson. After the general design elements were conceived by Paul and Berlin, they were given to the Kalamazoo plant to execute.

In Ted McCarty's version, Gibson developed the model in Kalamazoo. The carved, arched, violin-style top contour was hardly a new idea. It had been Orville Gibson's concept and it was the foundation of the Gibson company's existence. It was a natural, obvious design for Gibson's first solidbody for two reasons. First, it was an extension of Gibson's legacy as the originator of archtop guitars and mandolins. And more important to McCarty with his engineering background, it was a design that required more sophisticated equipment than a common band saw to produce, and competitors – particularly Fender – would have to expend considerable time and money if they wanted to copy it. McCarty's crew made prototypes with a solid maple body before settling on a lighter-weight mahogany body with a maple top cap.

The stories converge at the Delaware Water Gap, a resort area in the Pocono mountains of northern Pennsylvania where Les Paul and his wife Mary Ford were performing. Ted McCarty brought the finished prototype to Paul. Some parts of the story become clear at this point. The guitar did have Paul's combination tailpiece,

The golden touch

When Gibson saluted Les Paul's achievements in an ad (right), he and his wife, Mary Ford, were one of the most popular recording acts in the world. He would soon put down The Log for the new Gibson Les Paul Model that debuted in 1952. The first version of the model featured a gold-top finish, chosen by Paul to outclass and outshine the rather dull "blond" finish on Fender's Telecaster and hopefully attract a more showy kind of player. Ironically, two of the first artists to adopt the gold-top were the rather more down-to-earth bluesmen John Lee Hooker (below) and Freddie King (opposite right). The early gold-top (below) features Paul's unsatisfactory tailpiece arrangement that was to be changed within a year.

△ 1952 Les Paul gold top

THE GIBSON ELECTRIC GUITAR BOOK

Les Paul set the stage for his new Gibson model with a hit recording of 'How High The Moon,' which spent nine weeks at #1 in 1951. This early 1953 ad (below) for the Les Paul gold-top helped the company towards sales of 2,245 units of its "new sensation" during that year. Although few players bought Les Pauls in order to play like him, his signature models proved to be perfect for rock 'n' roll in the 1960s. By the end of the century, Gibson had sold over a million Les Paul guitars and Paul was still playing and enjoying the fame brought by the guitars that bear his name.

▷ 1952 Les Paul gold top

so he did have at least that much involvement in the design. But it was obvious that Paul did not have hands-on involvement, because the tailpiece was installed upside-down. The strings wrapped around the crossbar that acted as a bridge, and they were supposed to wrap over the top of the bar. Unfortunately, the prototype had a neckset angle so shallow that the strings had to wrap under the bar. In theory, it was a perfectly playable guitar, but to a guitarist, it felt as if something was fundamentally wrong. Many guitarists used the palm of the right hand to mute the strings as they crossed the bridge, and even if they didn't use that technique, they were accustomed to using the top of the bridge as a reference point for their right hand. With this new bridge configuration the strings seemed to be in the wrong place, and palm muting was next to impossible.

Paul fixed the problem immediately by heating up a screwdriver on his stove and using the hot blade to gouge out a channel in the top of the guitar to accept the bridge crosspiece. With the bridge essentially embedded in the top, the strings could now go over the bridge. That was good enough for Paul, at least for the moment, and he and McCarty then worked out a contract.

Some additional light would be shed on the origins of the finish color and the arched top a few years later when Gibson presented Les Paul with a guitar for his own personal use. It was black, the color of a tuxedo, which Paul later said was one of two colors he originally had in mind for his signature model. The top of this personalized guitar was not carved; it was by his request flat – evidence that it was Berlin or McCarty who had come up with the concept of an arched top on the original Les Paul Model.

When Les Paul signed his endorsement agreement with Gibson in 1952, he was the most famous guitar player in the world. Radio audiences had been hearing his lighting-fast technique for well over a decade, but that was only the beginning of his artistic persona. In 1948, he exploited the new technology of magnetic recording tape by overdubbing six guitar parts on the song 'Brazil,' and it went to No. 22 in the pop charts. In 1950, he added the voice of his wife Mary Ford to his arsenal of musical and production weapons, and the result was a series of pop hits that made him part of the most popular recording act of the early 1950s. The introduction of a Les Paul signature model followed on the heels of 'High High the Moon,' Les and Mary's No. 1 hit of 1951 and a NARAS (the Grammy Award organization) Hall of Fame recording. In 1953, Les and Mary hosted their own television show, giving the new guitar model more publicity and credibility than any amount of advertising could buy.

The Gibson Les Paul Model debuted in 1952 with a list price of $249.50 including case. Among its new features were rectangular, cream-colored pickup covers, soon to be referred to as "soapbars." Cosmetically as well as functionally, it was a well-designed guitar except for Paul's combination bridge/tailpiece. Paul's fix for the problem – gouging out the top of the guitar so the bridge could be lowered – was not an acceptable solution, and the production model was set up the way McCarty had brought it to Paul, with strings wrapping underneath the bridge. The cause of the problem was the angle of the neck, and it took Gibson over a year to redesign the neck joint to increase the string height over the body. With that change Gibson introduced a new wraparound bridge without the trapeze element; it was anchored on the top with two bolts. Despite the bridge problem, the Les Paul Model was an immediate success, selling 1,716 in 1952 and 2,245 in 1953. That was more than any other Gibson electric except the ES-125 and, more important, it equaled or surpassed Fender's production of Telecasters in the same period.

Les Paul's success as a Gibson endorser is one of the greatest ironies in the history of music. His playing style was jazz-influenced pop. He always went for a "brilliant" tone, closer to what the Fender players on the West Coast country scene were looking for than the warm, rich tone that most pop and jazz guitarists (and Gibson players) preferred. His guitar would become an icon for rock 'n' roll music, but his playing style was decidedly not rock 'n' roll – no one's was in 1952 – and he disliked rock music throughout his long career. His talent was recognized and highly respected by other guitarists, but unlike Charlie Christian and dozens of other of his contemporaries, he did not inspire "disciples." Among the few photos of artists playing gold-top Les Pauls are bluesmen John Lee Hooker and Freddie King, hardly the upscale musicians that the gold-top finish was designed to attract (and they most likely bought their guitars used), but they obviously found the Gibson solidbody to be superior for reducing feedback in club performances, where small amplifiers would be pushed to their limits.

Did Gibson really need Les Paul to sell its new solidbody guitar? Without Les Paul's notoriety to make an initial splash, the model might not have ever gotten off the ground. However, as Les Paul's record sales began to decline in the second half of the 1950s – his last Top 10 record was in 1955 – Gibson's Les Paul guitar sales remained steady. Like Converse's Chuck Taylor All Stars basketball shoes, developed by a now-obscure pro basketball player of the 1920s, Gibson's Les Paul guitars were increasingly bought by people who had no aspirations to play like Les Paul and, eventually, by people who had never heard a note of his music.

Regardless of whether Les Paul's name was responsible, the new model sold well enough to indicate that solidbodies would not be just a flash in the pan. The potential for higher sales was not all that good for the gold-top model, however, because it was too expensive. As the electric hollowbody line illustrated all too clearly, the fancy models brought the company prestige while the plainer, more affordable instruments paid the bills. Consequently, by the end of 1953, Gibson had built prototypes for a new Les Paul model that could be bought for $99.50 – less than half the price of the gold-top. The Les Paul Junior, as it would be called, did away with the carved maple top cap and featured a simple "slab" mahogany body, no less a "plank" than the Fenders that Gibson people had derided only a few years earlier but distinguishable from a Fender by a classic Gibson Sunburst finish.

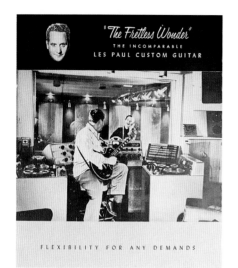

"The Fretless Wonder"
THE INCOMPARABLE
LES PAUL CUSTOM GUITAR

FLEXIBILITY FOR ANY DEMANDS

△ 1956 Les Paul Junior

In the **Gibson** galaxy of stars!

JOHNNY GRAY longtime radio favorite with Don McNeil's Breakfast Club . . . staff guitarist for ABC . . . recording artist . . . and "first call" man of many combos and recording studios, plucks the strings of a Les Paul Custom model Gibson to meet his exacting demands for tone and response. For guitars and amps, it's Gibson only for Johnny.

Gibson INC.
KALAMAZOO, MICHIGAN

In 1954 Gibson introduced two new Les Paul models at either end of the price scale. The Les Paul Junior (above), offered beginners or musicians on a budget a more affordable Les Paul. The Junior had a mahogany body with no maple top cap, an uncarved "slab" top, and a single pickup. At the other end of the range, the Les Paul Custom (opposite page) featured low frets, extra binding, mother-of-pearl inlays, upgraded pickups, and smart black finish. Custom players included Frannie Beecher (above) and session man Johnny Gray (right).

◁ 1954 Custom prototype

◁ 1954 Les Paul Custom

Les Paul, Mary Ford
and their Gibsons

ENTERTAIN ON RADIO AND TV

"AT HOME"

A prototype for the Les Paul Custom (far right) is a bit rougher than the production version, but all the elements are there, most important of which is the tune-o-matic bridge that is still standard equipment on most Gibson electrics. The "Black Beauty" was so attractive that Les Paul and Mary Ford (far right) apparently forsook their gold-tops for the model. One artist who did not forsake the gold-top was New Orleans bluesman Eddie "Guitar Slim" Jones (above), whose guitar features the original-style trapeze tailpiece.

(Fender was going in the opposite direction, upgrading its "plank" Telecaster to the highly modernized, countoured-body Stratocaster.) Where the gold-top Les Paul Model had a bound top, bound fingerboard, trapezoidal inlays, pearl logo, and two cream-colored soapbar P-90 pickups, the Junior had no binding anywhere, dot inlays, decal logo, and a single, black-covered "dog-ear" P-90. Still, it was a Gibson and it followed the expected sales pattern, starting with 823 in 1954, its first, partial year of production, and growing to 2,839 in 1955.

At the same time, Gibson came up with an elegant, more expensive Les Paul. The Les Paul Custom was more heavily bound and had large block inlays of mother-of-pearl, just as Gibson's L-5 acoustic had. The headstock inlay was the five-piece split-diamond from the Super 400. Les Paul's personal influence was manifest in low frets, designed for speedy play, and a black finish color. The pickups were black soapbars but the neck pickup had been upgraded with Alnico V magnets, and the pickup was distinguished by its rectangular polepieces. The extra features cost $100 over the price of the gold-top Les Paul.

The most important feature on the Custom was a new bridge. The stud-mounted wraparound bridge that had replaced the original combination trapeze style on the gold-top Les Paul Model had been an improvement in terms of solidity, but it did not improve on the limited capability for intonation adjustments. Like the trapeze style, the wraparound allowed for adjustment of the angle and the overall height of the bridge, but there was no way to adjust the strings individually. The Fender Telecaster, on the other hand, had three separate bridge-saddles that could be adjusted for string length as well as for height. The Les Paul Custom introduced the Gibson tune-o-matic bridge, designed by Ted McCarty, featuring six individual saddles – one for each string – that could be adjusted for string length. The entire unit could be raised or lowered. The strings were anchored in a separate "stopbar" tailpiece secured by two studs into the top. When asked how a non-musician could come up with such an effective improvement in bridge design, McCarty answered with one word: "Engineering." Whether it was McCarty's engineering background or, as one former Gibson employee claimed, an idea that was mailed to McCarty by a man in prison, McCarty patented the tune-o-matic. It quickly became standard equipment on the gold-top Les Paul and eventually on most of Gibson's electric models, where it remains the standard Gibson bridge to this day. The Les Paul Custom sold about half as well as the lower-priced Les Paul Model, but with shipments of 875 in 1955, its first full year of production, it still ranked with the midline hollowbody, the ES-175, in sales.

One more model completed the Les Paul quartet in 1955. Reasoning, apparently, that if one pickup was good, then two should be better, Gibson introduced a two-pickup version of the Junior called the Les Paul Special. It had several other extra features, including a bound fingerboard, a pearl logo and, most noticeably, a yellowish finish described variously as "Limed Mahogany" or "TV Yellow," the latter in reference to the fact that the lighter color would show up better on the black-and-white televisions of the day (although it would have been just as easy to offer any of the other Les Pauls in the same color). Priced between the Junior and Standard at $169.50, it sold in numbers, predictably, in between the Junior and Standard.

Les Paul's music, and that of all his peers on the pop charts of the early 1950s, was about to be overpowered by a revolutionary sound called rock 'n' roll. Although Gibson would be slow to recognize and react to rock 'n' roll, Gibson guitars were there at the beginning, even at the roots of the new music, in the hands of bluesmen such as B.B. King and T-bone Walker, and rock pioneers Bill Haley And The Comets. And on July 5th, 1954, at a moment that would change not just American music but American culture, Gibson was there.

The location was Sun Studios, aka Memphis Recording Service, where a 19-year-old delivery truck driver was auditioning for a chance to make a record. A lead guitarist and bass player had rehearsed with him the day before and were playing with him at the audition. After an unremarkable series of performances of standard tunes, the guitarist and bassist were packing up when Elvis Presley started "cutting up" with a supercharged version of the blues tune 'That's Alright.' The guitarist plugged in his Gibson ES-295, which would later be called "The Guitar That Changed the World," and they cut the record that did change the world.

The guitarist was Scotty Moore. Born Winfield Scott Moore near Humbolt, Tennessee, in 1931, he was living in Memphis after serving in the U.S. Navy. He had played a Gibson acoustic prior to his military service but while stationed in Japan, he had played cheap Japanese copies of Fenders. Upon his return to civilian life he bought one of the new Fender Esquires, but the thin body never felt right to him. "The problem was, I couldn't stand up and hold the dern thing," Moore said. "It was okay when I was sitting down. I had just gotten used to holding one under my arm like [his old Gibson flat-top]."

One day in 1953 he was walking along Union Street in downtown Memphis and passed by the O.K. Houck Piano store, which was the Gibson dealer in Memphis. They had just put a gold-colored electric guitar on display. "I said, 'My god, where did that come from? It's beautiful,'" Moore recalled. "I walked in and said, 'I don't care whose it is, where it came from, I want it.' And I got it."

The guitar was *not* the new Les Paul; it was a hollowbody archtop – essentially an ES-175 – and that quality was especially appealing to Moore. "I could hear it without even plugging it in," he said. "Just the overall sound of it ... The Fender depended strictly on the amplifier, but the Gibson, you sit and play it by itself." The finish was clearly inspired by the Les Paul, but it went a step farther. Where the Les Paul was gold on the top only (except for occasional all-gold examples), this new guitar was gold all the way around, including the back, sides and neck. Gibson had introduced it in 1952 and named it the ES-295.

Moore played his ES-295 for two or three years, but by the time of the Elvis sessions that produced 'Mystery Train' in July 1955, he had "moved up a notch," he

All shook up

On July 5th, 1954, the 19-year-old Elvis Presley walked into Sun Studios in Memphis and cut his version of the blues tune 'That's Alright.' Music would never be the same again. Ironically, "The Guitar That Changed The World", as Scotty Moore's instrument came to be known, was not one of the new Les Pauls but a hollowbody archtop introduced by Gibson in 1952 – the ES-295 (below). Essentially a glorified ES-175 with all-over gold finish and floral pickguard, the ES-295 featured the trapeze bridge/tailpiece that did not work on the Les Paul but worked fine on an archtop because it allowed room for the strings to wrap over the tailpiece. Scotty traded-in his ES-295 for an L-5CES in July 1955.

◁ 1952 ES-295

THE GIBSON ELECTRIC GUITAR BOOK

▷ 1957 Les Paul TV

Such was Les Paul's popularity that, in 1953, he and wife Mary were given their own television show called *At Home*. The show became a regular showcase for Gibson guitars, and the Les Paul TV model (far left) – a Junior with a Natural or, later, Limed Mahogany finish – was introduced in 1954 to capitalise on this. The Les Paul Special (left) followed in 1955, effectively a two-pickup version of the Junior. It adopted the Junior's un-carved "slab" top, but gained fingerboard binding, the same finish as the TV model, and was positioned towards the bottom of the Les Paul pricelist. The shape of the Junior, TV, and Special bodies was later changed (see page 62).

◁ 1955 Les Paul Special

said, to the bigger sound of a Gibson L-5CES. Two years later, Elvis was making movies in Hollywood, with Moore playing lead guitar on the soundtracks and L.A. session musician Tiny Timbrell playing rhythm guitar. Timbrell was also Gibson's artist relations representative for the Los Angeles area, and he officially hooked up Moore with Gibson. The result was a new Super 400CES in Natural finish that Moore played on the soundtracks to *Jailhouse Rock* and *King Creole*. In 1964, he got another Super 400CES, this one with black finish and the pointed cutaway that the model sported in the 1960s. He used that guitar on his solo album, *The Guitar That Changed the World* (a claim that he was always too modest to make), and that's the guitar that Elvis "borrowed" from Moore to perform 'One Night With You' on Elvis's 1968 "comeback" television special.

With traditional-style hollowbody electrics and modern solidbodies well-established, Gibson came up with an appealing variation in 1955 – a thin-depth hollowbody electric. The ES-175 shape, with its pointed cutaway and laminated maple body, provided the base model for the ES-225T (T for Thin), which initially had only a single pickup. On the high end, Gibson enlisted Billy Byrd and Hank Garland, Nashville session guitarists who also had a taste for jazz, to endorse a thinline guitar with a carved spruce top. The Byrdland was trimmed out much like an L-5, but it featured a shorter, 23½-inch scale to accommodate esoteric jazz chords that required wide stretches of the left hand. The ES-350T completed the thinline trio of 1955 as a less-fancy 17-inch model with a laminated body and the shortened scale of the Byrdland. Although the ES-350T never gained the notoriety of the Byrdland, it was the guitar Chuck Berry played in the mid to late 1950s as he "wrote the book" on rock guitar licks. The thinline selection was expanded a year later to include a two-pickup version of the ES-225 and a thin version of the most popular ES model, the 125. Gibson hit the sweet spot with the thinline ES-125T, and by the end of the 1950s, it had surpassed the full-depth ES-125 in sales.

In 1957, Gibson introduced a breakthrough in pickup design – the double-coil "humbucker." In Seth Lover's patent application, filed in 1957 and granted in 1959, the Gibson engineer got right to the point. His goal was " ... to provide a magnetic pickup for a stringed instrument which is not affected by adjacent electrical devices and which does not pick up and transmit to the amplifier the hum of such devices." It was a godsend to electric guitarists, who had been dealing with electrical interference (from amps, rheostats and virtually any source of electro-magnetic signal in proximity with a pickup) since the invention of the pickup itself.

Lover, a Kalamazoo native, was originally hired at Gibson in 1941 by Walt Fuller, the man who developed Gibson's first pickup. He left Gibson for the U.S. Navy but was rehired by Ted McCarty in 1952 to develop pickups and amplifiers. The theoretical solution to the "hum" problem was almost as well-known as the problem itself: Two coils of wire with currents traveling in opposite directions will cancel out electrical interference. Dating back to the beginnings of electrical amplification, some loudspeakers had used a horseshoe magnet with a coil at each end to cancel hum. In the guitar world, Lover cited in his patent a reference to Armand Knoblaugh's 1938 patent (assigned to the Baldwin piano company), which featured a pair of coils in a stacked configuration (a configuration that Gibson would feature in its P-100 pickup in 1990). In working on Gibson amps Lover developed a tone circuit with hum-canceling capability, and in 1955 he started building pickups with two coils placed side by side with a single magnet slipped in between.

The humbucker sat fully developed in Lover's office until 1956, when a competitor (probably Gretsch) showed a prototype humbucker at a trade show. By the end of the year, Gibson's humbucker debuted on a Hawaiian model, and that version featured three coils – a full-length center coil framed by two half-coils. It was February 1957 before the standard double-coil humbucker began appearing on Gibson's high-end Spanish electrics. Gibson also took the opportunity to upgrade the Les Paul Custom to three pickups (a two-pickup version remained optional). The Les Paul Model (gold-top) also received the upgrade to humbucker, marking the beginning of its classic period of production.

Gibson put a "Patent Applied For" sticker on the underside of the humbuckers, and when the patent was granted in 1959, McCarty was reluctant to make it easily accessible. For three more years the pickups continued to carry the "PAF" stickers. Finally, in mid 1962, the stickers had a patent number, but McCarty still tried to throw competitors "off the scent" of the humbucker. Anyone requesting a copy of patent 2,737,842 – the number on the sticker – would receive Les Paul's patent for the combination bridge/tailpiece. Lover's humbucker patent was in fact 2,896,491.

By the end of 1957, Gibson appeared to be sitting pretty. The humbucking pickup represented the first (and perhaps still the only) major improvement in pickup design since the invention of the electric guitar. Gibson hollowbody electrics were the preferred models in the country music center of Nashville. Jazz players still followed Charlie Christian's example and played Gibsons. And Gibson had gotten in on the ground floor when rock 'n' roll music began its ascendance. Scotty Moore was exclusively a Gibson man playing with Elvis. Bill Haley And The Comets had hit with 'Rock Around The Clock' in 1955, featuring a wild solo by Danny Cedrone playing a Gibson ES-300; although Cedrone had tragically died just days after the recording session when he fell down a flight of stairs and broke his neck, his replacement, Frannie Beecher, as well as Billy Haley, played Gibsons.

The first sign of impending trouble for Gibson came at the end of 1957, when Elvis received his draft notice. In the meantime, Buddy Holly had his first hit in the summer of 1957 with 'That'll Be The Day,' and in January 1958, as Elvis's draft board was deferring his induction until he completed filming *King Creole*, Holly appeared on the Ed Sullivan television show. In a time before music videos and entertainment channels, TV appearances by rock 'n' rollers were few and far

Archtop excellence

Although the era of the solidbody guitar was well underway by 1955, Gibson's archtop electrics were still the preferred style of the best-known guitarists. Gibson expanded its archtop offering with an improved version of the three-pickup ES-5 with "Switchmaster" pickup selection (right). Top Nashville players Hank Garland and Billy Byrd were enlisted to create the short scale Byrdland. In the meantime, Chuck Berry (below) began creating the lexicon of rock 'n' roll guitar licks on his Gibson ES-350T.

◁ 1957 ES-5 Switchmaster

Sun Records rockabilly Carl Perkins (right) was one of many pioneering guitarists who shaped the sound of rock 'n' roll with a hollowbody electric, in this case a Gibson ES-5 Switchmaster. With individual tone and volume controls for each of the three pickups, plus a selector switch, the Switchmaster offered guitarists a great improvement over the ES-5's original system, which controlled pickup selection only by volume controls.

◁ 1957 Byrdland

◁ 1957 ES-350T

between. It was the first glimpse that many Americans would have of Holly, and what they saw was a modern, curvy, white-colored electric guitar – a Fender Stratocaster. A torch was being passed – or grabbed – not only from Elvis to Holly but from Scotty Moore's Gibson to Holly's Fender. Elvis reported for duty to the U.S. Army in March 1958, and newspapers across the country ran a photo of him in a barber's chair, losing his sideburns and getting his hair cut short. It was almost as big a turning point in music as when he first strummed the rhythm to 'That's Alright,' because his music would never be the same again.

In Kalamazoo, if Ted McCarty was not alarmed it was only because Holly's appearance confirmed what he had been feeling for several years – Gibson's electric line needed a shot in the arm. The Gretsch company, based in New York, had signed Chet Atkins as an endorser and introduced the first of several Atkins signature models in late 1954. In 1955, Gretsch had introduced flashy finish colors – including orange, white, green, red, and yellow. Gibson had the gold-top Les Paul Model, the black Custom, and the just-introduced TV Yellow Special, but everything else remained traditional Sunburst or Natural. Fender had introduced a model in 1954 that is still considered by many to represent perfection in solidbody guitar design – the Stratocaster. The Stratocaster's sleek, sculpted body lines made Gibson's Les Pauls look not just conventional but old-fashioned. But what really set McCarty off was the talk going around the industry. He had heard that Leo Fender had called Gibson a stodgy old company that never had a new idea. Well, McCarty was working on a lot of new designs – some outlandish and some ingenious.

The first record of McCarty's new ideas went public on June 20, 1957 at the U.S. Patent Office in the form of three design patents – D181865, D181866 and D181867 – for electric guitar bodies. Although Hawaiian guitars had been made in various shapes since the 1930s, the farthest that Spanish-style models had strayed from tradition was the Fender Stratocaster, which still had lower bouts and upper bouts delineated by a "waist." McCarty's designs threw tradition out the window, but as yet they were only ideas – not guitars.

That changed on February 21, 1958, when an unknown person at Gibson made a most extraordinary entry into the shipping logs. The shipment of five new instruments to CMI headquarters, presumably for approval or possibly for photography for sales literature, marked the beginning of a legendary era in the history of Gibson electrics. "Flying V in Korena" was the most radical in that group of entries – it was the first of McCarty's patented trio of "modernistic" solidbody designs. "ES-335T" was the most innovative of the new models – a "semi-hollowbody" electric guitar, in which McCarty succeeded in combining Gibson's f-hole archtop tradition with the performance qualities of the newer solidbody concept. "EB-2" as the model number might suggest, was Gibson's second electric bass; this one was built on the semi-hollowbody of the ES-335. "Dbl neck Mandolin" was not a single- or double-neck mandolin, rather it was a double-neck electric guitar with a standard scale on one neck and a shorter scale on the second neck. The body was unique – hollow with a carved spruce top and no soundholes, a style previously used only on two experimental electric basses in the pre-World War II period.

The least innovative and, at the time, least important of the five entries is the one that garners the most interest today: "LP Cherry." Unlike the other entries, it was not a new model, and it was not even a significant change in the existing Les Paul Model. Up until then, the Les Paul Model had the gold-top finish with a walnut stain on the back, sides and neck. A change to Cherry finish was a bit of a downgrade, actually, as Gibson was also changing the finish on the lowly Les Paul Junior to Cherry at the same time. Several examples of "Cherry" Les Pauls from this period have a "shaded" look – a subtle Sunburst similar to the "Shaded Mahogany" finish that Gibson used on some mandolins and guitars in the 1910s and '20s. These Cherry examples were also shaded on the back of the body and neck. Later in 1958, Gibson settled on the now-classic Cherry Sunburst top finish with a yellow center section of the top and a uniform Cherry stain on the back, sides and neck. With this change, the model name also changed from Les Paul Model to Les Paul Standard.

The Flying V and its companions, the Explorer and Moderne, caused the biggest buzz in 1958, and the buzz continues today. If there had ever been any doubt, these three proved once and for all that if a guitar had a solidbody, there were virtually no constraints on the shape of that body as long as it could provide a secure framework for the strings and electronics. McCarty and his staff went through numerous designs before settling on the three. One early version had a triangular body, but it felt heavy and cumbersome, so a wedge was cut out of the lower end, leaving it in the shape of an inverted V. The peghead repeated the inverted V motif, and it was also accentuated by a flat, top-mounted tailpiece that allowed the strings to anchor through the body. With its arrowlike look, the model was named the Flying V.

A second model started off looking as if the designers had had a tug of war. The lower bass bout was pulled out at an angle, almost as far as the player's right elbow. Diagonally opposite, the upper treble bout appeared to have lost most of its substance in the battle, and it was narrow and protruded outward – downward to the player – at an odd angle. The headstock was symmetrical and in the shape of a V. This model was named the Futura but it never made it out of the prototype stage. The upper treble bout was enlarged and the angles revised so that it was in balance with the lower bass bout. The peghead was redesigned with a scimitar-like shape with all the tuners on the same side; the curves of the headstock did not complement or reflect the angular body design, but it was a more functional design than the V-shape. The revised model was named the Explorer.

The third model looked like a genetic accident. The bass-side half of the body was essentially that of the Flying V. The treble side had a shorter fin, and the middle

Tune-o-matics and humbuckers

As important and successful as the original Les Paul Model was, it did leave room for improvement in a few areas. Paul's trapeze-style combination bridge and tailpiece worked well on archtops but not on the Les Paul Model, and Gibson replaced it by the end of 1953 with a stud-mounted bar that allowed the strings to wrap over it. Then Gibson president Ted McCarty designed an improved bridge that allowed for individual saddle adjustments. Dubbed the tune-o-matic, it debuted on the Les Paul Custom and appeared on the gold-tops in 1955. In 1957, when Gibson replaced the original single-coil "soapbar" pickups with the new double-coil humbuckers, the evolution of the Les Paul was complete.

◁ 1954 Les Paul gold-top

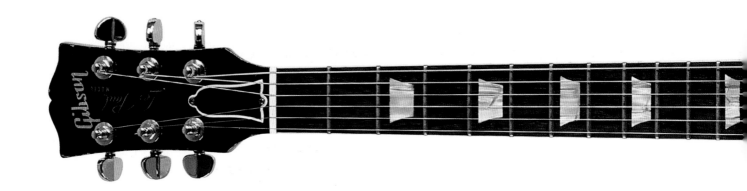

◁ 1957 Les Paul gold top

▽ 1957 Les Paul gold top left-handed

part appeared to have been scooped out, which made for an unusually small-feeling body. The headstock was an asymmetrical blob that not only looked bad, it had the tuners so misaligned with the strings that string guides were necessary. This one was called the Moderne, and the trio was called the Modernistic guitars.

Gibson had been using African limba wood on the Skylark lap steel model since 1956. It had a grain pattern very similar to mahogany but was much lighter in color. The "Limed Mahogany" or "TV" finish had proven to be popular on Gibson's Les Paul Special, and African limba was light enough that it could be used with only a clear coat of lacquer, saving Gibson several steps in the finishing process. It was also lighter in weight than mahogany, which made it suitable for the Flying V and the Explorer. Gibson made up a catchy name for it – Korina (it may have been Korena initially, or the ledger entry person may have simply misspelled it) – and used it for all three of McCarty's new Modernistics.

The Korina Trio, as they have come to be called, debuted at the annual NAMM (National Association of Music Merchants) trade show, held at the Palmer House hotel in Chicago. McCarty succeeded in his desire to shock the industry. Forrest White, production manager for Fender, said he thought some of Leo Fender's designs were crazy, but the new Gibsons topped Fender in that respect. McCarty was not so successful with sales, however. The Flying V was the first model to go into production and the only one of the three to be pictured in the 1958 catalog. Gibson shipping totals show 81 shipped in 1958, a respectable amount for such a radical design.

Unfortunately, by the time Gibson was ready to ship Explorers, the Flying Vs were still hanging on dealer's walls or being displayed in store windows as curiosity pieces. Shipping totals don't even list the Explorer by name. The only listing is the ambiguous "Korina (Mod. Gtr.)." Dealers were apparently unwilling to invest any more money in these new guitars because Gibson only shipped 19 of them in 1958. It is assumed that these were Explorers because no Modernes have ever turned up. The next year was worse, with 17 Flying Vs and three Explorers shipped, and then the Korinas disappeared, at least for a few years.

What happened to the Moderne? An artist's rendering survives in Gibson archives. And of course McCarty's drawing for the design patent survives (and provided the template for the "reissue" in the early 1980s). In separate interviews in 1993, Ted McCarty, longtime Gibson employee Julius Bellson and Fender's Forrest White all said they remembered seeing the Moderne on display at the Palmer House in 1958. However, according to Jim Deurloo, who started working for Gibson in 1956 and went on to become plant manager before co-founding Heritage Guitars, the Moderne was simply "a good old myth." To make a prototype, he explained, they had to have a "soft tool" to shape the body, and the soft tool was never developed for the Moderne. Furthermore, he added, "The first Flying Vs and Explorers were in a rack in the hallway coming out of the office for going on five years, and there never was a Moderne in that rack."

McCarty's ES-335 was everything the Korinas were not. It was well-designed and innovative in a practical sense rather than being a display of design for design's sake. And it was highly successful commercially because it perfectly balanced tradition with modern design. The arched top, though laminated rather than solid, was Orville Gibson's original concept, and the f-holes, introduced by Gibson in the 1920s, were by now a traditional element of guitar design. The thin body was a recent innovation that was fast gaining acceptance, and the double-cutaway body created a unique modern look and also offered the player maximum access to the upper frets. The heart of the design was underneath the top – a solid block of wood that ran down the center of the body. Thanks to the solid center block, the vibration of the top of the guitar was reduced to practically nothing, making the ES-335 function like a solidbody, which to guitarists meant less feedback and more sustain. A pair of humbucking pickups ensured that the power-potential of the semi-hollowbody could be exploited.

Before the year was out, the ES-335 was doing well enough to warrant a family of semi-hollowbodies. The ES-345 (the first of which didn't make it out the door until 1959) featured stereo wiring, allowing the player to run the pickups through separate amps, and a six-position "Varitone" switch that progressively cut out midrange tones. It also featured upgraded ornamentation, including double-parallelogram inlays and gold-plated hardware. The ES-355, debuting at the end of 1958, took the ornamentation a step higher with pearl block inlays and more layers of binding. It started out without the stereo and Varitone features, but they became standard in 1959. As usual, the least expensive ES-335 was the most successful, but in this case that success was due in part to the fact that players ultimately did not want the stereo and Varitone. The semi-hollow design made for a highly versatile electric guitar, illustrated by the diverse artists who have played guitars from the 335 family, including rock pioneer Chuck Berry, blues legend B.B. King, studio ace Larry Carlton, rock icon Keith Richards, and jazzer Lee Ritenour.

The EB-2 of 1958 presented the semi-hollowbody concept in the form of a bass. It replaced Gibson's first attempt at an electric bass, the solidbody EB (named EB-1 when it was revived in later years). The EB debuted in 1953, shortly after the Les Paul Model, and it had a unique, violin-shaped body with a carved top. A hollowbody violin-shaped bass, made by the Hofner company of Germany, would do quite well in the 1960s in the hands of The Beatles' Paul McCartney, but the violin shape did not work for Gibson. Nor would the semi-hollowbody EB-2, as it turned out. Like the EB and most of the basses that would follow, it had a 30-inch scale, compared to the 34-inch scale of the highly successful Fender Precision. Bassists never warmed up to the "thuddy" tone of the short scale Gibsons, and Gibson would always struggle in the bass market.

The double-neck guitar of 1958 was not the first double-neck electric, nor was it even Gibson's first. Twenty years earlier, still in the era of the "Charlie Christian" pickup, Gibson had made an instrument with an electric Hawaiian neck and an

The shape of things to come

The Gibson Flying V was the first of Ted McCarty's trio of "modernistic" solidbody designs. Made of lighter "Korina" wood, these designs were meant to add a more futuristic aspect to Gibson's image. They created a buzz when launched in 1958 but didn't sell well and were immediately abandoned. In the mid 1960s, guitarists such as Albert King (above), Lonnie Mack, The Kinks' Dave Davies, and Jimi Hendrix, in search of a distinctive looking guitar with a powerful sound, started using Flying Vs. The renewed interest created a demand for Gibson to reissue the model in 1965.

△ 1959 Flying V

The 1958 Explorer (right) was even more radical and even less successful than the Flying V. Some were made with a V-shaped headstock (far right), a carryover from the Futura prototype. Unsurprisingly, after such disappointing sales of the Flying V and Explorer, the third of McCarty's trio, the Moderne, never made it into production. In the meantime, Gibson was thinking about a new finish for the Les Paul Model and tried out a Cherry stain (below) on a handful of guitars.

◁ 1963 Explorer

▷ 1958 Explorer

◁ 1959 Les Paul Standard in cherry finish

Electric Spanish neck. The concept lay dormant, however, until 1955, when two of southern California's hottest country guitarists, Joe Maphis and Larry Collins, started playing double-necks made by Semie Moseley (founder of Mosrite guitars). As Gibson had done with the original Les Paul Model, the company designed its first double-neck to incorporate traditional Gibson designs that would not be easily copied by competitors. In this case, the design came from a pair of electric basses made in the prewar era that featured a carved spruce top with no soundholes. Gibson initially offered two double-necks by custom order only. The model with the standard neck and short 6-string neck was named the EMS-1235 (EMS for Electric Mandolin Spanish) and a model with 6-string and 12-string necks was called the EDS-1275 (D for Double-neck). In practice, any combination of guitar, mandolin or banjo necks was available by custom order.

The double-neck body shape quickly changed as the upper bass horn was reduced in size. This was not a planned design change, but a result of an equipment operator falling asleep on the job and allowing the metal pattern to heat up to the point were it cracked. The pattern was trimmed of the damaged part, and double-neck bodies featured the new shape for a short time. Less than 100 double-necks with the hollowbody were sold before they all changed to SG-style solidbodies in 1962.

There were more changes in the electric line in 1958. The Les Paul Junior was upgraded and modernized to become the first Gibson solidbody with a double-cutaway body, and a Cherry stain finish replaced its Sunburst finish. (The Les Paul Special would follow suit a year later with a double-cutaway body and optional Cherry finish.) In the hollowbody line, a sort of top-shelf ES-175 called the L-4C was offered in limited production. Like the high-end L-5CES and Super 400CES, it featured a solid, carved spruce top. Its pickup made it unique for the period – a reissue of the prewar "Charlie Christian" style.

The least expensive Les Paul Junior had been outselling all the other Les Paul models put together, so it followed that an even cheaper solidbody electric would do even better. That theory, along with the success of Fender's low-priced Musicmaster, gave rise to the Gibson Melody Maker of 1959. Although it did not bear the Les Paul name, it was essentially a junior version of the Les Paul Junior, with the Les Paul's single-cutaway shape but the cost-cutting features of a thinner body and a narrow headstock trimmed of its "wings." The pickup, too, was thinner; it had no polepieces and was housed under an oblong plastic cover. The original MM had a single pickup, and there was also a ¾-scale version; a double-pickup model joined the family a year later. The theory proved correct; by the mid 1960s, after going through a progression of double-cutaway body shapes, the Melody Maker became Gibson's best-selling solidbody.

The changes and innovations of 1958 – particularly the success of the ES-335 and the new looks for the Les Paul line – would seem to have ensured more than two years of security and stability for Gibson, but McCarty was on a roll. In 1961 he gave the Les Paul line a makeover that made the sweeping changes of 1958 look like a mere tune-up. The seed had been sown in 1958 with the Les Paul Junior's move to a double-cutaway body, which was followed in 1959 by the Les Paul Special. Shortly afterward, the Special lost its silkscreen signature on the headstock, and Gibson began referring to it as SG, for Solid Guitar.

Today, with the Cherry Sunburst Les Paul Standard revered by collectors and players alike, it seems unthinkable to abandon the model after one or two years of sagging sales, but that's what McCarty did – to the entire Les Paul family. On the other hand, yearly makeovers were a way of life in the automobile industry, and McCarty, with his interest in engineering and his location only a few hours from Detroit, would prove to be more than just an interested observer of automotive design (with the Firebird line of 1963).

The new Les Pauls of 1961 bore little resemblance to the Les Pauls of 1960. The body was only about half as thick, with double-cutaways that ended in pointed horns. The pickup configuration, ornamentation and model names did carry over from the earlier line. The Custom still had three humbuckers, bound ebony fingerboard with pearl block inlays, five-piece headstock inlay and gold-plated hardware. The Standard had two humbuckers, bound rosewood fingerboard with pearloid trapezoid inlay and nickel-plated hardware. The Special had two P-90s and a bound fingerboard with dot inlays. And the Junior had a single P-90 and an unbound fingerboard.

The Custom, Standard, and Junior were still called Les Pauls, although Paul's influence was negligible by this time. He and Mary Ford had their last chart hit in 1961, 'Jura (I Swear I Love You),' which only reached No. 37. Although Paul himself was pictured in a catalog with one of the new style Les Pauls, he has claimed he never liked the new design. According to Ted McCarty, McCarty and his wife had had a social relationship with Les Paul and Mary Ford, but that relationship had cooled by the early 1960s. The only logical reason to put the Les Paul name on the new models was simply that Paul's endorsement agreement still had a few years to run, and Gibson had no other models to put his name on. By late 1963 Paul's contract ran out and was not renewed, and his name was dropped from the guitars, which became SG models from that point onward.

The solidbody basses also changed over to the SG body, although they retained the EB model designation. Predictably, the inexpensive single-pickup EB-0, which had started out in 1959 with the rounded-horn double-cutaway body of the Les Paul Junior, was the most popular, outselling all the other basses put together through the 1960s. The EB-3, with two pickups was a distant second. Although EB-0 would not go down in history as a great or desirable bass, Gibson sold over 15,000 of them in the 1960s. The SG guitars put up larger sales figures during the same period – 18,000 Specials; 23,000 Juniors; 21,000 Standards – but the EB-0 was by far the most commercially successful bass Gibson would ever make.

The SG bodies of 1961 served notice that Gibson intended to be a part of the

Semi-hollows and Sunbursts

Gibson president Ted McCarty melded Gibson's archtop tradition with modern solidbody functionality and created the semi-hollowbody electric guitar in 1958. The original ES-335 model quickly spawned more highly ornamented versions including the ES-345 (right) and the ES-355, which Gibson clinician Andy Nelson demonstrated in ads (right) and at Gibson dealerships. A less profound but equally noteworthy innovation of 1958 was the change in finish on the Les Paul Model to Cherry Sunburst (below), at which time the model name was changed to Les Paul Standard.

Gibson thin-body guitars feel just right

Whenever guitar players get to talking about their favorite instrument there's one thing they'll always say: *the feel is right!* And that's just what they've all been saying about Gibson's great new series of thin-body electrics. Yes, every one of these models—each with the Gibson *wonder-thin silhouette*—really does have that certain "feel" to it. And fitting so close and comfortably to your body, it'll let you reach many chords easily you've never played before.* You'll find the slender Gibson neck feels just right in your hand, and it's so easy to finger. That extremely fast, low action will make the strings seem feather-light to your touch. If you haven't done so already, be sure to find out all about this new all-star line of light-weight low-action thin-body Gibsons . . . each model so easy to handle, so easy to play. All have that quick response, balanced tone that always says instantly—Gibson.

Gibson INC.

KALAMAZOO, MICHIGAN

the Gibson wonder-thin silhouette . . . only 1¾" to 2⅛" thin . . . in a full series of Gibson guitars, priced from $145 to $605.

* *Especially with Gibson's beautiful, cherry-red ES-355T double cutaway model, you'll reach right down to the very last fret with the greatest of ease (shown here, along with the GA-400 amp, by Gibson artist-enthusiast, Andy Nelson).*

◁ **1959 ES-345**

◁ **1958 Les Paul Standard**

The ES-335 came out of the chute with no need for improvement. Although Gibson did meddle with the specs in the '60s and '70s, demand for early examples with dot-inlaid fingerboard prompted the company to revert to the original style (below); it remains in production as the archetype of the semi-hollow guitar. Such was the appeal of the semi-hollowbody that it even featured on Gibson's amp flyers (right). B.B. King played an array of Gibsons, including this thinline hollowbody ES-330 (bottom), before settling on an ES-355.

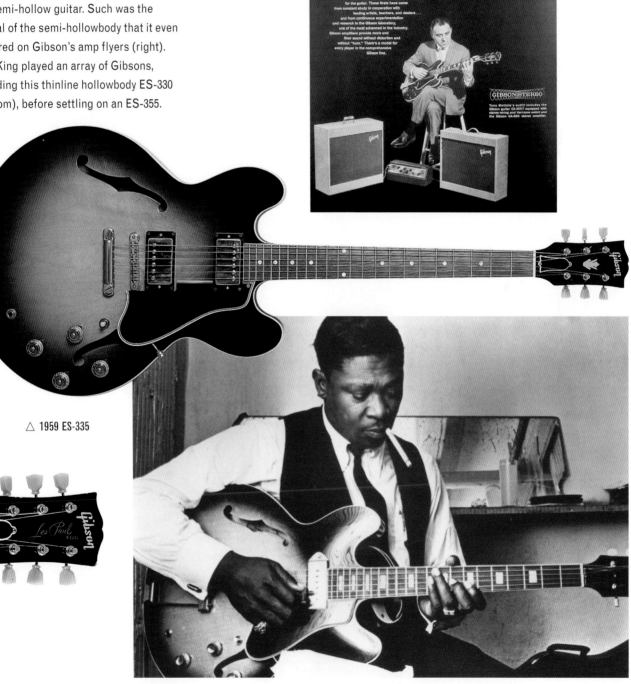

△ 1959 ES-335

new rock 'n' roll music played by younger guitarists, but McCarty did not ignore the more traditional models. Even as he was dropping Les Paul, he remained well aware of the benefits of association with a respected artist, and he set about creating an identity for Gibson hollowbody electrics. In that quest, he took the high road. Instead of a radical design makeover to catch the eyes of young rockers, he presented the hollowbodies as elite models endorsed by elite jazz guitarists.

The first was Johnny Smith. His only major hit record was his 1952 recording of the standard 'Moonlight in Vermont,' but he set the standard for smooth "chord-melody" jazz guitar stylings. Smith's personal guitar was a 17-inch, single-cutaway archtop made by John D'Angelico of New York. It was a fully acoustic guitar with a "floating" DeArmond pickup attached to the end of the fingerboard so that it did not in any way impede the vibration of the top. The upstart Guild company (founded in 1952) had signed him as its first artist and introduced a signature model in 1956, and his Guild was similar to his D'Angelico. When he moved to Gibson in 1961, Gibson made a closer copy of his D'Angelico, including a 25-inch scale (standard Gibson scale was 24¾ or 25½ inches). Gibson outfitted the Johnny Smith with its best pickup, a scaled down humbucker that "floated" on top of the guitar. Controls were mounted in the pickguard. In ornamentation, the Smith model was top-of-the-line, with the split-diamond fingerboard and headstock inlays of Gibson's previous top model, the Super 400CES. A two-pickup version of the Smith was added in 1963.

Where Johnny Smith was reserved, Barney Kessel was hip. Many Americans first got a glimpse of the bearded guitarist as the only white musician in the 1944 Academy Award-nominated short film *Jammin' the Blues*. A disciple of Charlie Christian, he played and recorded with just about every style of jazz bandleader, including Charlie Barnet, Benny Goodman, Artie Shaw, Charlie Parker, and Oscar Peterson before going solo in 1953. Through the 1950s he split his time between making his own albums and being a first-call studio guitarist. He played a customized Gibson, essentially an ES-350 with pearl dot fingerboard inlays and a Charlie Christian pickup, and it was featured prominently on Julie London's 1956 recording 'Cry Me a River.'

Kessel brought not only a hip jazz style but a cool new guitar design to the Gibson archtop electric line in 1961 – a full-depth, double-cutaway hollowbody with pointed horns. In a nod to acoustic tradition, the top was spruce, but it was laminated (although occasional examples were made with solid spruce top and solid maple sides). Gibson gave Kessel two versions: the Barney Kessel Regular had double-parallelogram fingerboard inlays, the "crown" peghead ornament, and nickel-plated hardware; the Barney Kessel Custom had unique bowtie-shaped inlays, a musical note on the peghead and gold-plated hardware.

Gibson's next signature artist was an unusual choice. Tal Farlow had been one of the top bebop jazz guitarists in the 1950s, but unlike Smith and Kessel, he had never had any success or interest in popular music. And by the time his signature model was introduced in 1962, he had been out of the music business and working as a sign painter for four years. His model was based on his personal ES-350, but with humbucking pickups. He added several unmistakable cosmetic touches: inlaid binding material in the cutaway bout to simulate a scroll, upside-down "pineapple" (acoustic J-200-style) fingerboard inlays and a double-crown inlay on the peghead. The Gibson Tal Farlow was further distinguished by a light brown Sunburst finish called Viceroy Brown.

Gibson broke the string of jazz signature artists in 1964 with Trini Lopez, a singer whose pop hits featured folk songs performed to the energized beat of a strummed electric guitar. The Dallas native had moved to Los Angeles intending to join the Crickets, Buddy Holly's band, after Holly's death. When that opportunity fell through he began playing solo, and he was discovered by Frank Sinatra in a nightclub fronting a three-piece band. An album called *Live at P.J.'s* put Lopez on the charts in the summer of 1963 with a supercharged version of 'If I Had a Hammer.' Lopez never pretended to be a great guitarist, but his style was effective and unique. There had been rhythm roles for electric guitars, to be sure, exemplified by the chugging, boogie-based figures of Chuck Berry, but virtually no one played a full-strum, acoustic rhythm style on anything but an acoustic until Trini Lopez. It was a sort of "people's style" – easy to learn, with the potential to carry the folk music boom over to the electric guitar. Lopez's popularity was rewarded with two distinctly different Gibson signature models.

The Trini Lopez Standard was built on the semi-hollowbody design of the ES-335. Lopez's personal features were diamond-shaped soundholes and a headstock with six-on-a-side tuners – essentially a Fender headstock. Diamonds may have suggested elegance, but the decal peghead logo kept the price down on the Lopez Standard. The second model, the Trini Lopez Deluxe, used the full-depth double-cutaway body of the Barney Kessel as a starting point. Like the Lopez Standard, it featured diamond soundholes and a Fender-style peghead and, in addition to the standard Gibson electronics (two humbuckers, four controls, three-way switch), it had a standby switch on the upper bass bout.

Gibson introduced both Lopez models in 1964, and they outsold all of the other signature models - in some years, they outsold all the other models – for the remainder of the 1960s. In the late '60s, Lopez turned to acting, appearing most notably in the film *The Dirty Dozen*, and his last record to make the Top 20 was 'Lemon Tree' in 1967. Although he continues performing to a worldwide fan base today, his Gibson models barely survived into the 1970s.

In the meantime McCarty still felt he had something to prove to the world of solidbody guitar design. His modernistic designs for the Flying V, Explorer and Moderne had not gotten off the ground, so called in outside help. Gibson had had success in the late 1940s with the Hawaiian guitars designed by the Barnes & Roenecke firm. This time around, McCarty looked to legendary automotive

The Incredible Jazz Guitar of

Wes Montgomery

"...whatever he does comes alive, the mark of a true artist"

A self-taught master of the jazz guitar, until recently Wes had done all of his playing (except for two years with Lionel Hampton) in and around his native Indianapolis. He didn't cut his first record album until late in 1959.

But the Montgomery sound had long been known and respected among professional musicians. And, once "discovered," the news of this man from Indiana spread to jazz enthusiasts everywhere.

What is the Montgomery sound? It's an exciting quality that makes Montgomery music come alive. It's a terrific swing, the ability to build solos dramatically, to climax after climax. A sense of rightness. A smooth, easy, flowing style. It's the sound of great jazz . . . from a guitar.

Most of all . . . the Montgomery sound is a soft, delicate, exceedingly sensitive kind of music that is created deep within his being. Yes, Wes Montgomery plays a truly incredible jazz guitar. And his guitar is a *Gibson*

Gibson, Inc.
Kalamazoo, Michigan

Solid Body ELECTRIC GUITARS

SG CUSTOM
Players call it the "Fretless Wonder" for its extremely low frets and fast action. Now it's more wonderful than ever with new body design and new features.
FEATURES: Ultra thin, hand contoured, double cutaway body, gold-plated metal parts. New extra slim, fast, low-action neck—with exclusive extra low frets—joins body at 22nd fret. One-piece mahogany neck, adjustable truss rod. Ebony fingerboard, deluxe pearl inlays. Adjustable Tune-O-Matic bridge. Three powerful humbucking pickups with unique wiring arrangement. Two sets of tone and volume controls. Three-position toggle switch. New Deluxe Gibson Vibrola. 12½" wide, 16" long, 1⅜" thin, 24¾" scale, 22 frets.
SG Custom White finish
0537 Faultless gold plush-lined case
ZC-SGC Deluxe zipper case cover

SG Standard
An established favorite with completely new modern styling . . . with thinner, lighter weight, contoured body, and deep double cutaway that provides ease access to all 22 frets.
FEATURES: Ultra thin, contoured, double cutaway body. Nickel-plated metal parts and individual machine heads with deluxe buttons. Slim, fast, low-action neck—with exclusive extra low frets—joins body at 22nd fret. One-piece mahogany neck, adjustable truss rod. Rosewood fingerboard, pearl inlays. Adjustable Tune-O-Matic bridge. Two powerful humbucking pickups with separate tone and volume controls which can be pre-set. New Deluxe Gibson Vibrola. Three-position toggle switch to activate either or both pickups. 12½" wide, 16" long, 1⅜" thin, 24¾" scale, 22 frets.
SG Standard Cherry finish
0537 Faultless gold plush-lined case
ZC-SGC Deluxe zipper case cover

SG SPECIAL
Two ways new! A lovely new finish in white or Gibson's cherry red . . . an ultra-modern, new sculptured shape. Outstanding for its tone, versatility, and low fast action at a modest price.
FEATURES: Ultra thin, contoured, double cutaway body, nickel-plated metal parts, enclosed individual machine heads. Slim, fast, low-action neck—with exclusive extra low frets—joins body at 22nd fret. Rosewood fingerboard, pearl dot inlays. One-piece mahogany neck, adjustable truss rod. Combination metal bridge and tailpiece, adjustable horizontally and vertically. Two powerful pickups with separate tone and volume controls which can be pre-set. Three-position toggle switch to activate either or both pickups. 12½" wide, 16" long, 1⅜" thin, 24¾" scale, 22 frets.
SG Special White finish
0537 Faultless plush-lined case
315 Archcraft plush-lined case
118 Durabilt case
ZC-SGC Deluxe zipper case cover

◁ 1960 Les Paul Junior

◁ 1966 SG Special

◁ 1961 SG Standard/Les Paul Standard

▷ 1961 SG/Les Paul Junior

During 1958, Gibson changed the shape of the Junior, Special, and TV to this new double-cutaway style (left) with a Cherry stain or yellow "TV" finish. The extra room at the top of the neck was designed to give easier access to higher frets. The seeds were sown for what was to become the SG (for Solid Guitar) range, with twin cutaways, sharp horns and bevelled edges. The Les Paul name remained on the new models until 1963, when Les's endorsement agreement ran out. Gibson changed the name of the range to SG but the basic elements that distinguish the four models remained: three humbuckers and pearl block inlay on the Custom, two humbuckers and trapezoid inlay on the Standard, two single-coils and dot inlay on the Special, one single-coil on the Junior. This example of the Standard (above left) features an unusual and short-lived sideways-action vibrato, operated with an in-and-out action, rather than the customary up-and-down movement.

designer Ray Dietrich to create a new line of solidbody guitars. In the early 1920s, Dietrich's Le Baron Carrossiers (French for coachbuilders) in New York pioneered the concept of designing a car completely on paper before proceeding with building. His designs in the 1930s for Packard and Chrysler helped define the Classic Era of automobiles. By the 1960s, Dietrich had retired in Kalamazoo. McCarty knew Dietrich's cars, and he asked him to take a shot at a guitar.

Ray Dietrich may have been a designer of Classic Era cars, but his guitar went in the opposite direction – literally reversing conventional designs. He made the upper treble horn longer than the bass horn (possibly using the Explorer as inspiration), and he put all the tuners on the treble side of the peghead. So that the player didn't have to make an awkward reach to turn the tuners, he used banjo-style machines with the shaft extending from the back of the headstock; this also made for a sleeker visual look, with the tuner buttons no longer protruding from the side of the headstock. Always conscious of the overall view, Dietrich drew up a smaller pickup than the standard humbucker, and he eliminated the screw poles to achieve a smoother look. Most important was the "neck-through" design, with the neck extending through the body. It wasn't an altogether new idea (Rickenbacker's 1950s solidbodies were neck-through), but it achieved a unity of design as it tied modern aesthetics to the very essence of the solidbody guitar.

Gibson named the new model the Firebird, drawing a connection to Ford's popular Thunderbird model (the Pontiac Firebird automobile would not be introduced until 1967). Like the Les Pauls and SGs, the Firebirds were offered with four different levels of ornamentation and features, but unlike the other lines, the Firebirds were simply named I, III, V and VII. The even numbers were filled by the Thunderbird II and Thunderbird IV basses. All featured the smaller pole-less pickups, soon to be known as mini-humbuckers.

The Firebird had one fundamental problem and that was Fender's Jazzmaster. Although Leo Fender had not patented the body designs of the Telecaster, Stratocaster or Precision Bass (the three models that formed the foundation of the company's success), he was granted a patent for the Jazzmaster in 1959, a year after the model's introduction. It was a typical design patent in that it consisted of drawings and a general claim to "the ornamental design for an electric guitar, substantially as shown and described." It mentioned no specific elements of the design, but the drawing clearly showed an asymmetrical body with "offset" body waists, a design that would make the guitar a little more comfortable to play when sitting down. It was a small distinction, but virtually every solidbody electric guitar – not only Fender's but even Ted McCarty's bizarre Explorer – had body waists that lined up. The Gibson Firebird's odd body shape makes it difficult to tell whether its waists line up or are offset, but Leo Fender thought they were offset and let Gibson know it.

McCarty honored Fender's wishes and redesigned the Firebirds. The new version, which began replacing the originals in 1965, had none of the angular flair of the Dietrich designs. The neck-thru-body design was abandoned for a conventional glued in neck, and the body appeared to have been pushed into a more squat, rounded shape. The bass-side horn was now longer than the treble-side horn – another element that returned to conventional design standards – and, yes, the waists lined up with each other. In the process, the Firebird's unique poleless mini-humbuckers were lost on models I and III, replaced with P-90s. These new Firebirds became known as the non-reverse models, and they quickly faded from sales reports.

By the mid 1960s, Ted McCarty had nothing left to prove at Gibson, and the job was beginning to wear on him. His personal relationship with Les Paul (as well as the company's relationship with Paul) had deteriorated and ended. Despite record production of over 100,000 instruments in 1965 (including the Epiphones that were made in the Kalmazoo plant), the corporate office was harder than ever to deal with. CMI's expansion, particularly its expansion plans for its Lowry Organ division, had taxed its solid, income-producing divisions. On the accounting books, Gibson had always sold instruments to CMI at 33 percent of list price, and CMI then sold to distributors at a standard wholesale price. Now, M.H. Berlin was squeezing Gibson down to a price of only 25 per cent of list.

McCarty had had a relationship with Paul Bigsby, the California maker of vibrola tailpieces and occasional solidbody guitars, since the early 1950s. It was McCarty who suggested and furnished the design for a rotating arm for the Bigsby vibrola. By 1965, Bigsby was ready to get out of the vibrola business, and he offered to sell it to McCarty. McCarty bought the company and asked his second in command, John Huis, who had worked for Gibson since the 1930s, if Huis would be interested in going into business together. Huis agreed without even knowing what business he would be in. He immediately resigned from Gibson to oversee the moving of Bigsby from California to Kalamazoo. It was a conflict of interest for McCarty, although Gibson was not a big customer of Bigsby, having developed its own vibrato units. As McCarty knew it would, his purchase of Bigsby drew the ire of M.H. Berlin, and he parted ways with Gibson in 1966.

McCarty continued to make Bigsby vibrola tailpieces to the guitar industry. (He also bought the Flex-Lite company which made flexible-neck flashlights that were popular with fishermen and hunters.) His only ties to Gibson were as a vendor, but he became associated with Gibson competitor Paul Reed Smith, first as a consultant and eventually with a signature model. His reign at Gibson was quickly recognized as a Golden Era, and he enjoyed the respect and attention of the guitar world right up to his death in 2001 at age 91. Gibson CEO Henry Juszkiewicz, who had not been pleased by McCarty's association with PRS, paid his respects to McCarty in an official statement: "Ted McCarty was the architect of a golden period in Gibson's history," Juszkiewicz said. "During his 18-year tenure, he helped to reestablish the company's historic leadership in the industry through a

More signatures required

In 1964, Trini Lopez became Gibson's first non-jazz signature artist. His Trini Lopez Standard featured a thin ES-335 double-cut archtop with rounded horns, diamond-shaped soundholes and six-on-one-side tuners. A full-bodied Deluxe model was the one Trini himself played (right). Gibson also signed up jazz great Tal Farlow, whose signature model (below) was based on his personal ES-350.

◁ 1964 Tal Farlow model

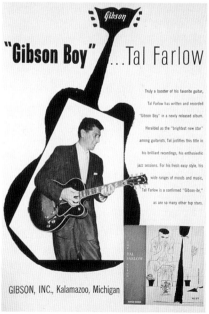

◁ 1961 Barney Kessell Custom

A former guitarist for the Chico Marx band, Barney Kessel (left) brought Gibson not just his heavily Charlie Christian-influenced jazz chops but also a cool new archtop design in 1961 – a full-depth, double-cutaway hollowbody with pointed horns, available with Regular or Custom (left) ornamentation. Kessel went on to become one of the most in-demand and most-recorded jazz guitarists of all time, playing on hundreds of records and film soundtracks over the next 40 years. Kessel advocates included Bryan MacLean, songwriter and rhythm guitarist with '60s psychedelic rockers, Love (below).

number of musical innovations that still resonate today. Gibson mourns the loss of one of its great leaders, and will fondly remember Ted as a member of the Gibson family."

The Ted McCarty era, from 1948–66, was more than a Golden Era for Gibson. It was an act that no one has yet to follow. Gibson would continue to try to advance the electric guitar after McCarty left, with new pickups, solid-state electronics, new body styles and even digital electronics. But the electric models that are the foundation of Gibson's success today – the Les Paul, SG, Firebird, Explorer, Flying V, and ES-335 – are all McCarty models. With the exception of the "solidbody acoustic" design that Chet Atkins would bring to Gibson in 1982, not a single new model developed and introduced by Gibson since McCarty would be successful.

The Golden Era for Gibson electrics may have ended with Ted McCarty's departure, but the story was just beginning to get interesting. The challenges ahead for Gibson – cheap imports, technological advances in general and electronic keyboards specifically – would be broader and more threatening than those McCarty faced. Not only was the future of Gibson shaky, the future of the electric guitar itself was in jeopardy.

McCarty had essentially given M.H. Berlin a year's notice but, when McCarty left, Berlin replaced him with an accountant. It's unlikely that Berlin or anyone else in the instrument business remembered back 42 years to the appointment of Guy Hart (the man McCarty had replaced) to the position of general manager, but the situations were similar. In 1923, the strong, charismatic, founding partner Lewis Williams left Gibson, followed by acoustic engineer Lloyd Loar a year later. Hart, a conservative caretaker type, took over and rebuilt the company. Unfortunately, history did not repeat itself in 1966. An accountant was not the solution, as sales began to fall from the peak McCarty had reached in his last full year. Within a year Berlin went looking for an experienced executive. He found one in Stan Rendell, a production specialist who had started his career in the radio business and, since 1963, had been CMI's vice president of manufacturing.

Rendell faced a serious problem everywhere he turned: production efficiency, product quality and a fickle market. On the line, the steelworkers union, which had organized Gibson's workforce during World War II, had become so powerful that it seemed as if the union, not the company, controlled production. Although Rendell couldn't force out the union, he did move non-guitar production – amplifiers and strings – out of Kalamazoo to a separate facility in the Chicago area, so that the remaining jobs were more closely related.

As typically happens in times of booming production, Gibson was taking shortcuts to achieve production goals, such as using wood that had not been dried long enough. In the case of the ES-335, with its three-ply laminated body, the trapped moisture caused the finish to check before the guitars left the factory. Gibson had been covering up the problem with a Sparkling Burgundy metallic finish. Rendell identified the problem and bought kilns to properly dry the wood.

Predicting what guitar players would buy was a more difficult problem, and Rendell dumped that task on CMI's sales department. Up until that time, Gibson had decided what guitars to make, and then it was CMI's task to sell them. Under Rendell, CMI had to deliver purchase orders to Gibson or Gibson would not make any instruments. While that move may have absolved Rendell of responsibility for unsold instruments, it could only made things worse in the long run by putting more control in the corporate office.

The record production year of 1965 was based largely on a surge in acoustic guitar sales as a result of the folk music boom. Sales slipped in 1966, and it didn't take an industry insider to look at the popular music scene and see that the immediate future did not look so good for Gibson electrics. The company's biggest signature artist, Trini Lopez, turned out to be a flash in the pan; his hits stopped and his movie career fizzled by the end of the decade. Gibson's only other truly popular signature artists, the Everly Brothers, who endorsed an acoustic flat-top, had enlisted in the U.S. Marine Corps just before the arrival of The Beatles, and their career never recovered.

The Beatles had arrived in 1964, giving a boost of credibility to Gretsch, Rickenbacker, and Hofner, which were the instruments played by George Harrison, John Lennon and Paul McCartney, respectively. Since 1962, Lennon and Harrison had actually used a Gibson electric model prominently on numerous records, but that guitar was a J-160E, the dreadnought-sized acoustic flat-top with a built-in pickup. Their J-160Es were heard primarily in acoustic mode and weren't seen by the public to any significant degree until Lennon and wife Yoko Ono's second bed-in for peace in Montreal in 1969, by which time Lennon had stripped the finish and drawn pictures of himself and Yoko on the guitar. Harrison played an SG Standard briefly in 1966, and he, Lennon, and Harrison all played Epiphone Casinos, which were made by Gibson, and millions of Americans saw McCartney with his Epiphone Texan acoustic performing 'Yesterday' on the Ed Sullivan show, so the Gibson company – but not so much the Gibson brand – benefited from The Beatles.

The only other band that rivaled The Beatles in the mid 1960s was The Rolling Stones, and the enduring image of the Stones from that era features blond-haired Brian Jones with his white Vox guitar. The Stones' Keith Richards was most often pictured in the early years playing Sunburst Epi Casinos (single and double pickup versions). The two guitarists changed instruments often, and they often played Gibsons, with Jones playing an original-style reverse-body Firebird and later a non-reverse version, and Richards playing a Sunburst Les Paul Standard (with a Bigsby vibrola) and a black Les Paul Custom. The problem for Gibson was, except for non-reverse Firebird, Gibson did not make those models anymore.

A quick look around at the new wave of rock stars confirmed that the discontinued-Gibson syndrome was widespread by the late 1960s. Mike

Fire in the air

△ 1961 Firebird I reverse body

The Firebird I (above) was the least expensive in a family of four new models created in 1963 by famed automotive designer Ray Dietrich. In contrast to the classic stylings of his cars, Dietrich's guitars went head-on against conventional design with reversed body shape and headstock shape. He also specified neck-through-body construction to eliminate the standard glued neck/body joint. Even in the Firebird's second version, with a less radical "non-reverse" body shape (top), it still made a strong, anti-establishment statement that appealed to rebellious rock 'n' roll guitarists such as Brian Jones of The Rolling Stones (above). A pair of basses – the Thunderbird II (with one pickup) and Thunderbird IV (two pickups) – complemented the guitar range.

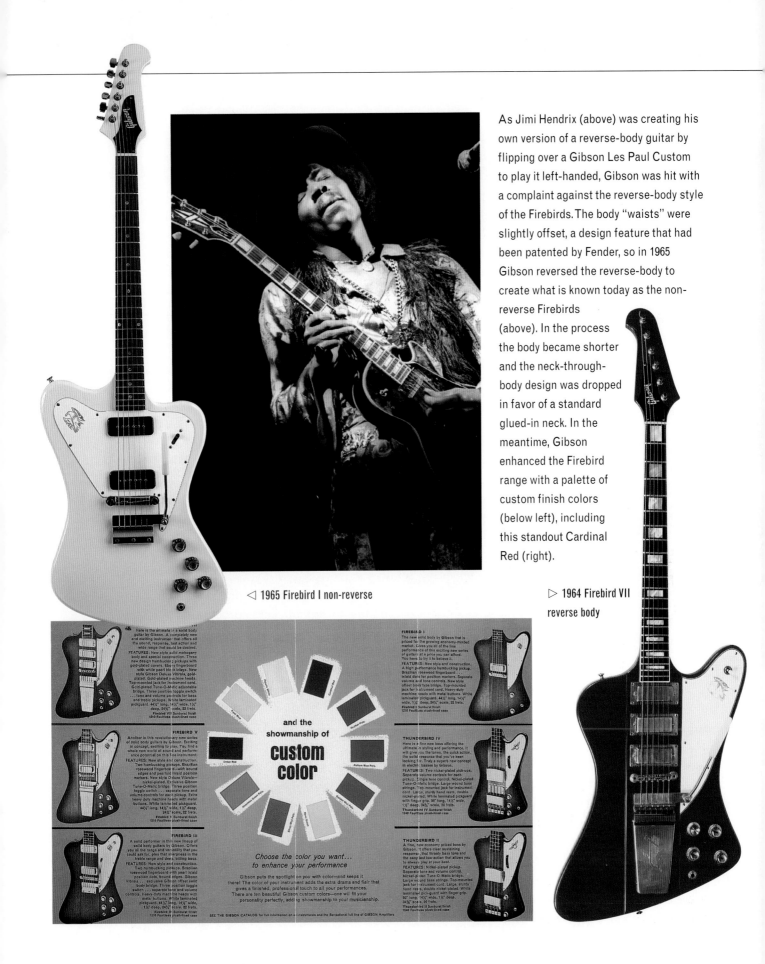

As Jimi Hendrix (above) was creating his own version of a reverse-body guitar by flipping over a Gibson Les Paul Custom to play it left-handed, Gibson was hit with a complaint against the reverse-body style of the Firebirds. The body "waists" were slightly offset, a design feature that had been patented by Fender, so in 1965 Gibson reversed the reverse-body to create what is known today as the non-reverse Firebirds (above). In the process the body became shorter and the neck-through-body design was dropped in favor of a standard glued-in neck. In the meantime, Gibson enhanced the Firebird range with a palette of custom finish colors (below left), including this standout Cardinal Red (right).

◁ 1965 Firebird I non-reverse

▷ 1964 Firebird VII reverse body

Bloomfield, a white Chicago-based blues guitarist, had brought blues to rock 'n' roll, using first a Fender Telecaster, then a gold-top Gibson Les Paul with P-90 pickups, then a Les Paul Standard with humbuckers. In England, a succession of guitarists emerged from the Yardbirds group and further established this new, blues-based rock guitar style for the coming generation of guitarists. Eric Clapton, Jeff Beck, and Jimmy Page all played Les Paul Standards with humbuckers. Yes, Gibson guitars were driving the music that would dominate the remainder of the century, but the sad truth was, Gibson no longer made any of those models.

A new model in 1968 suggested that Rendell's purchase-order system truly put the responsibility on someone in the Chicago office, specifically someone who was a fan of Mike Bloomfield during his gold-top Les Paul period, because that's what Gibson brought back. The new Les Paul of 1968 featured not only the gold-top finish but also the soapbar P-90 pickups of the 1952–56 models. Curiously, at the same time, Gibson did reintroduce the right version of the Les Paul Custom – not the 1954–57 version with the Alnico V and P-90 pickups but the later two-humbucker version.

Although someone – if not everyone – at Gibson quickly realized that the P-90 was the wrong version of the Les Paul to reintroduce, the company's next move made sense only in a manufacturing context. By the end of 1969, Gibson replaced the P-90s with humbuckers, all right, but they were the mini-humbucking pickups that Gibson relegated to Epiphones (and in the poleless configuration, to Firebirds); they were one of the features that kept the Epiphone models at a level of prestige slightly below the Gibson models. There was a simple, practical explanation as to why they would suddenly appear on a Gibson: They fit the hole for a P-90. Gibson had already routed out a supply of Les Paul bodies for P-90s, and when the order came to change to humbuckers, production manager Jim Deurloo noticed that the mini-humbuckers would fit the P-90 routings, so the requirement could be fulfilled – at least in a technical sense, since the mini-humbucker was technically a humbucking pickup – without re-routing the bodies. In addition to the already-routed bodies, there may well have been a surplus of mini-humbuckers since Epi production had fallen to the point that the production was about to be moved overseas. The Les Paul suddenly became in essence a "buildout" model, designed to use up overstocked parts. Although it was a step down from a Les Paul Standard, Gibson used a classic marketing ploy and presented it as a step up by calling it the Les Paul Deluxe.

By the end of 1969, Led Zeppelin had hit with 'Whole Lotta Love' featuring Jimmy Page laying the groundwork for heavy metal guitar on his vintage Sunburst Les Paul Standard. On the more populist side, Creedence Clearwater Revival were having hit after hit, beginning with 'Proud Mary' in early 1969, with leader John Fogerty playing not only an electric rhythm part but also some very accessible solos on an older Sunburst Les Paul Standard. No Les Pauls had ever had mini-humbuckers before that time, and there was certainly no demand from players for the minis – or even gold-tops, for that matter. The Les Paul Deluxe, with gold top finish and mini-humbuckers, illustrated how production efficiency in Kalamazoo was taking priority over the demands of the marketplace. Gibson still was not making the guitars that rock stars were playing.

The Les Paul Deluxe sported several new construction features. The body, which had always been a single piece of mahogany with a maple top cap, was now four pieces. The mahogany piece appeared to have been sliced in half with a thin maple laminate inserted, which made for more efficient use of wood supplies. Another change occurred across the entire Gibson line – the one-piece neck was replaced with a three-piece neck, which was maple on Les Pauls. A year later, in 1970, a volute was added to the back of the headstock where it joined the neck. Although the neck changes made for a stronger neck, and the "sandwich body," as it came to be known, did not affect the guitar's performance, these were changes to tradition that would eventually be perceived as signs of an undesirable era in Gibson history.

Shipping totals from 1969 and the early 1970s should have been a signal that something was wrong with the Les Paul Deluxe. Yes, it was selling well enough to qualify as a success, with steady growth to a peak of 10,000 units in 1973. But the Custom was keeping pace, topping 8,000 units in 1973. Historically, when the difference had been primarily in ornamentation, the Standard had outsold the Custom by more than two-to-one. Now, a higher percentage of players were willing to pay the extra price for a Custom in order to get the full-size humbuckers. More and more influential guitarists were showing up with vintage Les Pauls, including Duane Allman and Dickey Betts of The Allman Brothers Band (who first hit the charts in 1971) and Billy Gibbons of Z.Z. Top (debuting on the charts in 1972). The only prominent guitarist to play the Deluxe was the Who's Pete Townshend, who started playing them around 1971 and used a series of them that he modified and numbered. Although the original P-90-routed bodies that gave rise to the Deluxe had long since been used up, Gibson stayed with the Deluxe.

With the return of Les Paul models, Les Paul himself returned with a presence and influence on guitar design that hadn't been there since the first Les Paul in 1952. This time around, Paul took a hands-on role in design, and his personal preferences were manifest in two new models in 1969, the Les Paul Personal and Les Paul Professional. They had the familiar single-cutaway body shape of the originals, although they were an inch wider and almost an inch longer, and they had identifiable trimmings from the original line, such as block fingerboard inlays and split-diamond peghead inlay on the Personal, and trapezoid inlays on the Professional. The biggest differences were in the electronics, however. Paul had always preferred low impedance pickups, so that he could plug his guitar directly into a mixing board in a recording studio. He also loaded his new models with extra features, such as a microphone mount on the Personal and a pickup phase control on the Professional.

Welcome back, Les

▷ 1970 Les Paul Deluxe

Sell Kalamazoo to a beginner buying his first guitar and amplifier.

It could keep him from buying his second from somebody else.

By the late 1960s a new wave of influential blues-rock guitarists, among them Jeff Beck (below), were playing the single-cutaway, carved-top Les Paul models that hadn't been offered since 1960. In 1968, Gibson brought back the Les Paul, but with single-coil P-90 pickups (opposite, bottom). Players wanted humbuckers, so Gibson created the Les Paul Deluxe (left), which was fitted with mini-humbuckers because the bodies had already been routed for P-90s. In the meantime Charlie Whitney of Family (opposite) popularized Gibson's doubleneck EDS-1275, and Gibson counter-attacked the influx of cheap Japanese imports by reviving its pre-World War II budget brand – Kalamazoo (above).

THE GIBSON ELECTRIC GUITAR BOOK

L-5 CES

The inherent quality, versatility, and rich, impressive appearance of the L-5 CES have won acclaim from the most discriminating artists. Guitarists everywhere praise the slim, comfortable neck, the fast, easy-playing action and quick response. A beautiful modern deep cutaway guitar with hand-graduated, carved top of select close-grained spruce, arched back of highly figured curly maple with matching rims . . . white-and-black ivoroid binding, stunning pearl-inlaid peghead, gold-plated metal parts, and deluxe individual machine heads.

- Slim, fast, low-action neck joins body at 14th fret
- Three-piece curly maple neck, adjustable truss rod
- Ebony fingerboard, pearl block inlays
- Adjustable Tune-O-Matic bridge
- Exclusive L-5 adjustable tailpiece
- Twin, powerful humbucking pickups with separate tone and volume controls which can be preset . . .
- Three-position toggle switch to activate either or both pickups

17" wide, 21" long, 3⅜" deep . . . 25½" scale, 20 frets

L-5 CESN Natural finish
L-5 CES Sunburst finish
600 Faultless plush-lined case
ZC-6 Deluxe zipper case cover

ES-175D

The Florentine cutaway design provides easy access to the entire fret range. Easy to play and comfortable to hold, it produces a brilliant distortion-free tone. Beautiful arched top and back of select maple with matching rims, black-and-white ivoroid binding, exclusive tailpiece, nickel-plated metal parts, and individual machine heads with deluxe buttons.

- Slim, fast, low-action neck joins body at 14th fret
- One-piece mahogany neck, adjustable truss rod
- Rosewood fingerboard, pearl inlays
- Adjustable rosewood bridge
- Twin, powerful humbucking pickups with separate tone and volume controls which can be pre-set (double pickup models)
- Toggle switch activates either or both pickups on double pickup models

16¼" wide, 20¼" long, 3⅜" deep . . . 24¾" scale, 20 frets

Double Pickup Model
ES-175DN Natural finish
ES-175D Sunburst finish

Single Pickup Model
ES-175 Sunburst finish
515 Faultless plush-lined case
303 Archcraft plush-lined case
103 Durabilt case
ZC-5 Deluxe zipper case cover

ES-125

The unusual all-around performance, appearance, and value of the Gibson ES-125 has made it one of Gibson's most popular models. Only the best in parts and workmanship are used in this outstanding instrument. Made with arched top and back of select maple, mahogany rims with ivoroid binding, and nickel-plated metal parts.

- Slim, fast, low-action neck joins body at 14th fret
- One-piece mahogany neck, adjustable truss rod
- Rosewood fingerboard, pearl dot inlays
- Adjustable rosewood bridge
- Powerful pickup with individually adjustable polepieces
- Separate tone and volume controls
- Full body size

16½" wide, 20¼" long, 3⅜" deep . . . 24¾" scale, 20 frets

ES-125 Sunburst finish
515 Faultless, plush-lined case
303 Archcraft plush-lined case
103 Durabilt case

L-5 CES   ES-175 D   ES-125

◁ 1968 Les Paul gold top

◁ 1968 Les Paul Custom

The recording convenience that low-impedance pickups provided turned out to be a benefit that guitarists did not want. Most guitarists considered their amplifier to be a vital part of their sound, and in a recording situation, they plugged into the amp and put a microphone on it. They didn't want the "pure" signal of a guitar plugged directly into a mixing board, nor did they want a mount for a vocal mic on their guitar. After two years of slow sales of the Les Paul Personal and Professional, Gibson rolled them into a single model and renamed it the Les Paul Recording. It still had some of Les Paul's gimmickry, including the phase control and a 10-position "decade" tone control that warranted its own instruction book, listing settings for various popular tones. Most important to a working musician, it had a built-in transformer so a player could choose high- or low-impedance output. The Les Paul Recording was far from the most popular Les Paul, never topping 2,000 a year in sales, but it lasted through the 1970s.

Les Paul took advantage of his new status as a Gibson guitar designer and offered his ideas for semi-hollowbody and flat-top electrics as well. His faith that the low-impedance pickup worked in any type of guitar was manifest in the Les Paul Jumbo of 1969, a dreadnought-size cutaway flat-top with a low-impedance pickup installed between the fingerboard and the soundhole. Paul has said that he wanted the pickup hidden in the fingerboard, and that Gibson actually made some prototypes that way, although the pickup was so wide that it couldn't possibly have fit the way Paul envisioned it. Placed at the end of the fingerboard, however, the pickup was also so large that the soundhole had to be moved closer to the bridge. It simply wasn't a workable design, not to mention the fact that it was a type of guitar – a flat-top acoustic – that Les Paul had never played at any time in his 25-year professional career, and it only lasted to 1973.

The Les Paul Signature, introduced in 1973 was Paul's version of an ES-335, and it was more successful than the Jumbo. The asymmetrical double-cutaway body had a rounded upper bass horn like the 335, but the treble side cutaway was more pointed like a Les Paul Standard. Inside, Paul has said that he intended for it to have neck-through body construction (although that would have been difficult to engineer on a guitar with an arched top); it ended up with only a T-shaped center block. The Signature had Paul's signature electronics: low-impedance pickups (with two jacks for low or high-impedance output) and the in/out phase control. The body had Paul's signature finish color: gold. But neither the Les Paul Signature guitar nor its bass counterpart lasted very long – 1977 was the last year for the guitar, 1979 for the bass – although the bass became a favorite of Jefferson Airplane's Jack Casady, and it was successfully reintroduced in the 1990s under the Epiphone brand as Casady's signature model.

The Les Paul Standard was not the only late-1950s model that Gibson revived in the late 1960s. The Flying V had originally been made in such small numbers for such a short time, it's a wonder anyone remembered it. Its only notoriety came in 1963 when Lonnie Mack used a 1958 Flying with a custom-installed Bigsby vibrola to serve up the fiery tones of 'Memphis,' his hit instrumental version of the Chuck Berry classic. Gibson brought the V back in late 1965 in a more production-friendly version, with the three knobs mounted on a pickguard that covered a routed cavity (the original configuration required a "shotgun" rout from the jack to the neck pickup cavity). The body was mahogany rather than the original Korina wood, and the headstock was a little stubbier, but it was still radical enough to fit the personality and music of a guitarist such as Jimi Hendrix. Hendrix had three of them: a 1967 that he painted in a paisley pattern, a 1969 that remained in its original Sunburst finish, and another 1969 that was custom made for him with black finish, Trini Lopez-style split-diamond fingerboard inlays, and left-handed setup. While Hendrix was destroying Fender Stratocasters onstage and setting them on fire, as he did at the Monterey and Miami pop festivals, he seemed to have more respect for his Gibsons. He was playing his custom lefty Flying V onstage at the Isle of Wight Festival, his last filmed performance, three months before his death in 1970.

Despite Rendell's efforts to improve production and the increasing number of rock guitarists playing Gibsons, the numbers didn't lie. And the numbers looked bad as the 1960s came to an end. Under McCarty, Gibson had grown by leaps and bounds through the first half of the 1960s. Shipments from the Kalamazoo plant (including Epiphone models) were 35,000 in 1961, then 40,000 in 1962, 54,000 in 1963, 93,000 in 1964, and topped at 102,000 in 1965. In 1966, the year McCarty left, shipments fell to 83,000. By the last year of the decade the total was down to 59,000 instruments.

Not everything was down. The Super 400CES surged at the end of the decade. The Johnny Smith remained strong, as did Byrdland and L-5CES. The upper models in the SG line – the SG Standard and Custom – also rose in the late 1960s, possibly a result of Eric Clapton's widely seen use of an SG Standard with Cream in 1968 and Hendrix's appearance on *The Dick Cavett Show* in 1969 with a white SG Custom. But sales of midline models such as the ES-335, ES-330, and ES-125 steadily declined. And the low-end models – the ones that paid the bills – went into a power dive. For example, Gibson shipped 3,570 SG Juniors in 1965 but only 751 in 1969. At the entry level, the situation was even worse: almost 11,000 Melody Makers shipped in 1965 but not even 1,000 in 1969.

Almost half of the shortfall could be attributed to Epiphone, whose shipments fell by more than 85 per cent from 1965 to 1969, clearly the victim of cheaper guitars that had begun to flow from Japan. But even with Epiphone removed from the totals, Gibson-brand shipments were down 24 per cent from mid decade. The crunch was felt at CMI, where M.H. Berlin, possibly looking too far ahead to the coming era of electronic keyboards, had invested heavily in a new factory for Lowry organs. Consequently, CMI's stock price was depressed, making the company a sitting duck for a takeover.

The takeover move came from the most unlikely of places – Ecuador. ECL,

A personal touch

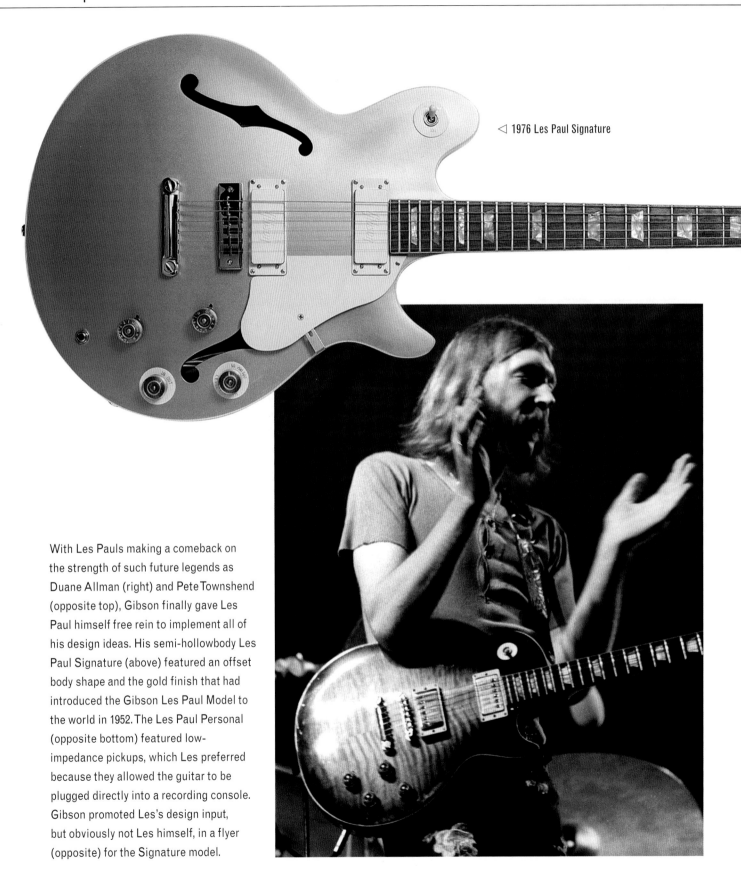

◁ 1976 Les Paul Signature

With Les Pauls making a comeback on
the strength of such future legends as
Duane Allman (right) and Pete Townshend
(opposite top), Gibson finally gave Les
Paul himself free rein to implement all of
his design ideas. His semi-hollowbody Les
Paul Signature (above) featured an offset
body shape and the gold finish that had
introduced the Gibson Les Paul Model to
the world in 1952. The Les Paul Personal
(opposite bottom) featured low-
impedance pickups, which Les preferred
because they allowed the guitar to be
plugged directly into a recording console.
Gibson promoted Les's design input,
but obviously not Les himself, in a flyer
(opposite) for the Signature model.

THE GIBSON ELECTRIC GUITAR BOOK

◁ 1969 Les Paul Personal

which stood for Ecuador Company Ltd., had started in the railroad business and by the 1960s was also known for making concrete and beer. Norton Stevens, son of the founder, was looking to invest in a North American company, and CMI gave him the opportunity. At the end of 1969, ECL bought CMI and moved headquarters to Chicago. Stevens combined "Norton" with "Berlin" and came up with Norlin as the name for the new company.

The incongruity of a beer and cement outfit creating the instruments that shaped America's musical culture was evident in the Gibson guitar models of the early 1970s. SGs. Inspired presumably by the questionable success of the Les Paul Deluxe, Norlin discontinued the SG Standard in 1971 and replaced it with the SG Deluxe. It featured a cruder SG body, with unbeveled edges in the cutaways, along with the wing-shaped pickguard of a Les Paul, controls on a semi-circularly plate and a Bigsby vibrola as standard equipment. Norlin quickly discovered that there was no magic in the Deluxe name and, by late, 1972 it was replaced by a new SG Standard, this one stripped down a bit with an unbound fingerboard, small rectangular pearloid fingerboard inlays and, after a few months of production, black plastic-covered humbuckers. It would struggle along with that configuration through 1980.

The SG Custom made it through the transition almost intact. Its white finish (though thickly applied and prone to deep finish checking) had been replaced by the plain brown "walnut" stain by 1969. For a brief moment in 1972, it got the wing-shaped pickguard of a Les Paul, along with a semi-circular control plate, but it returned quickly to its original configuration, and Norlin left it alone until discontinuing it after 1979.

The SG Junior and Special bit the dust immediately after the Norlin takeover. A two-P-90 SG reappeared in 1971 as the SG Pro, which was essentially the same as the Special but with a semi-circular control plate and wing-shaped pickguard. It gave way a year later to a new SG Special with black plastic covers on mini-humbucking pickups, and that version was shipped to the end of the decade.

Meanwhile the Melody Maker series, the least expensive of the solidbodies, gained the SG model name but, with ever-changing specs, they had no clear identity. In 1971, they were the SG-100 (one pickup), SG-200 (two pickups), and SG-250 (same as SG-200 but with Sunburst finish). They were specified with an oblong, black plastic-covered pickup but some were made with P-90s. By the end of 1972 they were the SG-1, SG-II and SG-III with black-covered mini-humbuckers. Gibson listed them only through 1973 but apparently overproduced them so that they were still shipping as late as 1979.

From today's perspective, with late-1950s-style Les Pauls the lifeblood of the Gibson company, it's hard to see why there was any confusion about what guitarists wanted in the early 1970s. They were buying up old Les Paul Standards. Why would Gibson not admit it and make a Les Paul Standard again? One possible explanation is that the 1950s Les Pauls (and early-1960s SGs, too) were perceived in the early 1970s as dated – not cool and not superior to the newer models, just yesterday's news. However, the reintroduction of the humbucker version of the Les Paul Custom concurrent with the gold-top, P-90-equipped Standard pokes a hole in that theory. Regardless of the reason, Gibson's only concession to the obvious demand was to change the finish on the Deluxe from gold-top to Cherry Sunburst in 1971. As demand continued to grow, Gibson did start making Standards and selling them "under the table." There are plenty of Les Pauls from 1972–75 with full-size humbuckers and "Standard" on the truss-rod cover, and they're even listed in shipping totals – 2,218 in 1974. Dealers were ordering them, and Gibson was making them, but still not listing them. Finally in late 1975, the Standard returned officially, although surprisingly the Deluxe continued.

With the Les Paul Custom and Standard re-established, the obvious move would be to bring back original versions of the lower-priced models, the Special and Junior. Again, Gibson's actions defy explanation. The Les Paul Junior, which in the 1950s had outsold the other three models put together, was never produced in the Norlin era. The Special did come back but not without some false starts. A single-cutaway version was made briefly around 1972, leaving no trail in company literature, but there is evidence of its existence in the guitar that reggae legend Bob Marley played for years. The Les Paul 55, introduced in 1974, was a single-cutaway Special in every way except that it said "Les Paul Model" rather than "Les Paul Special" on the headstock, and it lasted through 1980. In 1976, the double-cutaway version reappeared in a limited edition as the Special Double Cutaway, although it, too, said "Les Paul Model" on the headstock, and it continued as a regular production model.

Despite Norlin's apparent confusion, Gibson's sales did grow a bit in the early 1970s, giving Norlin the confidence to expand Gibson production. The trend among many businesses at the time was to build in the south, where labor was cheaper and labor unions were not strong. Nashville, in addition to being located in a right-to-work state, was centrally located with three interstate highways that offered easy distribution to the eastern, southern and Midwestern states. Norlin bought a piece of land in an industrial development near the airport and broke ground in 1974, but it was 1976 before the first Les Paul Deluxes and Les Paul Customs came off the line. The plant was intended to make the solidbody L-6S guitar and L-9 bass, too, but in an ominous sign of the future for guitarmakers, by the time the plant went online the production requirement was only half of the plant's capacity, and part of the workforce was assigned the task of assembling Pearl drums.

Through the first few years of the 1970s, Norlin's constant changing of Gibson models yielded a sense of disorganization that was reflected in the Gibson "catalog," which didn't actually exist as a single volume but consisted of separate pamphlets for each model line. In 1975 Gibson seemed to regroup, reorganize, and gather all its forces in an attempt to upgrade the brand's image and recapture its

Special guitars, special music

While Gibson Les Paul Standards were defining and dominating mainstream rock and roll, innovative and adventuresome artists found their creative voices with other Gibson models. In Jamaica, Bob Marley (right) used a Les Paul Special to provide a pointed rhythmic punctuation that identified reggae music. Meanwhile in southern California, Frank Zappa (opposite) also found the single-coil pickups of a Special – in his case an SG Special – to be the right vehicle for his experiments on the borders of rock, jazz and classical music.

◁ 1968 Les Paul Custom

THE GIBSON ELECTRIC GUITAR BOOK

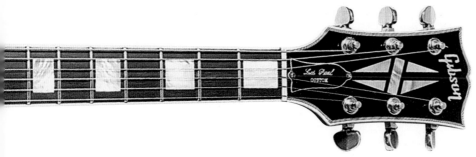

Even though the original Les Paul Model sported the rich look of a gold finish, the Custom (left) was always the epitome of elegance in the Les Paul range. The tuxedo-black finish, specified by Les himself, set off the gold-plated hardware and mother-of-pearl inlays, inspiring the nickname "Black Beauty." Low frets – another of Les's specifications, tailored to his lightning-fast playing style – made for a fast neck and inspired yet another nickname, "The Fretless Wonder."

former glory. A huge catalog presented a trimmed-down model line in high style, with an embossed vinyl cover and thick pages. Full-page images of artists playing Gibsons led off each of the model sections (which were also published in 8.5-inch x 11-inch size as individual pamphlets), and they featured such luminaries as B.B. King playing an ES-355 and Carlos Santana playing an L-6S.

In mid decade Gibson indeed looked once again like a classy company. The L-5S (S for solidbody) had been introduced in 1972 as an upscale solidbody, trading on the reputation of the Style 5 designation just as the ES-5 and L-5CES had done at the beginning of the Ted McCarty era. The L-5S was 16 inches wide and featured a maple top cap, although most had three pieces of maple rather than the book-matched two-piece top of the classic Sunburst Les Paul Standard. Ornamentation was typical L-5, with pearl block fingerboard inlays, flowerpot peghead inlay and gold-plated hardware. It started out with Les Paul's beloved low-impedance pickups but switched to humbuckers in 1974.

In the middle of the solidbody line, the L-6S had introduced a thin, single-cutaway body of solid maple in late 1973. In that sense, it was the realization of what Les Paul had wanted his guitar to be more than 20 years earlier, when he compromised with a maple top and lighter weight mahogany back. However, the designer behind the L-6S was not Les Paul but Bill Lawrence. Born Willi Lorenz Stich in Germany, Lawrence had started his career as a jazz guitarist and after moving to the U.S. gained a reputation for custom pickups. Gibson brought him aboard in 1972 to redesign the SG's electronics to offer more tonal possibilities, and he ended up with the L-6S as his personal project. His goal was a guitar that could sound like a Fender Telecaster or Stratocaster as well as a Gibson, and he added a rotary switch so that the player could achieve those sounds by putting the pickups out of phase or in parallel or series configuration. The model also featured his new "Super humbucker" pickups with ceramic magnets and distinctive five-sided covers.

The L-6S was an instant hit. With sales of over 5,000 in 1974, it ranked behind only the Les Paul Deluxe and Les Paul Custom. It was successful enough to spawn a second, less expensive model in 1975 – the L-6S Deluxe. At that time the original model became the L-6S Custom. As the offshoot model illustrated, "Deluxe" in Gibson terminology usually meant just the opposite. The L-6S Deluxe did not have the rotary selector switch but did have strings anchoring through the body, a unique feature on a Gibson.

Three more related models also appeared in 1975, and they introduced the bolt-on neck to Gibson. The Midnight Special had standard humbuckers. The Marauder had a humbucker and a single-coil blade pickup designed by Lawrence. The S-1 had three of Lawrence's single-coils. Latin-rock guitarist Carlos Santana was impressed enough with the L-6S that he dressed up in a dapper white suit and posed with the guitar for print ads and for the 1975 catalog. With Santana's help, all of these models lasted through the decade, which would turn out to be a long life span for a Norlin model.

On the hollowbody side, the Howard Roberts signature model appeared in 1974. This unique guitar – a cutaway hollowbody with a round soundhole – had been a highlight of the Epiphone line in the 1960s. Roberts was never a household name but as a top Los Angeles session player, he was still active and well-known in guitar circles.

The cream of the 1975 lineup was the Citation, the ultimate carved-top guitar. Conceived and originally introduced in 1969, it was now the showpiece that represented Gibson tradition. The 17-inch cutaway body was made with spectacularly figured maple. Pearl fleur-de-lis inlays adorned the headstock, the back of the headstock and the wooden pickguard. It came with one or two floating pickups.

A year later, the same degree of opulence carried over to the Les Paul Line with a model simply called The Les Paul, which was a study in maple and rosewood. Curly maple was the main them, on the back of the guitar as well as the top. Rosewood accents included the pickup covers, cavity coverplates, bindings and the center section of a three-piece ebony and rosewood fingerboard. The limited edition serial number was engraved into a small, oval mother-of-pearl medallion on the back of the peghead. And just in case The Les Paul didn't provide enough fancy ornamentation for Les Paul buyers, the Les Paul Artisan, also introduced in 1976, featured a fingerboard and peghead with the "hearts and flowers" inlay pattern previously reserved for classic Gibson banjos.

With the Citation, the Howard Roberts, The Les Paul, the L-5S, and the "right" Les Paul – the Standard – Gibson appeared to have regained a good sense of the guitar market and, more important, of the company's historic identity in the upper echelons of guitar makers. The line-up may have been strong, but the guitar market was weakening as popular music began abandoning the guitar for electronic keyboards.

The 1975 catalog was the last hurrah for Stan Rendell at the helm of Gibson. That year the corporate office appointed a financial analyst as executive vice president of Gibson and Rendell, the president, was ordered to report to his v.p. He balked and the order was rescinded, but the writing was on the wall, and he left Gibson to form his own string company in 1976. Norlin brought in Bob McRann, an executive from the record business, who lasted three years before being replaced by Marty Locke, a CMI veteran who had most recently run the Lowry organ division.

In 1976, the most encouraging sign for Gibson was the continuing interest in, and Gibson's reintroduction of, the Les Paul Standard. In reality, however, Gibson only went half the way. The real demand was for vintage-style Les Pauls, and dealers had to force Gibson to manufacture them. It started in 1974 when Chris Lovell, one of the owners of Strings and Things music store in Memphis, called Kalamazoo and custom-ordered some Les Pauls with late-1950s specifications, including a one-piece mahogany body, small headstock, uniform binding depth

When old is better than new

The S-1 (below) and L6-S (below left) represent Gibson's mistaken belief in the 1970s that new guitar designs would inherently be better than established models. German-born Bill Lawrence created thinner, maple solidbodies and armed them with pickups of his own design. The company enlisted the help of jazz guitarist Al DiMeola and rocker Ron Wood (then with The Faces), who even got his bandmate Rod Stewart to join him in an ad, but when the 1970s ended, so did most of Gibson's new models of the '70s. Although Gibson's financial condition fell steadily through the 1970s, the presence of Gibson guitars in rock 'n' roll remained strong, as many artists ignored the new models and stuck with the tried and true. Tony Iommi (below) powered the heavy metal sound

◁ 1976 S-1

of Black Sabbath with a left-handed SG. Mick Ronson (below) used what was fast becoming the rock 'n' roll standard – the Les Paul Standard – to enhance the music of David Bowie, Bob Dylan and Ian Hunter. And Stephen Stills (left) handled lead guitar work for Crosby, Stills, Nash & Young, as well as for his subsequent solo career, with a reverse-body Firebird I.

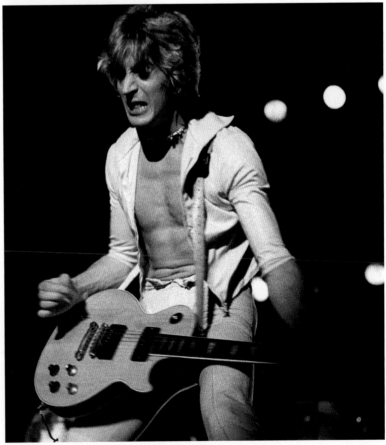

through the cutaway, a deeper "dish" in the top contour and, of course, humbucking pickups. (The Les Paul Deluxe and unofficial Standard at that time had the "pancake" three-piece mahogany back, a larger headstock than the originals, thicker binding through the cutaway and a flatter top contour.) Lovell also ordered the curliest-grain maple top available and, because Gibson's Cherry Sunburst finish had drifted so far off from that of a 1959 Les Paul, he ordered the guitars unfinished and applied the finish at his shop.

Strings and Things' orders were not voluminous – only 28 guitars from 1974–78 – but for an independent store in the pre-internet age, average sales of five or six units per year of a custom-ordered model were significant. Their initial order contributed heavily to Gibson's recognition of a demand for the older Les Paul Standard. It was the first step toward the past, as well as the future of the Gibson company.

In 1978, a second dealer began ordering Sunburst Les Pauls with vintage specs. Jimmy Wallace, a salesman at Arnold & Morgan in Dallas, visited the Kalamazoo plant and picked out the most highly figured maple tops from stock that Gibson had held back. He sold the first batch of guitars mostly to Japanese customers and then ordered more.

By this time regular-production Les Pauls were being made in the Nashville plant, so all the Kalamazoo plant could do was to produce a special run of 1,500 Les Pauls with flamed tops. The Les Paul Kalamazoo of 1979, identifiable by "KZ" on the truss-rod cover, had virtually no vintage specs except the flamed top, but it may have spurred the Nashville plant into developing a new Les Paul with more vintage specs. In analyzing the growing appeal for vintage Les Pauls, it was obvious that the headstock size, binding depth, carving pattern, wood grain and finish color made absolutely no difference in performance. The appeal of the originals was based on the pickups and, when Gibson engineer Tim Shaw looked into the 1950s pickups, literally, he found some fundamental differences. For starters, the current magnets were slightly smaller than the originals (the change had occurred in the early 1960s). That difference alone made the originals more powerful. The other difference was the coil wire. Gibson still used the same gauge (#42) but had switched from enamel-coated to polyurethane-coated, which had a different thickness, which resulted in a different number of "turns" around the bobbin, which produced a different output. Because poly-coated wire cost a dollar more per pound than enamel-coated, Shaw was not allowed to change the wire, but he did find the original spec for the number of turns. The spec was 5,000 turns, but when Shaw asked Seth Lover, the inventor of the humbucker, about it, Lover responded with his famous comment: "We wound them until they were full."

Gibson introduced its version of a Les Paul reissue in 1980, calling it the Les Paul Heritage 80. It was a good start, with curly top, smaller headstock, thin binding in the cutaway, nickel-plated parts and Shaw's improved retro pickup, but it still had some body dimensions that were different from the originals, and it still had the three-piece neck of the current regular production guitars. For a one-piece neck, guitarists had to buy the fancier Heritage 80 Elite or the even fancier Heritage 80 Award, but the Elite had an ebony fingerboard and the Award had gold-plated hardware, so it would appear that Gibson still did not fully grasp what guitar buyers were looking for.

Dealers did know what guitar buyers wanted. By 1982 Jimmy Wallace had opened his own store and was ordering reissues with more accurate specifications than the Heritage 80. Orders also began coming in from Leo's Music in Oakland, California, and Guitar Trader in Redbank, New Jersey. Legend has it that the Kalamazoo workers responded with their own model, the Les Paul Standard 82, which was essentially a Heritage 80 with a one-piece neck and a Kalamazoo pedigree. Not to be outdone, the story goes, the Nashville facility came up with an even better model in 1983 and called it the Les Paul Reissue. Although the sequence of models is correct, the rivalry between the plants is exaggerated, according to Jim Deurloo, who developed the production processes and bought the machinery for the Nashville plant, and had been the Kalamazoo plant manager since 1977. "They tried to run Nashville at capacity," he explained, "so anything that was an overage in requirement, then Kalamazoo would make them."

The Les Paul Reissue still wasn't all that faithful to the originals. It was not specifically a 1959 Reissue or a 1960 Reissue, and it wouldn't have the small headstock of the originals for another year. It did not stop the dealers from ordering their own models, but it was the first model to carry the model name of Reissue.

The attention garnered by vintage Les Pauls in the late 1970s carried over to another model family from the 1950s – the Korina Trio. Gibson had been making Flying Vs of one sort or another since the late 1960s, but they strayed even farther from the originals than the Les Pauls did. The Flying V II of 1981, for example, had a five-layer body with beveled edges and boomerang-shaped pickups. Another 1981 offering, the Flying V CMT, sported a curly maple top cap. The Explorer had been offered with a mahogany body from 1975–79 and then brought back as the Explorer I in 1981 with an alder body and a Kahler vibrato.

In late 1981, Gibson began reissuing the 1958-style Flying V and Explorer in Korina wood and also "reissued" the never-produced third member of the trio, the Moderne. The V and Moderne were called Heritage models and featured a 1950s-style inked-on serial number, although the number began with a letter rather than a numeral. The V continued as the Korina Flying V in 1983. The Explorer came in the opposite order, first called the Korina Explorer (with an eight-digit number), followed in 1983 by the Explorer Heritage, with an inked number with the numeral 1 as a prefix. Curiously, the Firebirds didn't get the same degree of attention – only a limited edition version of the Firebird V in 1972 and the not-so-vintage maple-body Firebird 76 of 1976 (and again in 1980).

The glory of The Paul

◁ 1979 Les Paul 25/50 Anniversary

Once Gibson recognized the power of the Les Paul in rock music, the company began to pay tribute in the form of highly ornamented variations on the basic theme. The Anniversary celebrated the 25th anniversary of the model and Les Paul's 50th anniversary in show business with a highly flamed top and Super 400-style inlays. The Artist featured active electronics. The Heritage 80 launched a succession of reissues of the 1959 Sunbursts. And The Les Paul was simply the ultimate Les Paul.

◁ 1979 Les Paul Artist

Gibson

THE GIBSON ELECTRIC GUITAR BOOK

As the Les Paul Standard was becoming a cultural icon, Angus Young (left) of AC/DC rocked hard with a different kind of Les Paul, one of the early-1960s SG-body Standards. It would become as closely identified with the Australian guitarist as his schoolboy short pants, and Gibson eventually made it Young's signature model. New York glam rocker Johnny Thunders (opposite bottom left) filled his needs with the most basic Les Paul, the single-pickup TV model.

▷ 1980 Les Paul Heritage Standard 80

◁ 1978 The Les Paul

While the demand for older Gibsons was growing, it wasn't growing fast enough to stop the sea change in popular music. Electronic keyboards were taking over. Two of the biggest artists of the era provided irrefutable proof. Bruce Springsteen had emerged in 1975 and was hailed as the future of rock 'n' roll, exemplified by the powerful guitar line of 'Born to Run'; but in 1984 most of the lead instrumental lines on his #1 album *Born in the USA* were played on a synthesizer. In the same period, Edward Van Halen revolutionized guitar playing with his finger-tapping heavy metal style, and the group Van Halen covered one of the all-time heaviest guitar licks with their 1978 hit 'You Really Got Me,' but in 1984, while Springsteen had the #1 album spot, Van Halen had the #1 single with the total pop-synth sound of 'Jump.' That was bad news for all guitar makers, but it was especially bad for Gibson, since Springsteen and Van Halen had never played Gibsons in the first place.

Gibson did not just sit back and accept falling sales. Drawing from Gibson history, which indicated that lower-priced models always outsold the fancier versions, Gibson's Nashville plant manager, Whitey Morrison, created a series of stripped-down models called The Paul, The SG, and the 335S. They featured the essentials – two humbucking pickups – on a thin solid body with no ornamentation and plain brown-stain finish. The lack of ornamentation extended to the peghead, which was routed for an inlaid pearl logo but with no pearl actually installed. It looked somewhat like the result of a hot branding iron, and these models were given an identity under the Firebrand banner.

Gibson also drew on Norlin's resources to keep Gibson up to date with technology. Norlin had acquired the Moog synthesizer company in 1973, and Moog engineers were tapped to design a circuit board for a line of Gibsons called "Artist" models. Unfortunately, the new active electronics were debuted on a new model shape called the RD (presumably for Research & Development). Gibson had just failed miserably with an engineered acoustic series, the Marks, and should have realized that engineering alone has never sold guitars. To make matters worse, the RD body looked and felt like a crude, klunky version of the reverse-body Firebird. A Gibson with a circuit board didn't appeal to guitarists, and those who did buy them found that when the circuitry failed (as it often did) it was irreparable. Gibson also offered Artist versions of the Les Paul, SG, and ES-335, but with no more success than the RD series.

Possibly the strongest evidence of Gibson's desperation started with the Sonex in 1980. It had the familiar, tried-and-true body shape of a Les Paul but the body consisted of a wood core with a molded resin outer layer that was much like particle board. Marketing the body a "Multi-Phonic" didn't help. The neck for the first two years of the model's existence was imported from Japan. Gibson had made inexpensive models before and would make more after the Sonex, but the Sonex had a quality – or lack thereof – that went beyond inexpensive. It was simply a cheap guitar.

The Challenger and Invader of 1983 expanded on the cheap theme. The Challenger was essentially a Les Paul with a bolt-on neck, a feature that had been associated with the less expensive Fender guitars for over 30 years. The Invader was a Les Paul without the Les Paul designation, which is to say, without the royalty payment to Les Paul.

The standard-bearers of Gibson today – the Les Pauls and SGs – must have seemed old and dated in the early 1980s, because Gibson tried anything and everything to establish a new model. The Victory models of 1981 had a thick, double-cutaway maple body with the horns coming to a point. Available with two or three non-traditional humbuckers, they only lasted through 1984. The Futura and Corvus models of 1982 featured neck-thru-body construction and bodies shaped like a medieval battle ax. The 1982 Spirit offered a double-cutaway body but with a carved top like the higher-end Les Pauls, which might have been a good idea, had the same model not been offered in the Epiphone line three years earlier as the Genesis (Japanese-made) and the Spirit (Kalamazoo-made).

Through the Norlin era, the hollow and semi-hollow electric lines were largely ignored. The low-end ES-125 had slowed in the late 1960s and Norlin didn't continue it in either its full-depth or thinline versions. The thinline, fully hollow models, such as the ES-330 were out of production by 1975. Late in 1969, the cutaways on the Byrdland, L-5CES and Super 400CES reverted from pointed back to rounded, and the backs reverted from laminated one-piece to solid two-piece, and they continued unmolested. The ES-350T, the 17-inch thinline model, was quietly reintroduced in 1977 with a long, 25½-inch scale length (the earlier version had had a 23½-inch scale). The ES-175 body was changed from laminated maple to laminated mahogany in 1983, an odd and virtually meaningless move.

Several offshoots of the ES-335 made brief appearances. The ES-340 (1969–73) had a master volume control and pickup mixer control. The ES-240 appeared briefly in 1977 with a coil tap switch, and that feature immediately became standard on the ES-335. The ES-Pro debuted in 1979 with a pair of the overwound Dirty Fingers humbuckers, stopbar tailpiece and dot fingerboard inlay. Although its pickups were hotter than the standard humbuckers, it looked more like the original 1958 version of the 335, with stopbar and dots rather than trapeze and small blocks (which the 335 had had since the early 1960s). The Pro gained enough attention in the midst of the Les Paul reissue activity that in 1981 Norlin retrofitted the ES-335 with vintage specs (including nickel-plated hardware) and renamed it the ES-335 DOT. Called the ES-335 Reissue since 1990, it is still in production today

Elsewhere in the semi-hollowbody family, the ES-345 continued with no significant changes until it got a stopbar tailpiece in 1982, just before being discontinued. A slightly upgraded version with a coil tap and TP-6 fine-tune tailpiece appeared in 1978 with the slightly upgraded model name of ES-347. The ES-355 also continued unbothered through the 1970s and bit the dust in 1982. On

The scattergun approach

◁ 1980 Explorer Heritage reissue prototype

▷ 1981 Flying V-II

An SG. For half a G.

Here's a great old guitar tradition for a grand old price. Actually, half a grand. $499.50 to be exact.* "The SG" guitar by Gibson.

Gibson SG guitars have been playing sellout concerts and hit recording sessions ever since rock started rolling. And The SG is another example of what legends are made of. Its new pickup combination includes the famous Gibson Humbucking pickup in front. And in back, there's a new TGA™ Super Humbucking pickup. It turns out an incredibly powerful sound, while it turns on sizzling highs and midfrequencies. The SG's dense, solid walnut body adds more life to each note, with a long, lingering sustain.

Heavy as it sounds, The SG is a lightweight guitar that's easy to handle. The fingerboard's the finest—natural ebony. And the double cutaway is a cut above too—no other guitar design gives you easier access to all 22 frets. Of course, there's one more important reason to buy The SG—Quality.

For nearly twenty years, SG guitars have proven their worth with several million sellers. But, you don't have to have a million seller to afford one. The SG by Gibson. It can earn you a lot of bread. For just a little bread.

PAY $499 50

Gibson Quality, Prestige, Innovation. Yesterday, Today, Tomorrow. 7373 N. Cicero Ave., Lincolnwood, Illinois 60646 A Division of Norlin Industries 51 Nantucket Blvd., Scarborough, Ontario Canada

*Manufacturer's Suggested Retail List Price

As the 1980s began, Gibson seemed to shoot in every direction in hopes of bagging a successful new model. A glance back at the Golden Era of the McCarty years yielded a reissue of the Korina-body Explorer (far left), along with reissues of the Flying V and Moderne, but at the same time Gibson hedged its bets with a complete reworking of the Flying V, dubbed the Flying V II (near left). If that didn't work, maybe the solution was simply cheaper guitars, such as the no-frills The SG (above), with thinner body, no pickup covers and a plain brown finish.

◁ 1983 Corvus

◁ 1979 RD Artist

Gibson's desperation reached a peak with the Corvus (top) which, with a little sharpening of an edge, could double as a battleaxe. Aside from the logo on the headstock, there was little about the Corvus that was recognizable as a Gibson. The RD Artist (above) introduced solid-state, active electronics, which was not inherently a bad idea, but it sported a body shape that belonged with the Corvus in the what-were-they-thinking category. After all the shots had been fired, the model that remained standing – even in the hands of emerging guitarists such as Steve Clark of Def Leppard (right) – was the Les Paul Standard.

the lower end, the ES-320, with two single-coil Melody Maker-style pickups, made a short run from 1971–74, and the ES-325, with a pair of mini-humbuckers and only one f-hole, lasted only a bit longer, from 1972–78. One more oddball, the ES-369 appeared in 1982 only, featuring a neck with multi-colored binding (inspired by the ill-fated Mark Series acoustics) and a body with no f-holes.

The Les Paul Standard had some interesting but short-lived offshoots. The Pro-Deluxe (1978–91) gave the soapbar P-90 pickups one last shot. The Spotlight Special (1983–84), probably designed to use up small pieces of walnut and maple, sported a three-piece top with a walnut center section. The XPL (1984) was a Standard with an Explorer-style headstock. The K-II (1980) introduced a double-cutaway, carved top Les Paul, and the Double Cutaway XPL (1984–86) expanded on the concept with an Explorer headstock.

The variations on the Les Paul Custom seemed to make more sense: Alnico V and P-90 pickup (called the Custom '54, available in 1973), maple fingerboard (1975–81), nickel-plated hardware (1976 as a special edition, then a regular model from 1979 onward), three pickups (optional or made in special runs at various times), 25th anniversary edition with silver finish (1977, although 1979 would have been the 25th anniversary of the Custom), and in the reissue spirit of the early 1980s, the Black Beauty '82 with (inexplicably) trapezoid rather than block inlays.

One new Les Paul did stick – the Studio, a stripped-down version of the Standard with no binding and dot inlays but still with the carved top. Shortly after its introduction in 1983, Gibson expanded the line to include a Studio Standard and Studio Custom, which seemed like a contraction in terms, i.e., fancier versions of a stripped-down model. The Standard and Custom quickly fell by the wayside, but the basic Les Paul Studio model went on to rival the Les Paul Standard as Gibson's top-selling electric, and it remains in production today.

The SG Standard, after being replaced by the Deluxe, returned in 1972 and made it through the decade with only minor changes, but in the flurry of new models that began in 1980, the SG Standard and the SG Custom were eliminated. The SG Pro, with two soapbar pickups, replaced the Special in 1971 but was itself replaced by a new SG with mini-humbuckers in 1972. It gave way in 1978 to the SG Studio with full-size humbuckers, which didn't last into 1979. A new SG did appear in 1979; the SG Exclusive featured a coil-tap with a rotary control knob and lasted only one year.

The Q series featured new pickup configurations and a similar body shape to the Victory MV series but with a bolt-on neck. The idea, probably inspired by the popular "fat Strat" modifications (replacing one of the Stratocaster's three single-coil pickups with a humbucker), was to offer Gibson buyers a wider variety of pickup combinations than the standard Gibson double-humbucker setup. Four Q models debuted in 1985, along with a Les Paul Special 400 and SG Special 400 that were outfitted with the Q-400 configuration (one Dirty Fingers humbucker and two single-coils). The target group was clear from the Kahler vibrato that was optional or standard on all the Q models, but the target group of hard rockers did not respond, and the Q models barely lasted a year.

In 1980 Gibson made one of its longest-running artist relationships official with a B.B. King signature model. The blues legend had been playing Gibsons since the late 1940s, when he put a pickup on his acoustic archtop Gibson L-30. He had almost lost his life trying to save that guitar from a nightclub fire that had started when two men began fighting over a woman named Lucille, and he subsequently named all of his Gibson's Lucille to remind himself not ever to risk his life again for a guitar. Lucille was an ES-5 for a while, then a Byrdland, but by the time King's records started getting airplay on pop radio stations in the late 1960s, Lucille was an ES-355. By 1980, King was an icon of blues and popular music, and Gibson introduced two signature models – the B.B. King Custom and the B.B. King Standard, renamed Lucille Custom and Lucille Standard a year later. Both were essentially ES-355s with no soundholes (for less feedback), a TP-6 fine-tune tailpiece and "Lucille" on the headstock. The chrome-plated Standard only lasted through 1984, but the Custom, eventually called the B.B. King Lucille, remains in production.

A year after signing B.B. King, Gibson scored another artist relations coup when Chet Atkins brought Gibson a new idea for an amplified classical guitar with a solid body. Atkins carried a degree of respect and influence that is unmatched in the guitar business. He had been one of the world's most influential guitarists for over a quarter-century. As a record producer and head of RCA's Nashville office, he had been a prime force in shaping the Nashville Sound. And as a guitar designer and endorser, he had had successful Gretsch signature models continuously from 1954 until he became disenchanted with the quality of the product in the late 1970s. Moreover, Atkins was personally involved in the designs of his Gretsch models to a much greater degree than Les Paul had been with the original Gibson Les Pauls. Although Atkins had built his career on finger-picking an electric guitar, by the 1980s he was playing mostly nylon-string classical acoustic guitars, if for no other reason than his fingernails were so brittle that steel strings caused them to break. The only drawback to the acoustic classical was the same drawback every acoustic guitar has: In a live performance, the guitar has to be mic'd, and there is a limit to how high the volume can be turned up before it starts feeding back.

For Atkins' purposes, the classical guitar needed to be amplified. His initial solution was to develop and patent nylon strings with a steel core so that they would work with a conventional magnetic pickup. The result, however, would sound no different than any other electric guitar, with none of the tonal characteristics of a nylon string classical (or any other style of acoustic guitar, for that matter). For a truer acoustic sound, he looked to a piezo-electric pickup. Materials with piezo-electric properties produce an electric signal when they are physically compressed. The best spot on a guitar for a piezo-electric crystal was under the

The cream begins to rise

Although Gibson's fortunes continued to fall, the Les Paul continued to rise to the top of the guitar world. Gibson finally came up with a well thought out variation in the Studio, which was basically a trimmed-down, less expensive Standard, and a lightweight version called the Studio Lite (below). The original gold-top look – but, significantly, with the humbuckers that most players preferred – made a successful comeback (below left). Still, there was the occasional wild hair, such as the Spotlight Special (below right), with a decorative but inexplicable piece of walnut in the center of the body.

◁ 1992 Les Paul Studio Lite

△ 1983 Les Paul Spotlight Special

The original Flying V.

It broke the sound barrier in '58 with one great leap of imagination. And then defied over two decades of imitation.

Now the guitar that reshaped rock and roll is on the wing again, with all the original features—from a Korina wood body to gold-plated hardware—that made it one of the most sought-after collector's items in music history. Each instrument in this limited reissue will be specially serialized to ensure its lasting value.

Soar with a legend. The original Gibson Flying V.

Gibson.
Making history.
Yesterday, today, tomorrow.

▷ 1985 Alpha Q-3000

The Q-Series guitars marked the last gasp of the Norlin company with a misdirected attempt to join the competition with a distinctively un-Gibson look and various combinations of pickups. An advertisement for the new "original" Flying V provided a more accurate picture of where Gibson's future lay. And as always, had Gibson looked at working rock 'n' roll guitarists, such as Aerosmith's Brad Whitford (above), the answer to all the company's problems was right there in the form of a Les Paul Standard.

bridge saddle, in the direct path of the transfer of vibrations from the strings to the top of the guitar. It was hardly new technology – Gibson had tried it as early as 1960 with the C-1E classical – but it wasn't developed and perfected until the 1970s, primarily by Ovation and Takamine (spurred by a Baldwin acoustic/electric played by Atkins's cohort Jerry Reed).

A piezo-equipped acoustic could still feed back onstage, but Atkins knew how to fix that. In his early years as a Gretsch endorser, he had beefed up the bracing on his hollowbody model until the top and back braces actually came together, making the guitar perform more like a solidbody. For his electric classical, he took the concept all the way. He had Kentucky luthier Hascal Haile build a prototype on a solid plank of wood (much like Les Paul had done with The Log 40 years earlier), and he took it to Gibson. In December 1981, the first Gibson Chet Atkins CE models (CE for Classical Electric) introduced the new concept of a solidbody acoustic guitar. Actually, it wasn't fully solid. The mahogany back was routed with "tone chambers" so that some of the vibrations of the spruce top could be retained.

The CE had a 1 7/8-inch nut width, and Gibson also offered it with a 2-inch nut, called the Chet Atkins CEC. Although classical guitarists ignored it, pop artists who played classical guitars – such as Willie Nelson and Earl Klugh – were among the first to get one. It was only a moderate commercial success but Atkins's name brought much-needed prestige to Gibson's line, and his model family would expand quite successfully in the post-Norlin era.

Despite the best efforts of those in Kalamazoo and in Nashville, by the early 1980s it was obvious that the Nashville plant had been a mistake. As Jim Deurloo noted, "You know how marketing forecasts go. It's always straight up; the curve is always upward. It never ratchets up and down like the stock market does." As the Nashville plant was being built, the guitar market was not going up and down, it was going straight down. In the early 1970s, instrument makers sold well over 2 million instruments annually; by the early 1980s, the number was less than 1 million. After the Nashville plant opened, neither plant operated at full capacity, and the Kalamazoo plant began building wooden clock cases in an effort to stay afloat. Every one of Norlin's musical instrument divisions was losing money – Gibson alone was losing a million dollars a year – and Norlin had already unloaded some of those companies.

The heart and soul of Gibson was still at 225 Parsons St. in Kalamazoo, where the core group of guitar builders had stayed, and in 1983 Marty Locke told Jim Deurloo that he planned to close the Nashville plant. Apparently that was a riskier option than closing the Kalamazoo plant and, according to Deurloo, within three weeks one of Locke's strongest supporters at the Norlin corporate level left the company and Locke reversed himself. He announced that the Kalamazoo plant would close and all production would move to Nashville.

In June 1984, the last Gibson guitars left the loading dock of 225 Parsons St. If there was still any magic or mystique about Gibson in Kalamazoo, it remained there, as many Kalamazoo employees refused to uproot their families for an insecure future in Nashville. Among those were four key Gibson employees – Jim Deurloo, J.P. Moats, Bill Paige and Marv Lamb – who stayed not only in Kalamazoo but in the Parsons St. factory, where they formed the Heritage guitar company and found success as the company that, more than Gibson, continued the Gibson tradition.

It was the end of an era for Norlin as well as for Gibson. Norlin was taken over in 1984 by investors intent on getting out of the musical instrument business, and they succeeded by the first days of 1986 when they rid themselves of the last of Norlin's music-related divisions – Gibson. Despite a gloomy future for Gibson, there was still reason to believe in the company's survival. Jim Deurloo summed it up with an observation that could apply to many eras of Gibson history: "When the company changes hands and the person who started it is no longer there, companies go through a cycle. No matter what management or marketing tries to do, they just can't ruin the product because the people on the line keep doing the things they did. That's the only thing that saves the company – the people on the line keep on making the product."

Norlin's sale of Gibson ended one of the darkest periods in Gibson history, but with an inexperienced workforce in Nashville and new owners who had no experience at all in the musical instrument industry, Gibson's future looked anything but bright.

Henry Juszkiewicz, Dave Berryman and Gary Zebrowski didn't have all that much experience in any kind of business – the oldest had just turned 34 when they acquired Gibson – but they had the confidence that came with their Masters of Business Administration degrees from Harvard Business School (where they met), bolstered by success in their first business venture together. Juszkiewicz was born in Argentina but grew up in Rochester, New York; he earned an engineering degree at the General Motors Institute and worked for the auto giant before entering Harvard. Berryman, from Buffalo, New York, graduated from Boston College and worked in the accounting field before going for his Masters. Zebrowski, a native of Philadelphia, Pennsylvania, earned a double major from Dartmouth in mathematics and economics before going on to Harvard.

The three MBAs had gone their separate ways into the business world after Harvard but soon joined forces and bought a struggling company in Oklahoma City called Phi Technologies, which manufactured heavy-duty cassette tape decks for such clients as the Muzak "elevator music" company. They turned Phi Tech around and began looking at other companies to acquire. They were not particularly looking for music-related companies and weren't even aware that Norlin was trying to sell Gibson until a former classmate remembered that Juszkiewicz played guitar and tipped him off. Norlin had been asking $15 million for Gibson, and two years had passed with no takers. The Phi Tech group started negotiating in June 1985, and they finally closed the deal for a reported $5 million on January 15, 1986,

Blues legend B.B. King (above) was not the only artist to be featured in Gibson promotions in the 1970s and 1980s, but he was the one who ushered in a new era of signature models. He had been naming his Gibsons "Lucille" for 30 years when Gibson finally made the relationship official in 1980. The Gibson Lucille (opposite) was based on King's Gibson ES-355 semi-hollowbody, but with a fine-tune tailpiece and no soundholes in the body. Gibson promoted it in a wide range of catalog photos and advertisments.

B.B.'s got a new shade of blues.

Nobody's ever put the blue into blues like the legendary B.B. King. Or his Lucille.

But now there's a new lady in B.B.'s arms. The Gibson Lucille Custom. This lady sings blues in a different shade, with sleek new looks and slick new accessories. Like Gibson's Crank Machine Heads, with flip-out-and-wind-up levers that take the blues out of restringing. And the TP-6 Fine Tuning Tailpiece to keep every waiting note in tune.

The Lucille Custom was built to play tribute to the King of the Blues. You can feel it, from light azure to deep sapphire. And there's a Lucille Standard mod-el that will give you a whole new tone spectrum no matter what color your sound.

Both the Custom and Standard are dressed in style, with beautifully arched tops, the finest woods and that unmistakable Gibson craftsmanship. The same craftsmanship that's kept B.B. King true-blue to Gibson for more than thirty years.

The Gibson Lucille. Hold her in *your* arms. And find out what makes B.B. King a lady's man.

Gibson P.O. Box 100087
Nashville, TN 37210

For a full-color catalog, send $3.95 to Gibson Literature Dept. For a poster size reprint of this ad, send $2.00 to P.O. Box 100087, Dept. BB.

△ 1990 Chet Atkins
CE (Standard)

◁ 1998 B.B. King Lucille

Gibson scored a major coup in artist relations when Chet Atkins ended a long relationship with Gretsch and came over to Gibson in 1982. He brought with him a new kind of guitar, a solidbody acoustic, which used a piezo-electric pickup to produce acoustic guitar sounds without the feedback that accompanied acoustics played through a mic. The original CE model (for Classical Electric) spawned a successful steel-string version, the Chet Atkins SST. Gibson also enlisted graphic artists to design a series of custom finishes for Flying Vs and Explorers.

just days before the annual winter NAMM (National Association of Music Merchants) trade show.

With Juszkiewicz as Chairman and Chief Executive Officer and Berryman as President (Zebrowski left after a short period, trading his interest in Gibson for his partners' shares of PhiTech), the new owners had serious problems to deal with in every facet of Gibson's operation. They immediately cut some costs by eliminating 30 of the 250 jobs, most of them in management. The quality of Gibson instruments had become inconsistent during the Norlin years, but more important, the perception of Gibson quality had fallen. To make matters worse, in an attempt to generate more sales, first-quality instrument were being labeled as factory seconds so that the sales force could discount them.

The new owners had to restore quality on the production line without benefit of the expertise that had stayed in Kalamazoo. As difficult a task as that might be, it was easy compared to restoring the confidence of guitar buyers in the Gibson brand. To that end, Juszkiewicz made a risky move that went against conventional retail and marketing strategy of decreasing prices to spur sales. Instead, he increased the price of a Gibson. His reasoning was simply that a high-quality guitar cannot come with a cheap price, and that guitarists would buy into the reverse logic, that a higher price means higher quality. It was not a completely new concept. In the late 1970s, the Curtis Mathes television company advertised with a slogan that bordered on arrogance: "The most expensive television in America and darn well worth it." While the claim may have been true, the company was on a path to bankruptcy by the mid 1980s, the victim – like many American guitar companies two decades earlier – of cheap Japanese imports.

To help push guitarists across Juszkiewicz's leap of logic, he raised the quality of Gibson cases from the molded, black-plastic Protector (nicknamed the "chainsaw" case) to one an attractive brown leather-grain vinyl outer covering, pink plush lining and an inner "shroud" to protect the top of the guitar. To underscore these assertions of higher Gibson quality, he did away with his safety net and eliminated factory seconds altogether. Word quickly spread through the guitar world that if a Gibson guitar couldn't pass final inspection as a first-quality instrument, it went straight to the band saw and then to the incinerator.

Juszkiewicz didn't need an MBA to see that the models Norlin had developed weren't going to save Gibson, and they were all cast off except for the Les Paul Studio. He kept the tried and true models from the CMI years – the Les Paul Custom, Les Paul Standard, Flying V, Explorer, ES-335 DOT and the traditional hollowbody electrics – and expanded on that theme by reviving the single-cutaway Les Paul Junior (with P-90 pickup), the SG Custom, a vintage-style SG Standard called the SG Reissue, and a souped-up single-humbucker version of the lowly Melody Maker. Those provided a solid core group of traditional models, but Gibson needed new blood in the model line to represent the new blood in ownership.

Through what had become known as The Great Synthesizer Scare of the

Seventies, the guitars that survived and thrived were made by upstarts such as Charvel/Jackson and Kramer (the guitars Eddie Van Halen played), using the Fender Stratocaster as a starting point and then added a humbucking pickup in the bridge position and a "dive bomb" vibrato. By mid 1986, Gibson had one, too – the US-1. In addition to the "required" features, the US-1 had some unique Gibsonesque attractions, including the routed mahogany back (a la Chet Atkins CE) combined with the maple top (from the Les Paul). The hollow center was filled with lightweight but structurally strong balsa wood, which Juszkiewicz called Chromyte (in the same spirit that Ted McCarty renamed African limba wood Korina in 1958). The pickups looked like the HSS (humbucker, single-coil, single-coil) configuration of the popular "fat Strats," but the two single-coils were actually stacked humbuckers. A second, less expensive Strat-style guitar, the U-2 (later called the Mach II), joined the US-1 in early 1987, with a lightweight solid basswood body and a choice of HSS (with true single-coils) or dual-humbucker pickups.

Midway through 1987, Juszkiewicz went directly to the source of the Van Halen-style, modified-Strat guitars – Wayne Charvel, who had made the guitar that Eddie Van Halen used on the group's first album. Juszkiewicz asked him to design a Gibson, and he came up with a Strat-style body and bolt-on neck, HSS pickups (the singles were actually stacked-coils), three on-off switches, a coil-tap switch and Floyd Rose vibrato. Unbeknown to Charvel, Gibson put "Charvel" on the headstock. Charvel had sold the rights to his name along with his guitar company in 1978 to Grover Jackson, and after Jackson saw "Charvel" on a guitar at the 1987 summer NAMM show, he sued. Gibson removed "Charvel" and simply put WRC or WC on the truss-rod cover, but the model, along with two limited-run offshoots, the SR-71 with set neck and the WRC Showcase Edition with EMG pickups, died on the vine.

For guitarists still interested in the established models, Juszkiewicz conjured up a full slate of specials in 1987. From March through December, Gibson served up a series of Showcase Specials with custom finishes and EMG active electronics, one model each month, made in a limited run of 200 for U.S. distribution plus another 50 for international markets.

Also in 1987, the Chet Atkins electric solidbody classical, a Norlin model, yielded an unexpected benefit when Gibson strung it up with steel strings and called it the Chet Atkins SST. Its feedback-free performance capability quickly found its way onto rock and roll stages, most notably in the hands of Mark Knopfler and Dave Matthews, and it spawned more variations on the Chet Atkins solidbody acoustic theme. The CE Showcase edition was a guitar-of-the-month special in 1988, featuring a Sunburst finish. The Chet Atkins Celebrity of 1991–93 sported a black finish. The SST 12-string made a brief appearance from 1990–94 and included a flame-top offshoot (1993–95). The wide appeal of the SST was illustrated by a 12-string version with gold-top finish endorsed by Brett Michaels of the heavy metal

▷ 1998 Chet Atkins Country Gentleman

As new owners Henry Juszkiewicz and David Berryman took over Gibson in 1986, the company was poised to build upon its rich tradition and regain the reputation for electric guitars it had enjoyed in the 1950s and '60s. The semi-hollowbody ES-355 made a statement of tradition combined with modernism in the hands of Johnny Marr of The Smiths, just as it had in 1958. The introduction of the Chet Atkins Country Gentleman as a Gibson model represented the continuation of Atkins's worldwide influence. But Gibson's new owners couldn't resist an attempt to expand the image of Gibson guitars with the US-1, which combined the signature element of a classic Les Paul with a body that owed more to the Fender Stratocaster than any Gibson tradition. Once again, however, the key to Gibson's success could be clearly seen on rock 'n' roll stages, where new artists – such as The Scorpions and Cinderella (opposite) – continued to play old Gibson models.

◁ 1987 US-2

The Scorpions
Rock the World...
with
Gibson.

The Scorpions
hit America with a
rare blend of excep-
tional musicianship
and throbbing, raw
power. They are totally
original, just like the
instruments they play—
Rudolf's Flying V, Matthias'
Explorer, Francis' new
Explorer bass, Klaus' 335
DOT. All are originals bearing
the name of the company that
created them. . . . Gibson.
   Just like their music, the Scorpions don't settle for copies.
Having earned their way to the
top, they can have their choice.
But no thanks, they know what
they want. They buy Gibson.
They know when you're that
serious about your music, the
difference is worth it.
   Now you can order a special
Rudolf Schenker design finish
on your new Gibson Flying V.
Or how about a Matthias
top design finish on a new
Gibson Explorer? Both are
available now in Gibson's
Designer Series.

Gibson®
American-made. World-played.

"You Take Your Road—I'll Take Mine."
From Nobodys Fool/NIGHT SONGS ALBUM

Tom Keifer of
Cinderella

Photo Credit: THE WEISSGUY
© 1987 GIBSON GUITAR CORP.

I'll Play Gibson!

Gibson
USA

band Poison, offered from 1992–93 but produced in the extremely limited quantity of only two instruments. Gibson would later tout the Jimmy Page Les Paul as the company's first double-signature model, but the Chet Atkins SST 12-string Brett Michaels Edition was actually the first. On the classical side, the Chet Atkins Studio Classic, made only in 1993, and the Studio CE, introduced in 1993, refined the original CE design to incorporate more acoustic qualities by way of a hollow (routed) mahogany body and a spruce top with classical style fan-pattern bracing.

With the success of Atkins' solidbody electrics the next obvious step was to revive the traditional Atkins models that had been the backbone of Gretsch sales during Atkins's 25 years as a Gretsch endorser. Atkins was still active as a recording artist. A measure of his influence was the Chet Atkins Appreciation Society, which was formed as a fan club in the 1950s but by 1985 was holding an annual convention in Nashville (independent of Atkins's participation) featuring workshops, forums and Atkins-style performers. The Gibson Chet Atkins Country Gentleman, introduced in 1986, and the plainer Tennessean, introduced in 1990, gave these legions of Chet fans what they hadn't been able to get from Gretsch since the early 1970s – a top-quality semi-hollowbody Chet Atkins model. Special Atkins appointments included a single-cutaway body shape, a 25½-inch scale, a 1¾-inch nut width and a vibrola.

Not all the Gibson Chet Atkins models were as successful. The CGP, which stood for Certified Guitar Player, Atkins's self-awarded "degree," featured a carved mahogany top and was featured in a catalog in 1986 but never made it into production. The Phasar, an oddly shaped solidbody electric, was pictured in the 1988 catalog but only about six were made. The Chet Atkins (JS) Double was essentially the two-pickup version of the Johnny Smith full-depth hollowbody with floating pickups, and only a few prototypes with experimental pickups were made around 1990. The Chet Atkins Super 4000 of 2001, a thin-bodied version of the Super 400 with a floating pickup, was also produced only at the prototype level.

Atkins died in 2001, and his estate withdrew his endorsement from Gibson in 2005. His Gibson solidbody acoustic design lives on in a pair of models with chambered bodies, introduced in 2004 as the Americana Series: the Pioneer Cutaway, a dreadnought size model, and the Ranger, based on the smaller, prewar, L-00 flat-top model.

Gibson's new owners were helped in their turnaround efforts by a turnaround in the entire guitar market. From the low of under $100 million in annual sales in the early 1980s, the industry hit the $500 million mark by 1993 and was growing steadily. Gibson's sales, most of which were electrics, did even better, going from around $10 million in 1986 to $70 million in 1993.

Undeterred by the cool reception given the Strat-inspired Gibsons of 1986 and '87, Juszkiewicz and R&D head J.T. Riboloff set about designing a new model from scratch. They came up with a sleek body shape featuring cutaway horns that seemed to have been formed by a single continuous line. It was different enough to warrant a design patent, granted in 1993. The standard model featured a pair of humbuckers surrounding a new single-coil pickup designed by Riboloff and dubbed the NSX. A five-position switch offered ten different pickup combinations. The M-III debuted in 1991 with numerous variations, including the M-III-H with two humbuckers, and Deluxe versions with bodies of five-ply maple, walnut and poplar.

The M-IIIs went nowhere. Riboloff went back to work and came up with the Nighthawk, featuring a more conventional single-cutaway body shape but with more new, higher-output pickups and a full array of options. Upon its introduction at winter NAMM in January 1993, the Nighthawk won the top design award from *The Music Trades* magazine and won a small following among studio guitarists who appreciated its versatility. One of the Nighthawk's biggest fans was G.E. Smith, the bandleader on NBC's *Saturday Night Live*, but while he used it on sessions, he typically appeared on camera playing vintage Gibsons. It was a sign of the times – not a good sign for the Nighthawk but a good sign for Gibson.

Signs of a growing interest in historic Gibsons had been apparent since the late 1980s. The Custom Shop – which was actually an informal group of talented individuals within the regular production facility – had been receiving orders in the late 1980s for Sunburst Les Paul Standards with the thinner neck of a 1960 model. J.T. Riboloff took that spec and other classic appointments, such as nickel-plated hardware, inked-on serial number and a nicely figured top, and put them together with modern, hot ceramic-magnet pickups. The result was the Les Paul Classic, introduced in 1990 and an instant hit.

The Les Paul Classic's vintage features, such as a small headstock, push-in tuner bushings and aged fingerboard inlays, made a mockery of the Les Paul Reissue. In 1990, the Reissue had received an upgrade – perhaps "retrograde" is a more accurate word – in the form of the '57 Classic humbucking pickup with original "patent-applied-for" specs. Still, the Classic was a more accurate reissue than the Reissue. In 1991, the Reissue was moved to the Historic Collection (it had previously been listed as a regular-production Les Paul), and one of the distinctions between the 1959 and '60 originals was recognized by splitting the Reissue into two models – the Les Paul '59 Flametop Reissue with the fat, clubby neck and the '60 Flametop Reissue with the slim, fast neck. It was a small sign of big moves in store for the Historic Collection and the Custom Shop.

In addition to the Les Paul Classic, Riboloff was working on reissues of the original Flying V and Explorer, borrowing original examples from collectors so that such details as the thickness of the pickguard and the jackplate, the neck/body joint, etc., would be correct (which they were not on the Heritage Reissues of the early 1980s). Riboloff spec'd the guitars and luthier Phil Jones hand-built the prototypes. Initially, the 1958 Korina Flying V and the 1958 Korina Explorer were to be sold as a set, and the first few Vs had odd- numbered serial numbers while the Explorers had even numbers so that sets could have adjacent numbers, such as Flying #1 with Explorer #2, Flying V #3 with Explorer #4, etc. The list price was to be

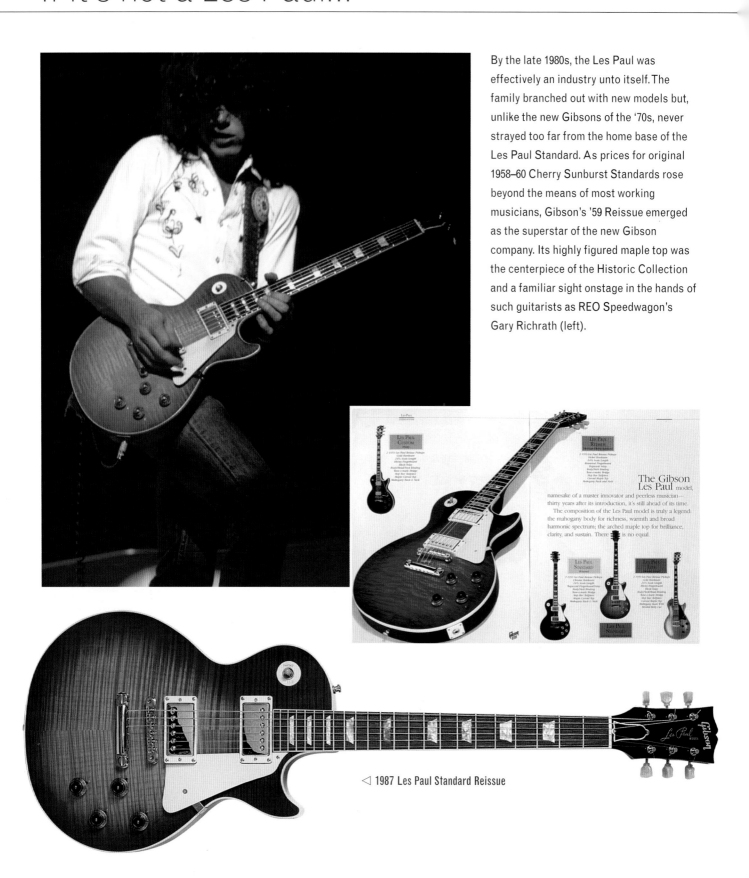

By the late 1980s, the Les Paul was effectively an industry unto itself. The family branched out with new models but, unlike the new Gibsons of the '70s, never strayed too far from the home base of the Les Paul Standard. As prices for original 1958–60 Cherry Sunburst Standards rose beyond the means of most working musicians, Gibson's '59 Reissue emerged as the superstar of the new Gibson company. Its highly figured maple top was the centerpiece of the Historic Collection and a familiar sight onstage in the hands of such guitarists as REO Speedwagon's Gary Richrath (left).

◁ 1987 Les Paul Standard Reissue

Gibson's growing success with Les Pauls made it difficult to establish new models that deviated from tradition. The M-III (below) had a distinctive, modern look and functionality. The Nighthawk (right) won an industry design award and featured a multitude of pickup options. However, Zakk Wylde, Slash, and Tony Iommi favored variations on established models (right). While Suede guitarist Bernard Butler's ES-355 (bottom right) showed the continued appeal of Gibson tradition.

▽ 1991 M-III Standard

◁ 1993 Nighthawk Special

$15,000 for the pair, but when they appeared on price lists they were priced individually at $10,000 each. Phil Jones continued to hand-make every Korina reissue that came out of the Custom Shop through the 1990s.

In the meantime in the vintage guitar market, a growing demand for original Sunburst Les Pauls had pushed prices into the $20,000–25,000 range. Buyers in that market were increasingly aware of every small detail of the original models and also aware of how many of those details were not accurate on Gibson's Flametop Reissue. Tom Murphy, who had joined Gibson in 1989, had a passion for vintage guitars, and he thought it disappointing and even embarrassing that Gibson seemed unable to match the original specs on one of its own models. Moreover, having attended vintage guitar shows, he knew that consumers would pay significantly more than the current Flametop Reissue price for a better reissue. He voiced that feeling at a meeting with the Nashville division's general manager Kurt Serafin and newly hired product manager Richard Head. They told him to bring a list of specifications that needed to be fixed on the Reissue, and he came back with 25 items.

The improved Reissue was not as difficult a sell to management as Murphy had expected. "A key factor was, Richard Head owned a real '60 'burst," Murphy said. "I didn't have to draw a picture for him. He was a key player. Kurt Serafin had no knowledge of the originals; he just wanted positive things to happen for the division." With Riboloff busy on other projects, the Les Paul Reissue project was handed to Murphy.

Murphy had luthier Keith Medley on the team to hand-built the prototypes, but putting the models into production would be challenging. For example, Murphy noted that on the originals, the silkscreened "Les Paul Model" on the peghead was applied on top of the final finish (after buffing), whereas Gibson's standard production procedure was to apply the silkscreen first, then the finish. Production engineer Matthew Klein noted that putting the silkscreen on top of the finish would leave it exposed to possible damage through the entire final assembly process. Murphy recalled, "Instead of Richard and Kurt going, 'Okay, we have to listen to Matthew,' Richard said, 'Well, they did it 30 years ago. We can do it now.' I said, 'I guarantee the consumer who's going to pay $5,000 dollars for this guitar would rather have fingerprints on it than lacquer shot over the logo.'"

The silkscreen was not the only production problem posed by the Reissue peghead. On the originals, the holly veneer was .030-inch thick; on standard 1990s Les Pauls the veneer was .060-inch thick, but when the workers tried to make the veneer thinner, the wood stuck to the jig and tore. Also on the originals, the Gibson logo was masked off and the veneer was sprayed black; on standard 1990s models the veneer was stained and then sprayed with clear lacquer so that the pearl Gibson logo did not have to be masked off. With similar obstacles at every turn, Murphy saw the potential for widespread negative reaction, and he called meetings with every production line. "It was sort of a pep talk and an orientation to the changes," he said. "I told them this guitar was a $5,000 guitar and an original was $25,000. This guitar was so important out in the market. If we make it, people will be so surprised. Their response was generally positive. They would be proud to be involved rather than resistant."

As the '59 Les Paul neared completion, rumors of "the replica" circulated through the guitar world, although Gibson referred to it by the code stamped inside the control cavity – R9. Introduced at the January 1993 NAMM show, the R9 and R7 ('57 Gold-top Reissue) featured a longer neck tenon (the extension of the neck into the body), a control cavity floor routed parallel to the top (rather than to the back of the guitar), a "deep dish" top curvature that had been reproduced from a digital map of an original, and numerous other small but important historic details. The R0, a 1960 reissue, was also introduced but wasn't actually available, since Murphy had not spec'd out the slimmer neck dimension, nor such differences as the double-ring tuner buttons and metal-capped control knobs. For the first orders of the R0, he took an R9 and simply shaved the neck down.

In the meantime, Henry Juszkiewicz moved to take full advantage of the surge in interest in historic Gibson models. In late 1993 he broke the Custom Shop off into a separate division with its own facility. Rick Gembar, who had owned his own custom furniture business, was brought in to manage the new Custom, Art & Historic division. In a brash financial move, Juszkiewicz convinced dealers to fund the venture with a Historic Collection membership fee of $10,000 (a loan, actually, that Gibson paid back with interest).

By the early 1990s, the market for new guitars had made a full recovery from the slump of the late 1970s and early '80s, and the market for vintage Gibsons was also booming. The Custom Shop's replica models offered an attractive alternative to guitar buyers who couldn't afford an original. With the Historic Collection models providing the lifeblood, the Custom division expanded in every direction. The Reissues grew into an array of models, representing almost every year and every Les Paul Model of the 1950s. Old Les Pauls spawned new versions of Les Pauls, such as the Elites with diamond-shaped soundholes and sparkle finishes, or the Ultima with elaborately inlaid fingerboards. Limited-run models linked Gibson with such lifestyle icons as Corvette automobiles, Donzi speedboats and Indian motorcycles. Art guitars created in-house by Bruce Kunkel sported painted imagery or relief carving to commemorate such historical attractions as Les Paul's life, the events of the 20th century and the birth of Jesus. And artist signature models, replicated famous guitars of influential stars or else featured their personal design touches.

The range of artist models included virtually everyone who was anyone. Among the replica models, The Allman Brothers Band was represented by three guitars: the 1957 Les Paul that Dickey Betts refinished in red, immortalized in the lyrics of Charlie Daniels' 'The South's Gonna Do It Again' (2002); Betts's 1957 gold-top (2001); and Duane Allman's Les Paul with his name in fretwire pressed into the

Artists, show your Gibsons

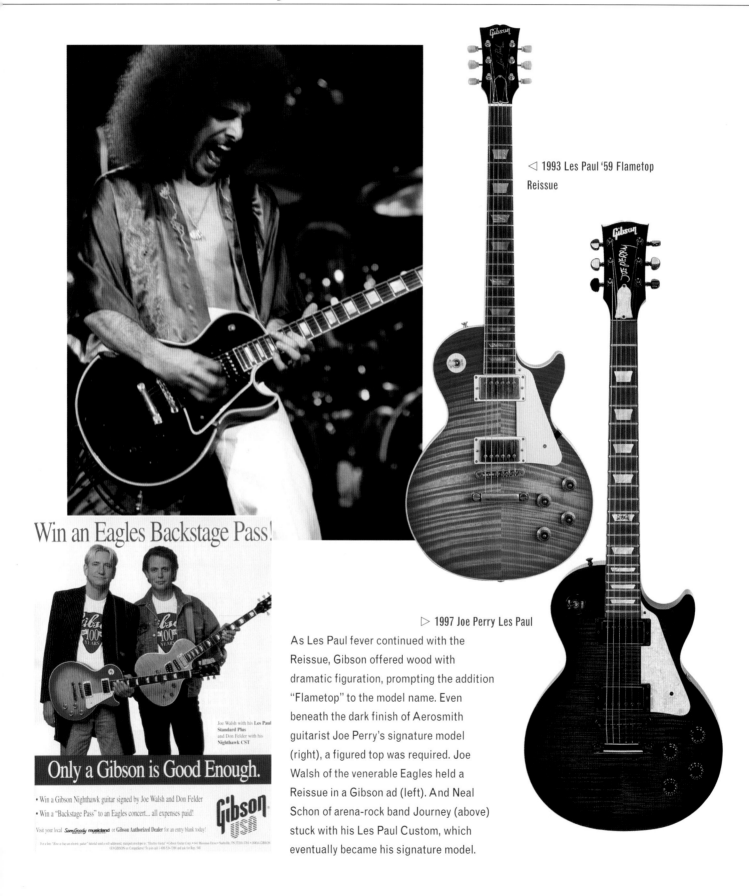

◁ 1993 Les Paul '59 Flametop
Reissue

▷ 1997 Joe Perry Les Paul

As Les Paul fever continued with the Reissue, Gibson offered wood with dramatic figuration, prompting the addition "Flametop" to the model name. Even beneath the dark finish of Aerosmith guitarist Joe Perry's signature model (right), a figured top was required. Joe Walsh of the venerable Eagles held a Reissue in a Gibson ad (left). And Neal Schon of arena-rock band Journey (above) stuck with his Les Paul Custom, which eventually became his signature model.

Jimmy Page, one of the most influential electric guitarists of the 1960s and '70s with Led Zeppelin, joined with Gibson to create a signature model (left) based on one of his personal highly customized sunburst Les Pauls. Pop/rock/R&B artist Lenny Kravitz customized another traditional Gibson model, the Flying V, for his signature model, adding a sparkle-black finish and a mirror pickguard. Gibson even teamed up with an American automotive icon, the Chevrolet Corvette, to create the first of many product-inspired guitars.

▷ 1995 Les Paul '60 Corvette

back (2003). Their fellow Southern rockers Lynyrd Skynyrd also had three Custom Shop guitars: the Les Paul that Gary Rossington nicknamed Bernice, complete with two screws in the headstock replicating a homemade repair job (2002); Rossington's early-1960s SG-style Les Paul (2003); and a Korina Explorer honoring the late Allen Collins (2003). A replica of reggae legend Bob Marley's heavily customized 1972 Les Paul Special (2002) featured an aluminum pickguard and aluminum, football-shaped switch washer, just like the original. Jimmy Page's 1959 Les Paul (2004) was recreated in every detail, and the first 150 examples were "Murphy-aged" – which by 2004 was the highest level of the Custom Shop's aging processes, with playing wear and weather checking personally executed by Tom Murphy.

Numerous artists created their own models. The Joe Perry (Aerosmith) model (1996) featured a curly top and a black stain finish along with some personalized electronics; Perry returned with a second model, the Joe Perry Boneyard (2003), sporting a "green tiger" finish that was picked out by his wife. Slash (Guns 'N Roses) also had two models – the first with a hand-carved snake on the top (1997), the second with two conventional pickups plus an acoustic-style transducer pickup (2004). Heavy metal guitarist Zakk Wylde checked in with five different models, two of them with his trademark black-and-white bullseye graphic (2000, 2004), one with a camouflage bullseye (2004), one with bottle caps adorning the top (2002) and one with a stripped, roughed-up top (2000). Ace Frehley of Kiss put a graphic of himself on the headstock of his model (1997), along with three double-white coil DiMarzio humbuckers. Peter Frampton's Les Paul Custom (2000) had a weight-relieved body and three pickups and custom wiring. Lenny Kravitz's Flying V (2002) sported a mirror pickguard and black sparkle finish. Neal Schon (Journey) checked in with an early-1980s style customized Les Paul (2005) featuring a Floyd Rose "dive bomb" vibrato and a pair of mini switches for pickup on/off and octave effect.

The Custom Shop developed its own aura and its own loyal clientele, and the annual Custom Shop party, featuring food, star entertainers and guitar giveaways, became a highlight of the summer NAMM shows in Nashville (and continued after NAMM left Nashville).

In 1994 Gibson celebrated its centennial year (not the 100th anniversary of the company's founding but of the oldest surviving instrument made by Orville Gibson) with a guitar-of-the-month series that topped all others. Each month a different model was produced in a maximum run of 101 guitars, numbered from 1894 to 1984. The serial number was applied to the stopbar tailpiece, and the numeral 1 was made with a row of diamonds. The dot over the letter "i" in the peghead log was also a diamond. A medallion with a portrait of Orville Gibson adorned the back of the peghead. The guitar came in a leather covered case, along with a framed 16 x 20-inch color photo of the guitar and a gold signet ring with the new Gibson Musical Instruments logo.

The new logo of 1994, which featured a pre-World War II-style logo in yellow-gold against the red background of a large guitar pick, elevated the Gibson name to a position as head of a family of brands. It ended the confusing distinctions between Gibson's sales and marketing arm, which Juszkiewicz had named Consolidated Musical Instruments (to tie in with the initials of Gibson's former parent company, Chicago Musical Instrument), and Gibson Guitar Corp., which was the official name of the parent company. Gibson Musical Instruments signaled the beginning of a push to make Gibson more than a musical instrument company.

Henry Juszkiewicz always had a "big picture" vision for Gibson. As soon as the company was on its feet he began acquiring or entering into joint ventures or distribution agreements with a wide range of instrument manufacturers. His vision extended beyond simply having a complete range of musical instruments to offer dealers; he saw Gibson ultimately as the dealer, too, with Gibson stores serving as a one-stop destination for all musical needs. He envisioned Gibson as a lifestyle company, increasingly involved in everyone's day-to-day lives as the company expanded from guitars to performance venues to home electronic products.

One product that emerged from Juszkiewicz's world view was the Smartwood guitar. In an increasingly eco-conscious world, it was obvious that supplies of Gibson's primary raw material – wood – were being depleted. Juszkiewicz aligned Gibson with the Rainforest Alliance, eventually serving on the organization's board of directors. The Rainforest Alliance promoted the use of Smartwood, its trade name for wood certified as coming from eco-friendly sources, and Gibson responded with the first guitar made entirely from certified wood – the Les Paul Smartwood of 1996.

The year 1996 seemed to be a year of realization that there was no use in trying to improve the electric guitar, so Gibson might as well have just fun with it. There was nothing fundamentally new about the guitars of 1996, but there was still plenty to look at, with no end to the finish colors and combinations of features that might catch the eye of a guitar buyer. The Les Paul Studio Gem series combined cream-colored soapbar P-90 pickups and gold-plated hardware with transparent finish colors inspired by gemstones, including ruby, emerald, green, topaz, sapphire and amethyst. The Landmark models were based on the Nighthawk body with a pair of Firebird-style mini-humbuckers and finish colors inspired by America's national parks - Glacier blue, Sequoia Red, Mojave burst, Navajo turquoise and Everglades green. A special run of just over 100 guitars featured tops with a 1960s-style tie-dye finish, each one unique and executed by artist George St. Pierre.

The All American series of 1996 offered not only unique combinations of features, they also offered unique pricing. At that time the lowest-priced electric was the Les Paul Special with a list of $1,239. With subdued finishes (Ebony, Wine Red or Dark Wineburst) and stripped-down ornamentation, the All Americans ranged in list price from $669 to $999. The All American I was an SG stripped down to the bare essentials – a humbucking pickup and a coil tap. The All American II

All in the family

By the mid 1990s, Gibson was cautious about straying far from the original Les Paul design. The double-cutaway body shape had been successful in the 1950s on the lower models, the Junior and Special, so Gibson tried it on a carved-top Standard. Helped along, no doubt, by a figured maple top, the DC (for double cutaway) gained a foothold. Gibson's commitment to renewable wood resources led to the Smartwood Les Paul. And the Les Paul continued to be the preferred guitar for all types of rock, as exemplified by James Dean Bradfield of Manic Street Preachers with his Les Paul Custom.

▷ 1997 Les Paul DC Pro

▽ 1998 Les Paul Smartwood Standard

THE GIBSON ELECTRIC GUITAR BOOK

Tony Iommi created some of the heaviest guitar lines in rock history as Black Sabbath's lead guitarist, and Gibson recognized his continuing influence with a signature model. It wasn't exactly like Iommi's SG Standard, however, since Iommi played left-handed. In the meantime, Huey Morgan of the hip-hop/rock group Fun Lovin' Criminals, used a Les Paul Custom, providing yet another example of the ubiquitous presence of Gibson Les Pauls in popular music.

▽ 1998 Tony Iommi Les Paul SG

had a double-cutaway shape similar to that of the early-'60s version of the Melody Maker, with rounded horns, and it came with a pair of single-coil pickups. These two models were initially offered in 1995 as trade show specials that dealers could sell for under $500. They were so successful that Gibson revived the concept and expanded it into a series of six models in 1996 featuring different body shapes. In addition to the original two, the series included The Hawk (a Nighthawk with no top cap or binding), an SG Special, an M-III with three humbuckers and The Paul II (with a thin body and carved top). Most of the All Americans lasted for only a year or two, but the original model survived to become a part of the next round of new models – or at least new model names. The All American SG became the SG-X in 1998, and in mid-year it sported summer colors such as Caribbean blue, coral or corona yellow.

Electric basses in the Juszkiewicz era had a few false starts and then followed Gibson tradition, reflecting the guitar line. In 1991 a series of Les Paul basses appeared, based on the Standard (with carved top) and Special ("slab" body), a seemingly obvious move that Gibson had only previously tried with the Les Paul Triumph, a bass version of the Personal/Professsional/Recording models. A similarly shaped pair of models, but with a semi-hollowbody and diamond-shaped soundholes, appeared briefly from 1991–93 as the EB-650 and EB-750. The EB-Z, apparently named in the spirit of the SG-X of 1998, was essentially an update of the EB-3 bass of the 1960s and '70s. For the most part the bass line of the 1990s and early 2000s maintained another Gibson tradition, and that was the inability of Gibson to convince bass players that Gibson was a bass company. The notable exception was the Thunderbird IV (with Firebird body and two pickups), which Juszkiewicz reintroduced upon his arrival in 1986 and which continues to be the only Gibson bass with anything approaching legendary status.

In 1999 Gibson's electric guitar production expanded into a multi-purpose facility located on Memphis' famous Beale Street. In addition to a restaurant, performance venue and museum, the Memphis plant produced the ES line of semi-hollow and hollowbody electrics). The facility struggled for several years until the factory operation was merged into the Custom division in 2005. The ES line continues to be made in Memphis under the Memphis Custom banner.

By the mid 1990s, Juszkiewicz realized that he was not going to make his mark in the guitar world with the M-III guitars or any other variation on traditional electrics. As an engineer and a techno-savvy individual, he was well aware of the digital revolution. In addition to playing guitar, he played around in a home-recording studio, and he would eventually buy a music software company, Opcode, in 1998. Clearly the future of music was digital, and the guitar was a dinosaur, a situation that Juszkiewicz viewed as an opportunity to change the electric guitar as we know it. The task of executing such a vision was given to Gibson Labs, a research center located in the San Francisco Bay area of northern California. He described his mission in 1994 in the book *Gibson Guitars: 100 Years of an American*

Icon. "We are ... using state-of-the-art technology to explore the very essence of sound," he wrote, "to find out what makes instruments sound good, and to use that technology and knowledge to create new sounds. We'll be utilizing technology – like giving an author a word processor – to give a musician a more versatile instrument and a more efficient way to make sounds."

Along the way to developing a digital guitar, the engineers at Gibson Labs developed a technology with the potential to revolutionize the entire consumer electronics industry – a technology that effectively supercharged the standard Ethernet cable so that it could carry more information at greater speeds over greater distances. Gibson announced GMICS (prounounced "gimmicks"), for Global Musical Instrument Communication Standard, in September 1999 at the Audio Engineering Society meeting in New York. Along with the announcement came the promise of a GMICS-based instrument to be unveiled at the February 2000 NAMM show in Anaheim, California, but when NAMM arrived, Gibson displayed only a "Top Secret" wooden crate. An instrument wouldn't be ready until the summer NAMM show in Nashville, and even then, it was not a Gibson. At a private demonstration in Henry's, Juszkiewicz's coffeehouse/nightclub on Broadway in downtown Nashville, Gibson Labs engineers fitted a "hex" pickup (with six individual pickups – one for each string) to guitarist Adrian Legg's personal custom-made instrument. While Legg played, Gibson Labs R&D director Stephen Woolley operated the "GMICS processor," panning the string signals in different combinations across a five-speaker setup. Also on display was an Epiphone hollowbody guitar with the back cut out and a GMICS circuit board installed.

The hex pickup itself was not digital. It used conventional magnet-and-coil technology and had been around since the 1980s. Gibson had offered it briefly as an add-on item in 1992. The outputs from the pickup went into an onboard digital converter, which sent out digital information in GMICS format via an Ethernet cable to the processor. The GMICS processor was not a processor in the sense of a digital workstation, rather it converted the signal back to analog and functioned as a mixer to feed it to the speakers.

The digital guitar and GMICS lay relatively quiet for two years and then came back with a splash at the Comdex technology convention in Las Vegas in November 2002. The technology was now called MaGIC – Media-accelerated Global Information Carrier – and the processor was now a "breakout box" named BoB. A keynote speech by Hector Ruiz, CEO of computer chipmaker AMD, ended with Ruiz being joined onstage by rock guitarist Slash and by Juszkiewicz, who played a Gibson digital guitar as they jammed on 'Knockin' on Heaven's Door.'

Gibson continued to "introduce" the digital guitar at every opportunity. The Scorpions' Rudolph Schenker tried it out at the Intel Developers Forum in 2003. Juszkiewicz played it on the CNN news network. Gibson clinician Chuck Yamek demonstrated it at the 2005 Consumer Electronics Show. It got to the point that

Dancin' with the one that brought you

Not all guitarists bought into the ever-curlier tops of the classic Sunburst Les Pauls, and Gibson gave these anti-establishmentarians a plain, stripped down Les Paul called the Raw Power. Outside the mainstream, artists such as Foo Fighters frontman Dave Grohl still preferred a modern version of a traditional Gibson, the slightly downsized

Firebird Studio. And even farther outside the mainstream, Gibson used a retro 1950s-style ad to draw attention to a new model; but despite its modern construction (routed back with integral braces), the ES-446 body style had no identity in current rock music and consequently simply had the look of an old guitar.

◁ 2000 Les Paul Standard Raw Power

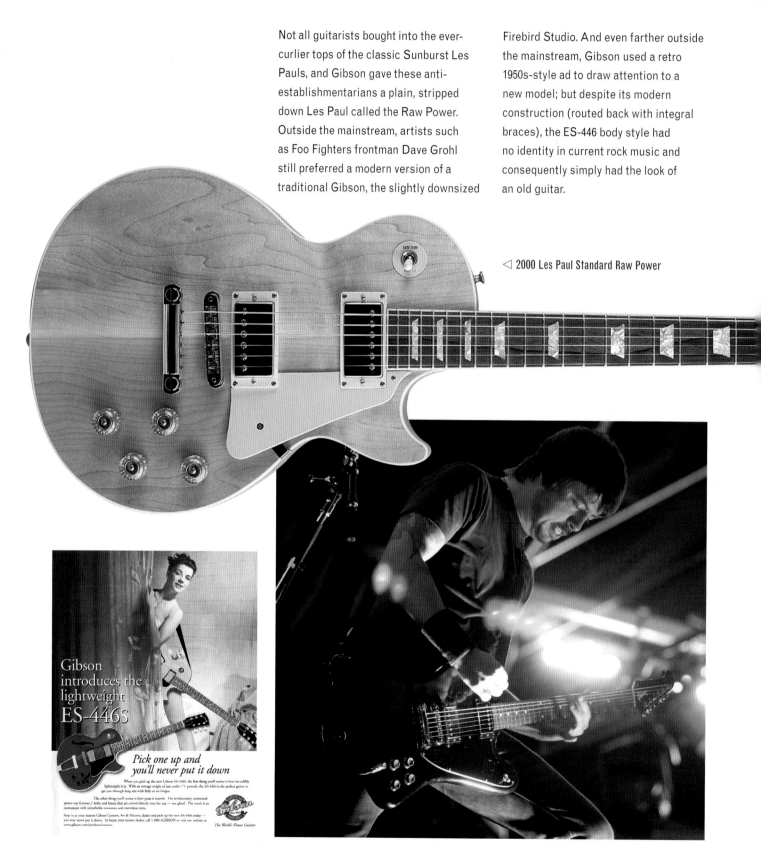

At the turn of the 21st century, Gibson ads touted reissues of models over 40 years old. While it may have been frustrating to those with a desire to push guitar design forward, it also reflected the preferences of guitarists such as Justin Hawkins of the Darkness, with his Les Paul Standard, and the phenomenal success Gibson was enjoying. Even the Firebird V (right), once a radical design that flew in the face of tradition, is now a mainstay of Gibson's traditional model offering.

▷ 1999 Firebird V

RED HOT. RAZOR SHARP.
THE LES PAUL SG STANDARD REISSUE

An Historically accurate rendition of the world's most distinctive solid-body guitar

Since the early 1960s, the Les Paul SG Standard has been Gibson's premier double-cutaway solid-body electric. The extra slim, fast, low-action neck, aggressive styling, and thin, lightweight mahogany body have made it a favorite among guitarists for decades.

Gibson's Custom, Art & Historic Division introduces

the Les Paul SG Standard Historic Reissue. This instrument has been engineered and manufactured to the same specifications as the original model and reflects the sharp contoured carving, dramatic scarfing and an overlapping heel neck joint. The peghead has been restored to its original specification and features a holly head veneer.

The Les Paul SG Standard Reissue is available with either a long Maestro tailpiece or stopbar tailpiece. Additionally, it comes with a rosewood fingerboard with trapezoid inlays, vintage-style tuners, and two '57 Classic humbucking pickups. For the ultimate vintage look, the Les Paul SG Standard Reissue comes with optional aged hardware.

Both models are available in the standard faded cherry finish and, for an additional charge, can be finished in TV Yellow or Classic White.

To find out more about the Les Paul SG Standard Historic Reissue, visit our website at www.gibsoncustom.com or find your nearest Historic Award Dealer by calling 1-800-987-2284, extension 700.

The World's Finest Guitars
WWW.GIBSONCUSTOM.COM

"Welcome to our annual reintroduction of the digital guitar" became a running joke at Gibson. After an initial positive response, the press was not so impressed. A 2004 article in *Wired* magazine quoted a product manager for rival Roland Corporation (which had partnered with Fender to create a synth-driving Stratocaster) with this observation: "MaGIC looks like a solution in search of a problem." Indeed, the problem or demand that the digital guitar supposedly filled was never in evidence. Its surround-sound capability was a novelty that no peforming guitarists used. Juszkiewicz noted that the hex pickup produced a cleaner sound and that the output from the humbuckers (aka "classic mode") was truer when delivered through the Ethernet cable than through a standard guitar cord, but again, no guitarists were demanding a cleaner, truer sound.

In January 2005, Juszkiewicz told *MacWorld* magazine: "It will definitely be for the bleeding edge player. It is indeed the future of Gibson and the industry. We are going to do it because it's the right thing to do." But Gibson still did not do it. Instead it was the Brian Moore company that did it, stealing Gibson's digital thunder in fall 2005 by shipping a guitar with a USB port that would connect the guitar directly into any computer. (Plugging Gibson's model into a computer would destroy the computer.) On the Create Digital Music website, writer Peter Kirn opined: "This thing is more likely to be useful than Gibson's digital offering, and, unlike the Digital Les Paul, the Brian Moore guitars are actually shipping. Sorry to beat up on you like this, Gibson, but my money is that this is what most 'digital guitarists' will want."

Finally, in November 2006, Gibson began shipping the digital guitar, now called the Digital HD.6X-Pro (HD for High Definition sound, 6X for six channels). It was a Les Paul, complete with "Les Paul Model" on the headstock, with some special ornamentation, including metallic blue top finish, knurled cylindrical tuners and metallic checkerboard fret markers. Bundled with the breakout box, plus hardware and software so that it could be used with a computer, it listed for $4,999.

In these early years of the 21st century, Gibson's electric line is one variation after another, but almost all are variations on the traditional themes of proven models. The model families are familiar – Les Paul, SG, Flying V, Explorer, Firebird, ES-335 and traditional hollowbodies. Within those basic model groups, the model count is now approaching 200 different variations.

Perhaps the biggest challenge for Gibson today is coming up with new variations and, possibly the most fun, coming up with new model names. Juszkiewicz shook up what had been called the Designer Series (Explorers, Flying Vs and Firebirds) in 2002 with a new name – the X-Factor Series. The X designation seemed natural for the Explorer, which became the X-plorer, but wasn't so natural for the Flying V, which became the V-Factor X. Complementing the aura of mystery that went with "X-Factor" were the Voodoo models, available in Flying V, SG and Les Paul versions, featuring a "Juju" finish, with blood red wood filler rubbed into the grain after an Ebony finish had been applied to the swamp ash body.

The X-Factor changes set the stage for a deluge of new models in 2006. The Menace, available in Les Paul and SG versions, expanded on that ominous theme, with flat black paint, "tribal" body carvings and a clenched fist inlaid in the fingerboard. On the opposite side of the attitude spectrum, the New Century models (Les Paul, SG, X-Factor, V-Factor X) reflected reality, literally, with a full-body mirror pickguard. The name of the Les Paul Goddess flattered its target audience of women guitarists, and the model featured a lightweight body and thinner neck. For the "bad girls" the Les Paul Vixen was a cheaper version of the Goddess, with opaque finish colors instead of the Goddess's Sunbursts. For automotive enthusiasts, the Les Paul GT offered monochrome flame finishes in such colors as Muscle Green and Daytona Blue, and the SG GT sported a white racing stripe and a massive chrome-plated tailpiece. The Vegas and High Roller used gambling references to convey the excitement – or maybe the risk – of a new body type, sporting an asymmetrical, semi-hollowbody with maple top and mahogany back.

After the scattergun approach of 2006, Gibson was more focused in 2007, emphasizing the digital guitar and the Les Paul BFG, a stripped-down, modified Les Paul with no binding (not even a truss-rod), a humbucker and a P-90 pickup, and the selector switch rewired to be a kill switch. The Custom division was similarly subdued, primarily promoting a new signature model from actor Kiefer Sutherland (of the hit TV series *24*), featuring a gold finish and upscale ornamentation on the routed-back 336-style guitar.

As Gibson passed the midway point in the first decade of the 21st century, the Gibson electric guitar passed its 70th anniversary in good health. Gibson's iconic models – as well as the company itself – have weathered the ups and downs of a fickle music market and the perils of ownership changes. Moreover, recent combinations and variations of features, along with catchy new model names, have accomplished what all the valiant (but failed) efforts to advance electric guitar design through the 1970s, '80s and '90s could not do. They've given Gibson electrics a youthful flair that has changed Gibson's identity from a staid, traditional company to one with a modern, fashionable sense of design. The stigma, which had started in the 1950s and inspired Ted McCarty to draw up the most radical guitars he could think of, has finally been lifted, but without sacrificing Gibson's foundation of tradition.

The only force that could stop Gibson electric guitars now would have to be a force strong enough to stop the electric guitar itself. That appears unlikely, as the electric guitar has endured where earlier popular instruments, such as the minstrel banjo, the mandolin and the tenor banjo, succumbed to "the next big thing. But if a new type of guitar or some other kind of instrument does suddenly make the electric guitar obsolete, whether the new technology is digital or something altogether different, Gibson, more than any other company, seems ready to embrace and lead the charge to the future.

Variations on a theme of success

◁ 2004 Les Paul Voodoo

◁ 2007 Les Paul BFG

With a stable of proven winners no other guitar maker can match, Gibson now finds continuing success in accessorizing established models rather than trying to reinvent the electric guitar. The Les Paul Voodoo sports campy features such as blood red wood filler and a skull on the fingerboard, while the Les Paul BFG was designed to look like a customized guitar. The X-plorer New Century dresses up the now-familiar angular design with a full-body mirrored pickguard. Even the new CS-336 relies on traditional elements to attract a following. Gibson has a model to fit almost every player's taste, as illustrated by Patrick Stump of Fall Out Boy (opposite) with a platinum-finish SG Special, and Andrew Stockdale of Wolfmother (left) with his customized, Bigsby-equipped SG. And even the futuristic, experimental nature of the Digital guitar was built on the most solid foundation available - a Gibson Les Paul.

◁ 2006 X-Plorer New Century

▷ 2006 Digital HD.6X-Pro

How to use this **reference section**

This reference section is broken down into nine main model groupings as follows:

Chet Atkins Models
ES Models
Explorer Models
Firebird Models
Flying V Models
Les Paul Models
SG Models
Other Models
Custom Models

Models are listed alphabetically within these groups except for Artist Signature models, which are listed separately at the end of each group. Artist models are listed alphabetically by last name (e.g. Jimi Hendrix = H).

Models with product or personality themes are listed under Custom models.

Production totals, where available, are from the personal records of Gibson employee Julius Bellson for the pre-World War II years (1937–41) and from Gibson shipping totals (1948–79).

Format of the model listings:
Model name (years of production) /
Later model name (years of production)
Quick identification keys
• Body specifications
• Neck specifications
• Electronic specifications
Production numbers (not all years and models available)

Related models (in alphabetical order), production years, specs and production numbers

CHET ATKINS MODELS

Chet Atkins 350XT: Prototype of Chet Atkins Country Gentleman.

Chet Atkins 3535: Original name for Chet Atkins Country Gentleman.

Chet Atkins CE (Standard) (1982–2005)
Single-cut solidbody classical, nylon strings
• 14½-inch wide, single cutaway, chambered mahogany back, spruce top (cedar optional (1994–95), simulated round soundhole, soundhole insert with signature and prewar script logo, rectangular bridge, multiple-bound top with brown outer layer, gold-plated hardware.
• 25½-inch scale, unbound rosewood fingerboard (ebony from 1996), 1.8-inch nut width (also specified as 1¹³⁄₁₆-inch and 1⅞-inch), slotted peghead, scalloped top edge of peghead, no logo (standard "dove wing" with logo from 1993).
•Transducer pickup, roller knobs recessed into upper bass side, individual trim pots accessible internally.

Chet Atkins CE Showcase Edition (July 1988 guitar of the month): Vintage Sunburst finish. Production: 200 for U.S., 50 for overseas.
Chet Atkins CEC (1982–2005): Ebony fingerboard, 2-inch wide at nut.
Chet Atkins CEC – True Cedar (2000–2005): Cedar top, ebony fingerboard, 2-inch wide at nut, Natural finish.

Chet Atkins CGP (1986–87)
Asymmtrical solidbody, 2 mini toggles, bolt-on neck
• Contoured mahogany body, flat-mount bridge/tailpiece with individual string adjustments, Kahler Flyer vibrato optional, gold-plated hardware, Wine Red finish.
• Bolt-on maple neck, ebony fingerboard, 25½ scale.
• 2 single-coil pickups tapped for normal and high output, 2 knobs (volume and tone), 2 mini-toggles for ohm tap, 3-way selector switch.
Production: Catalogued but few if any produced.

Chet Atkins Country Gentleman (1986–2005)
Thin single-cut archtop, red rectangular inlays
• 17-inch wide, rounded cutaway, thinline semi-hollowbody, tune-o-matic bridge, ebony bridge base with pearl inlay, Bigsby vibrato with curved tubular arm (optional from 1993), 7-ply top binding, 5-ply back binding, bound f-holes.
• Laminated maple neck, 25½-inch scale, 21 frets, unbound ebony fingerboard, red rectangular inlays positioned on bass edge of fingerboard, 1¾-inch nut width, unbound peghead, crown peghead inlay, metal tuner buttons.
• 2 humbucking pickups, 3 knobs (2 volume, 1 master tone) and 3-way selector switch on lower treble bout, master volume knob on cutaway bout.

Chet Atkins (JS) Double (1989–91): See Johnny Smith Double.

Chet Atkins Phasar (1987)
Double-cut asymmetrical solidbody, 2 narrow humbuckers
• Asymmetrical double cutaway solidbody.
• Rosewood fingerboard, 25½-inch scale, dot inlays, 6-on-a-side tuner arrangement.
• 2 narrow humbucking pickups with no visible poles, 2 knobs.
Production: 6 (3 with vibrato, 3 without).

Chet Atkins SST (1987–2005)
Single-cut solidbody acoustic, steel strings, Chet Atkins signature on body
• Single cutaway, spruce top, mahogany body with Chromyte (balsa) center, simulated round soundhole, soundhole insert with signature and prewar script logo (no soundhole from 1993, signature decal near fingerboard from 1993), rectangular ebony bridge (belly bridge from 1993), bound top, gold-plated hardware, Antique Natural, Alpine White or Ebony finish.
• Mahogany neck, 21 frets, 25½-inch scale, unbound ebony fingerboard, dot inlay (star inlay from 1993), 1¹¹⁄₁₆-inch nut width, solid peghead, scalloped top edge of peghead (standard "dove wing" peghead from 1991), no peghead logo or ornament (prewar-style script logo from 1991, star inlay from 1993).
•Transducer bridge pickup with built-in preamp, 2 knobs on top (knobs on rim from 1993).

Chet Atkins SST 12-string (1990–94): Star fingerboard inlay, scalloped top edge of peghead, prewar script logo, gold-plated hardware, Antique Natural, Alpine White, Wine Red or Ebony finish.
Chet Atkins SST 12-string Brett Michaels Edition (1992–93): Antique Gold finish. Production: 2.
Chet Atkins SST Celebrity Series (1991–93): Gold-plated hardware, Ebony finish.
Chet Atkins SST – True Cedar (2000–2005): Cedar top, Natural finish.
Chet Atkins SST w/flame-top (1993–95): Flamed maple top, Antique Natural, Heritage Cherry Sunburst or Translucent Amber finish.
Chet Atkins Studio CE (1993–2000, 2004–05): *Single-cut solidbody acoustic, nylon strings, Chet Atkins signature on body*

- Single cutaway (deeper cutaway from 2004), hollow mahogany back (sound port from 2004), spruce top (cedar from 2004), no soundhole, flared bridge ends (moustache bridge from 2004), gold-plated hardware, Antique Natural finish.
- 26-inch scale, unbound ebony fingerboard with treble-side extension, 1¹³⁄₁₆-inch nut width, slotted peghead, decal logo.
- Under-saddle pickup, controls on rim (slider controls on circular plate on upper bass bout from 2004), individual string volume controls accessible internally, signature on upper bass bout near fingerboard, multiple-bound top with black outer layer.

Chet Atkins Studio CEC (1993–2000, 2004–05): 2-inch nut width.

Chet Atkins Studio Classic (1991–93)
Single-cut solidbody acoustic, fleur de lis on peghead
- Single cutaway, hollow mahogany back, fan-braced spruce top, controls on rim, no soundhole, flared bridge ends, abalone top border, cocobolo wood bindings, top inlaid at end of fingerboard with rosewood and abalone fleur-de-lis (no top inlay, 1993), gold-plated hardware, Antique Natural finish.
- 26¼-inch scale, V-end ebony fingerboard (asymmetrical with treble-side extension, 1993), 2-inch nut width, small *CGP* inlay at 7th fret, no other fingerboard inlay, slotted peghead, peghead narrows toward top, rosewood peghead veneer, prewar style *The Gibson* logo in pearl (postwar logo, 1993), small fleur-de-lis peghead inlay.
- Under-saddle pickup, controls on rim.

Chet Atkins Super 4000 (1995, 1997)
Thinbody single-cut archtop, split-block inlays, floating pickup
- 18-inch archtop, carved spruce top, figured maple back and sides, Heritage Cherry Sunburst finish.
- 5-piece maple neck, ebony fingerboard, split-block inlays, 5-piece split-diamond peghead inlay.
- Floating full-size humbucking pickup.

Chet Atkins Tennessean (1990–2005)
Thinbody single-cut archtop, dot inlays, near edge of fingerboard
- 16¼-inch wide, 1⅝-inch deep, single rounded cutaway, laminated maple back and sides with Chromyte (balsa) center block, tune-o-matic bridge, stopbar tailpiece, clear pickguard with silver paint on back and model name stenciled in black, single-bound top and back.
- Unbound ebony fingerboard, 25½-inch scale, dot inlay positioned closer to bass edge of fingerboard, 1¾-inch nut width, clear plastic truss-rod cover back-painted silver, Chet

Atkins signature peghead decal, plastic tuner buttons.
- 2 humbucking pickups.

ES MODELS

ES-5 (1949–55)
Single-cut archtop, 3 pickups, 4 knobs
- 17-inch wide, rounded cutaway, rosewood bridge (tune-o-matic from 1955) trapeze tailpiece with pointed ends and 3 raised parallelograms, laminated beveled-edge pickguard, triple-bound top and back (5-ply from 1955), bound *f*-holes (a few early unbound), gold-plated hardware, Sunburst or Natural finish.
- 2-piece maple neck with stripe down center, pointed-end rosewood fingerboard with 5-ply binding, large pearl block inlays, single-bound peghead, black "stinger" on back of peghead, crown peghead inlay.
- 3 P-90 pickups (Alnico V specified, 1955), 3 volume controls, 1 master tone knob on cutaway bout.
Production: 911 (includes some ES-5 Switchmasters 1955).

ES-5 Reissue (1996–2006): 3 P-90 pickups.

ES-5 Switchmaster (1955–62)
Single-cut archtop, 3 pickups, 6 knobs
- 17-inch wide, rounded cutaway (pointed 1960–62), tune-o-matic bridge 1955, trapeze tailpiece (tubular with double loop from 1956), laminated beveled-edge pickguard, 5-ply binding, gold-plated hardware, Sunburst or Natural finish.
- 2-piece maple neck with stripe down center, pointed-end rosewood fingerboard with 5-ply binding, large pearl block inlays, single-bound peghead, black "stinger" on back of peghead, crown peghead inlay.
- 3 P-90 pickups (humbuckers from 1957), 6 knobs (3 volume, 3 tone), slotted pickup selector switch on cutaway bout.
Production: 498 (1956–71).

Switchmaster Reissue (1996–2006): 3 humbucking pickups.
Switchmaster Reissue Alnico (1996–2006): 3 Alnico V pickups.

ES-100 (1938–41)/ **ES-125** pre-WWII (1941–43)
Non-cut archtop, 1 pickup, prewar script logo in paint
- Full-depth hollowbody, 14¼-inch wide, X-braced carved spruce top, maple back and sides, flat back (arched from 1940), single-bound top and back, Sunburst finish.
- Unbound rosewood fingerboard (unbound from 1940), dot inlays, silkscreen logo.
- Blade pickup with white rectangular housing

(rectangular metal-covered with screw-poles from 1940), pickup in neck position (bridge position from 1940), 2 knobs, jack on side. Production: 585 (ES-100); 152 (ES-125, 1941).

EST-100 / ETG-100 (1940–41): 4-string tenor. Production: 19.

ES-120T (1962–70)
Thinbody archtop, pickup and controls in molded pickguard
- 16¼-inch wide thinline body, 1 *f*-hole, single-bound top and back, Sunburst finish.
- Unbound rosewood fingerboard, dot inlays, decal logo.
- Melody Maker pickup, knobs and jack all mounted in large molded pickguard.
Production: 8,895.

ES-125 pre-WWII. See ES-100.

ES-125 post-WWII (1946–70)
Non-cut archtop, 1 P-90 pickup, postwar logo, dot or trapezoid inlays
- 16¼-inch full-depth hollowbody of laminated maple (some with all-mahogany body), tortoise pickguard, trapeze tailpiece, single-bound top and back, Sunburst finish.
- Unbound rosewood fingerboard (unbound from 1940), pearloid trapezoid inlay (some with dot inlay from 1946, all with dot inlay from 1950), decal logo.
- P-90 pickup in neck position (earliest with no non-adjustable poles or no poles), 2 knobs.
Production: 32,940.

ES-125C (1966–70): Pointed cutaway, 1 P-90 pickup. Production: 475.
ES-125CD (1966–70): Pointed cutaway, 2 P-90 pickups. Production: 1,104.
ES-125T (1956–68): Thinline body. Production: 9,640.
ES-125T (¾-scale) (1957–68): Thinline body 12¾-inch wide, 22¾-inch scale. Production: 1,582.
ES-125TC (1961–69): Thinline body, pointed cutaway. Production: 5,234.
ES-125TCD (1960): 2 P-90 pickups. Production: 287.
ES-125TD (1957–63): 2 pickups. Production: 1,215.
ES-125TDC (1961–70): 2 P-90 pickups: Production: 5,556.

ES-130 full-depth (1954–56), **ES-135** (1956–57)
Non-cut archtop, 1 pickup, trapezoid inlays
- 16¼-inch archtop body of laminated maple, trapeze tailpiece with raised diamond, laminated beveled-edge pickguard, single-bound top and back.
- 1 P-90 pickup mounted 1-inch from fingerboard, 2 knobs.
- Mahogany neck, 24¾-inch scale, single-bound fingerboard, trapezoid inlays, decal logo, no peghead ornament, Sunburst finish.
Production: 556.

ES-135 2nd version (1991–2003)
Thinbody single-cut archtop, pointed horn, dot inlays
• 16-inch laminated maple/poplar/maple semi-hollowbody, 2¼-inch deep, pointed cutaway, f-holes (no f-holes from 2002), tune-o-matic bridge, trapeze tailpiece (stopbar from 2002), chrome-plated hardware (some gold-plated, 1998–99).
• Maple neck, unbound rosewood fingerboard, dot inlays, model name decal on peghead, decal logo.
• 2 P-100 stacked-coil humbucking pickups (humbuckers optional, 1998–2002, standard from 2003), 4 knobs, selector switch on upper bass bout.

ES-135 Gothic (1998–99): 2 humbucking pickups with no covers, black pickguard, ebony fingerboard, moon-and-star inlay at 12th fret, o other inlay, white outline of logo on peghead, black chrome hardware, flat black finish.
Swingmaster ES-135 (1999): 2 dog-ear P-90 pickups, ebony fingerboard, pearloid trapezoid inlays, optional Bigsby vibrato, Custom Coral, Daddy-O Yellow, Mint Green or Outa-Sight White finish.

ES-137 Classic (2002–current)
Thinbody single-cut archtop, pointed horn, trapezoid inlays
• 16-inch laminated maple/poplar/maple semi-hollowbody, 2¼-inch deep, pointed cutaway, f-holes, tune-o-matic bridge, multiply top binding, single-bound back, chrome- or gold-plated hardware.
• Maple neck, bound rosewood fingerboard, trapezoid inlays, *C* inlay at 12th fret, decal logo.
• 2 humbucking pickups, 4 knobs, selector switch on upper bass bout.

ES-137 Custom (2002–current)
Thinbody single-cut archtop, pointed horn, split-diamond inlays
• 16-inch laminated maple/poplar/maple semi-hollowbody, 2¼-inch deep, pointed cutaway, f-holes, tune-o-matic bridge, multiply top binding, single-bound back, chrome- or gold-plated hardware.
• 3-piece maple neck, bound ebony fingerboard, trapezoid inlays, pearl logo.
• 2 humbucking pickups, 4 knobs, rotary Varitone switch, selector switch on upper bass bout.

ES-137P (Premier) (2002–04)
Thinbody single-cut archtop, pointed horn, half-trapezoid inlays
• 16-inch laminated maple/poplar/maple semi-hollowbody, 2¼-inch deep, pointed cutaway, f-holes, tune-o-matic bridge, black body binding, chrome-plated hardware, metallic finishes.

• Maple neck, unbound rosewood fingerboard, half-trapezoid inlays, *P* inlay at 12th fret, decal logo.
• 2 exposed-coil humbucking pickups or 2 P-90 pickups, 4 knobs, selector switch on upper bass bout.

ES-140 (¾-scale) (1950–56)
Small single-cut archtop, pointed horn
• 12¾-inch wide laminated maple hollowbody, f-holes, pointed cutaway, trapeze tailpiece, single-bound top and back.
• 22¾-inch scale, dot inlays, Sunburst finish (Natural finish rare).
• 1 P-90 pickup.
Production: 2,385.

ES-140T (¾-scale T) (1957–67): Thin body. Production: 1,533.

ES-150 pre-WWII (1936–42)
Non-cut archtop, dot inlays, pearl logo
• Full-depth hollowbody, 16¼-inch wide, X-braced carved spruce top, flat back (arched from 1940), single-bound top and back, single-bound pickguard, Sunburst finish.
• Single-bound rosewood fingerboard (unbound from 1940), dot inlays, pearl logo.
• "Charlie Christian" blade pickup in hexagonal housing (rectangular metal-covered with screw-poles from 1940), single-ply binding around pickup and around blade (triple-ply 1938–9), 2 knobs, jack at tailpiece base.
Production: 1,629 (1937–41).

EST-150 (1937–39) / **ETG-150** (1940–42): Tenor neck, arched back, jack on side. Production: 95 (1937–41).
ESP-150 (1939): Plectrum neck, arched back, jack on side. Production: 1.

ES-150 post-WWII (1947–56)
Non-cut archtop, 17-inch wide, single P-90 pickup, dot or trapezoid inlays
• Full-depth laminated maple hollowbody, 17-inch wide, laminated beveled-edge pickguard, bound top and back.
• Unbound rosewood fingerboard (bound from 1950), dot inlay (trapezoid from 1950), silkscreen logo.
• P-90 pickup in neck position, jack on side.
Production: 3,447 (1948–56).

ETG-150 (1947–71): Tenor neck, electric version of TG-50 acoustic, 16¼-inch hollowbody, 1 P-90 pickup, laminated beveled-edge pickguard, bound fingerboard, dot inlays, no peghead ornament. Production: 476 (1948–60).

ES-150DC (1969–74)
Double-cut archtop, full-depth body, rounded horns
• 16¼-inch archtop body of laminated maple,

3-inch deep, Natural, Walnut, or Cherry finish.
• Rosewood fingerboard, small block inlays, crown peghead inlay.
• 2 humbucking pickups, 4 knobs on lower treble bout, master volume knob on upper treble bout Production: 2,801.

ES-175 single pickup (1949–72)
Single-cut archtop, pointed horn, double-parallelogram inlay, 1 pickup
• 16¼-inch wide, laminated maple body, pointed cutaway, laminated beveled-edge pickguard, rosewood bridge (tune-o-matic from 1977), hinged tailpiece with pointed ends and 3 raised parallelograms (T-center with zigzag tubes 1958–71), triple-bound top, single-bound back, Sunburst or Natural finish.
• Bound rosewood fingerboard, double-parallelogram inlay, crown peghead inlay, pearl logo.
• 1 P-90 pickup in neck position (some with 2 pickups and 3 knobs 1951–53; some with Alnico V pickup 1955, humbucker from 1957), 2 knobs.
Production; 9,964.

ES-175 double pickup (1951–53, 1971–91, 2006–current) / **ES-175D** (1953–70) / **ES-175 Reissue** (1991–2005)
Single-cut archtop, pointed horn, double-parallelogram inlay, 2 pickups
• 16¼-inch wide, laminated maple body (mahogany back and sides 1983–90), pointed cutaway, laminated beveled-edge pickguard, rosewood bridge (tune-o-matic from 1977), hinged tailpiece with pointed ends and 3 raised parallelograms (T-center with zigzag tubes 1958–71, hinged from 1991), triple-bound top, single-bound back, Sunburst or Natural finish.
• Bound rosewood fingerboard, double-parallelogram inlay, crown peghead inlay, pearl logo.
• 2 P-90 pickups (some with Alnico V, humbuckers from 1957), 4 knobs, toggle switch.
Production: 16,790.

ES-175 Aged Reissue (2002–04): Zigzag tailpiece, aged hardware.
ES-175CC (1978–79): Charlie Christian pickup, 3 screws into top, adjustable rosewood bridge, Sunburst or Walnut stain finish. Production: 489.
ES-175D CMT (1989–90): Curly maple top, bound ebony fingerboard, bound peghead, gold-plated hardware.
ES-175T (1976–79): Thinbody 1⅞-inch deep. Production: 1,063.
Swingmaster ES-175 (1999): 2 P-90 pickups, ebony fingerboard, pearloid trapezoid inlays, optional Bigsby vibrato, Custom Coral, Daddy-O Yellow, Mint Green or Outa-Sight White finish.

ES-225T (1956–58)
Thinbody single-cut archtop, pointed horn, dot inlay
• 16¼-inch wide, pointed cutaway, trapeze bridge/tailpiece combination with strings looping over bridge, laminated beveled-edge pickguard, single-bound top and back, Sunburst or Natural finish.
• Bound rosewood fingerboard, dot inlays, pearl logo, no peghead ornament.
• P-90 pickup in middle position, 2 knobs.
Production: 5,220.
ES-225TD (1956–59): 2 pickups. Production: 2,754.

ES-240 (1977–1978)
Thinbody double-cut archtop, rounded horns, same as ES-335 but with coil-tap switch
• Thin double-cutaway semi-hollowbody, rounded horns, tune-o-matic bridge, stopbar tailpiece.
• Bound rosewood fingerboard, small block inlays, crown peghead inlay, pearl logo.
• 2 humbucking pickups, 4 knobs, selector switch, coil-tap switch on lower bass treble bout near tone and volume knobs.
Production: 3.

ES-250 (1939–40)
Non-cut archtop, open-book inlays, Charlie Christian pickup
• 17-inch wide, carved spruce top, maple sides and arched back, triple-bound pickguard, large tailpiece, Sunburst or Natural finish.
• Bound rosewood fingerboard, open-book inlay (some with double-parallelogram, some with fancy pattern in rectangular inserts), 2-piece maple neck with center stripe, stairstep headstock (some with non-stairstep, bound or unbound), stinger on back of headstock, pearl logo (some with post-WWII logo).
• Triple-bound Charlie Christian pickup with 6 blades (some assembled post-WWII with P-90 pickup), 2 knobs, jack at tailpiece base.
Production: 70.

ES-295 (1952–58, 1990–2000)
Single-cut archtop, pointed horn, gold finish
• 16¼-inch wide laminated maple body, pointed cutaway, clear pickguard back-painted with white background and gold floral design, trapeze bridge/tailpiece combo with strings looping over bridge (Bigsby vibrola 1992–97, optional 1998), triple-bound top, single-bound back, gold-plated hardware, gold finish.
• Bound rosewood fingerboard, 19 frets (20 from 1955), double-parallelogram inlay, crown peghead inlay.
• 2 P-90 pickups with white covers (humbuckers from late 1958).
Production: 1,770 (1952–58).

ES-300 pre-WWII (1940–42)
Non-cut archtop, double-parallelogram inlays, prewar logo
• 17-inch wide, parallel-braced carved spruce top, most with dowel supports under bridge, carved maple back, tailpiece with pointed ends and raised diamond and arrows, triple-bound top (some single-ply) and back, bound tortoiseshell celluloid pickguard.
• 2-piece maple neck with stripe down middle, double-parallelogram inlay, single-bound peghead, black "stinger" on back of peghead, crown peghead inlay (some with 7-piece split-diamond), pearl logo.
• 7-inch slant-mounted oblong pickup with adjustable poles (4⅛-inch pickup from 1941), jack on side.
Production: 194 (1940–41).

ES-300 post-WWII (1945–52)
Non-cut archtop, double-parallelogram inlays, postwar logo
• 17-inch laminated maple body (a few early with 5-ply mahogany body), trapeze tailpiece with pointed ends and 3 raised parallelograms (early with plate tailpiece with 2 f-hole cutouts), laminated beveled-edge pickguard (early with bound tortoiseshell celluloid pickguard), triple-bound top and back, Sunburst or Natural finish (a few black, 1945).
• 1-piece mahogany neck, bound rosewood fingerboard, double-parallelogram inlay, bound peghead, crown peghead inlay, plastic keystone tuner buttons: mid 1946.
• P-90 pickup in neck position (2 pickups from 1948), 2 knobs (master tone knob added on upper treble bout, 1948).
Production: 826 (1948–56).

ES-320TD (1971–74)
Thinbody double-cut archtop, dot inlays, oblong pickups
• 16-inch double cutaway thinbody of laminated maple, tune-o-matic bridge, nickel-plated bridge cover with logo, black plastic pickguard, bound top and back (black-painted edges to simulate binding on Natural finish models), Natural, Walnut, or Cherry finish.
• Rosewood fingerboard, dot inlays, decal logo.
• 2 Melody Maker pickups with embossed Gibson logo, oblong metal control plate with 2 knobs and 2 slide switches.
Production: 664.

ES-325TD (1972–79)
Thinbody double-cut archtop, 1 f-hole
• 16-inch semi-hollow archtop, tune-o-matic bridge, trapeze tailpiece with pointed ends, single-bound top and back.
• 2 mini-humbucking pickups with no visible poles (polepieces from 1976), semi-circular plastic control plate, 4 knobs.
• Rosewood fingerboard, dot inlays.
Production: 2,445.

ES-330T (1959–63)
Thinbody double-cut archtop, P-90 pickup
• 16-inch hollow thinbody archtop of laminated maple, double rounded cutaways, tune-o-matic bridge, trapeze tailpiece, single-bound top and back, Sunburst or Natural finish.
• Neck joins body at 17th fret, bound rosewood fingerboard, dot inlay (small blocks from 1962), pearl logo, no peghead ornament.
• 1 black plastic-covered P-90 pickup in middle position (chrome cover from 1962).
Production: 2,510.

ES-330TD (1959–71) (1998–99): 2 black plastic-covered P-90 pickups, neck joins at 20th fret from 1968. Production: 21,379 (1959–75).

ES-333 (2003–05)
Thin double-cut archtop, rounded horns, no pickguard
• Thin double-cutaway semi-hollowbody of laminated maple/poplar/maple, tune-o-matic bridge, bound top and back, nickel-plated hardware.
• Bound rosewood fingerboard, dot inlays, no peghead ornament, decal logo.
• 2 exposed-coil humbucking pickups, 4 knobs

ES-335TD (1958–81) / **ES-335 DOT** (1981–90) / **ES-335 Reissue** (1991–98) / **ES-335 Dot** (1999–current)
Thinbody double-cutaway archtop, 2 humbuckers, dot or small block inlays
• 16-inch semi-hollowbody of laminated maple, 1⅝-inch deep, double-cutaway, rounded horns, tune-o-matic bridge, stop tailpiece (trapeze from 1964), Bigsby vibrato optional (most models with Bigsby have CUSTOM MADE plate covering original tailpiece holes; some without holes or plate), laminated beveled-edge pickguard extends below bridge (shorter guard from 1961, longer guard from), single-bound top and back, plain or figured top optional from 2006, satin or gloss finish optional from 2006.
• Single-bound rosewood fingerboard, neck-body joint at 19th fret, dot inlay (small pearloid blocks from 1962; some with single-parallelogram 1960s), crown peghead inlay (early with unbound fingerboard and no peghead ornament).
• 2 humbucking pickups, 2 tone and 2 volume knobs, 1 switch, coil tap switch 1977–81.
Production: 23,571 (1958–70); 26,781 (1971–79).

1959 ES-335 DOT Reissue (2002–current): Custom Shop model, dot inlays, plain top, nickel-plated hardware, single-ring tuner buttons.
1963 ES-335 Block Reissue (2002–current): Custom shop model, small block inlays, nickel-plated hardware, double-ring tuner buttons.
Custom Shop ES-335 (1995–2001): Figured maple back, long pickguard, thick 1959-style neck, replica orange oval label.

ES-335-12 (1965–70): 12-string, double-triangle peghead inlay with rounded points (sharp points from 1968). Production: 2,062.

ES-335 Block (1998–2000): Unbound ebony fingerboard, small block inlays.

ES-335 Centennial (Aug. 1994 guitar of the month): Cherry finish, serial number in raised numerals on tailpiece, numeral *1* of serial number formed by row of diamonds, letter *i* of logo dotted by inlaid diamond, gold medallion on back of peghead, gold-plated hardware, limited run of no more than 101 serial numbered from 1894–1994, packaged with 16 x 20-inch framed photograph and gold signet ring.

ES-335 CRR (1979): Country Rock Regular, 2 exposed-coil Dirty Fingers humbuckers, coil tap, brass nut, Antique Sunburst finish. Production: 300

ES-335 CRRS (1979): Country Rock Stereo, stereo electronics, master volume control, coil tap, TP-6 fine-tune tailpiece, brass nut, Country Tobacco or Dixie Brown (pink-to-brown Sunburst) finish. Production: 300

ES-335 Custom: See Custom Shop ES-335.

ES-335 DOT (1981–90): Dot inlays stopbar tailpiece, gold-plated hardware optional with white finish.

ES-335 DOT CMT (1983–85): Custom Shop model, highly figured maple top and back, 2 PAF humbucking pickups, full-length maple centerblock, mahogany neck.

ES-335 Gothic (1998): 2 '57 Classic humbucking pickups with no covers, black pickguard, ebony fingerboard, moon-and-star inlay at 12th fret, no other inlay, white outline of logo on peghead, black chrome hardware, flat black finish.

ES-335 Plain '60s Block (2005): Regular production model, plain top, block inlays, thin 1960s neck profile.

ES-335 Pro (1979–81): 2 Dirty Fingers humbucking pickups with exposed coils.

ES-335 Reissue (1990–current): Dot inlay (some limited runs with black binding, ebony fingerboard, small block inlays, 1998–99), stopbar tailpiece .

ES-335S: See 335-S.

ES-335 Showcase Edition (Apr. 1988 guitar of the month): EMG pickups, beige finish. Production: 200 for U.S., 50 for overseas.

ES-335 Studio (1986–91), ES-Studio (1991): No f-holes, 2 Dirty Fingers humbucking pickups with covers (earliest with exposed-coil PAF humbuckers, mahogany neck, unbound rosewood fingerboard (earliest with ebony), dot inlays, no peghead ornament, decal logo, Ebony or Cherry finish

ES-336 (1996–98) / **CS-336** (2002–current)
Thinbody double-cut archtop, smaller than ES-335, dot inlays
• 13¾-inch double-cutaway semi-hollowbody, routed mahogany back with solid center area,

arched (routed) maple top available with plain or figured grain, f-holes, rounded double cutaways, body lines similar to ES-335, back beveled on bass side, tune-o-matic bridge, bound top and back, chrome-plated hardware.
• Offset-V neck profile, bound rosewood fingerboard with compound radius, dot inlays, tapered peghead with straight string-pull (standard peghead from 2002), decal logo, Custom Shop decal logo on peghead, sealed-back tuners, inked-on serial number.
• 2 '57 Classic humbucking pickups, 4 knobs.

ES-340TD (1969–73)
Same as ES-335 except for maple neck (ES-335 has mahogany neck during ES-340 production period)
• 16-inch semi-hollowbody of laminated maple, 1⅝-inch deep, double-cutaway, rounded horns, tune-o-matic bridge, trapeze tailpiece, single-bound top and back, Walnut or Natural finish.
• 3-piece maple neck, single-bound rosewood fingerboard, small block inlays, crown peghead inlay.
• 2 humbucking pickups, 4 knobs, master volume control and master mixer control (rather than 2 volume controls).
Production: 1,561.

ES-345TD (1959–82) (2002) / **ES-345 Reissue** (2003–current)
Thinbody double-cut archtop, 2 humbuckers, double-parallelogram inlays
• 16-inch semi-hollow body of laminated maple, 1⅝-inch deep, double rounded cutaways, tune-o-matic bridge, stop tailpiece (trapeze from 1964, stopbar from 1982), laminated beveled-edge pickguard extends below bridge (shorter guard from 1961), single-bound top and back, gold-plated hardware.
• Single-bound rosewood fingerboard, neck-body joint at 19th fret, double-parallelogram inlay, crown peghead inlay (early with unbound fingerboard and no peghead ornament).
• 2 humbucking pickups, 2 tone and 2 volume knobs, 1 selector switch switch, stereo electronics with two jacks, Vari-tone rotary tone selector, black ring around Vari-tone switch (gold ring from 1960).
Production: 7,240 (1958–70); 4,348 (1971–79).

ES-346 (1997–98) / **Paul Jackson Jr. ES-346** (1999–2006)
Thinbody double-cut archtop, smaller than ES-335, double-parallelogram inlay
• 13¾-inch double-cutaway semi-hollowbody, routed mahogany back with solid center area, arched (routed) maple top available with plain or figured grain, f-holes, rounded double cutaways, body lines similar to ES-335, back beveled on bass side, tune-o-matic bridge, bound top and back, gold-plated

hardware, Emberglow, faded Cherry or Gingerburst finish.
• Offset-V neck profile, bound rosewood fingerboard with compound radius, double-parallelogram inlay, tapered peghead with straight string-pull, pearl logo, Custom Shop decal logo on peghead, sealed-back tuners, chrome-plated hardware, inked-on serial number.
• 2 '57 Classic humbucking pickups, 4 knobs.

ES-347TD (1978–85) / **ES-347S** (1987–93)
Thinbody double-cut archtop, 2 humbuckers, TP-6 tailpiece
• 16-inch semi-hollowbody of laminated maple, 1⅝-inch deep, double rounded cutaways, tune-o-matic bridge, TP-6 fine-tune tailpiece, laminated beveled-edge pickguard, single-bound top and back, chrome-plated hardware (gold-plated from 1987).
• Bound ebony fingerboard, large block inlays, bound peghead (multiply binding from 1987), crown peghead inlay, pearl logo.
• 2 humbucking pickups, 4 knobs and 1 pickup selector switch on lower treble bout, coil-tap switch on upper treble bout.
Production: 1,896 (1978–79).

ES-350 (also **ES-350 Premier**) (1947–56)
Single-cut archtop, rounded horn, double-parallelogram inlays
• 17-inch wide, rosewood bridge (tune-o-matic 1956), trapeze tailpiece with pointed ends and 3 raised parallelograms, laminated beveled-edge pickguard (early with bound tortoiseshell celluloid pickguard), triple-bound top and back, gold-plated hardware, Sunburst or Natural finish.
• 2-piece maple neck with stripe down center, single-bound fingerboard, double-parallelogram inlay, single-bound peghead, black "stinger" on back of peghead, crown peghead inlay crown peghead inlay, plastic keystone tuner buttons.
• 1 P-90 pickup (2 pickups from 1948), 2 knobs (master tone control added on cutaway from 1948, 4 knobs and toggle switch from 1952).
Production: 1,056 (1948–56).

ES-350T (1955–63, 1977–80, 1992–93, 1998–99)
Thinbody single-cut archtop, rounded horn, double-parallelogram inlays
• 17-inch wide body of laminated maple, rounded cutaway (pointed cutaway 1960–63), tune-o-matic bridge, tailpiece with W-shape tubular design, laminated beveled-edge pickguard, triple-bound top and back, Sunburst or Natural finish, gold-plated hardware.
• 23½-inch scale (25½-inch from 1977), single-bound fingerboard and peghead, double-parallelogram inlay, crown peghead inlay.
• 2 P-90 pickups (humbuckers from mid 1957).
Production: 1,041 (1955–63); 481 (1977–79).

ES-350T Centennial (Mar. 1994 guitar of the month): Vintage Sunburst finish, serial number in raised numerals on tailpiece, numeral *1* of serial number formed by row of diamonds, letter *i* of logo dotted by inlaid diamond, gold medallion on back of peghead, gold-plated hardware, limited run of no more than 101 serial numbered from 1894–1994, package includes 16 x 20-inch framed photograph and gold signet ring.

ES-355TD (1958–71, 1994, 1997, 2004)
Thinbody double-cut archtop, 2 humbuckers, block inlays
• 16-inch semi-hollowbody of laminated maple, 1⅝-inch deep, double-cutaway, rounded horns, tune-o-matic bridge, Bigsby vibrato (SW sideways-action vibrato optional, lyre vibrato 1963–68), multiple-bound pickguard extends below bridge, multiple-bound top, triple-bound back, single-bound *f*-holes.
• 2 humbucking pickups, mono circuitry standard but stereo with Varitone more common
• Single-bound ebony fingerboard, large block inlays, multiple-bound peghead, 5-piece split-diamond peghead inlay, Grover Rotomatic tuners.
Production: 3,151 (1958–70); 2,029 (1971–79).

ES-355 Centennial (June 1994 guitar of the month): Vintage Sunburst finish, serial number in raised numerals on tailpiece, numeral *1* of serial number formed by row of diamonds, letter *i* of logo dotted by inlaid diamond, gold medallion on back of peghead, gold-plated hardware, Vintage Sunburst finish, limited run of no more than 101 serial numbered from 1894–1994, package includes 16 x 20-inch framed photograph and gold signet ring.

ES-357 (1983–84)
Thinbody double-cut archtop, 3 pickups, Mitch Holder model
• 16-inch semi-hollowbody of laminated maple, 2-inch deep, curly maple top, no *f*-hples, TP-6 fine-tune tailpiece, single-bound top and back, Natural finish.
• 3-piece maple neck, bound ebony fingerboard, pearl block inlays, crown peghead inlay, bound peghead, gold-plated hardware.
• 3 P-90 pickups with black soapbar covers or humbucking covers (polepieces across center), 4 knobs (3 volume, 1 master tone), selector switch, mini-toggle switch for middle pickup control.
Production: 7 from Kalamazoo Custom Shop (1983); a few more made in Nashville (1984).

ES-369 (1982)
Thinbody double-cut archtop, narrow peghead, prewar script logo
• 16-inch semi-hollow archtop body of laminated maple, tune-o-matic bridge, TP-6 tailpiece, single-ply cream-colored pickguard, single-bound top and back.
• Single-bound rosewood fingerboard, pearloid trapezoid inlays, snakehead peghead, old-style script logo.
• 2 Dirty Fingers pickups with exposed coils, 4 speed knobs, 1 selector switch, 1 mini-toggle coil-tap switch.

ES-446s (2003–04)
Thinbody single-cut archtop, pointed horn, spruce top
• Single pointed cutaway, carved spruce top with integral braces, mahogany back, f-holes, tune-o-matic bridge, trapeze tailpiece.
• Unbound rosewood fingerboard, dot inlay.
• 2 humbucking pickups, 4 knobs, selector switch on upper bass bout.

ES-775 Classic Beauty (1990–93)
Single-cut archtop, pointed horn, slotted-block inlay
• 16¼-inch wide, figured laminated maple body, pointed cutaway, gold-plated hardware.
• 3-ply maple neck, bound ebony fingerboard, slotted-block inlay.
• 2 humbucking pickups, 4 knobs, selector switch.

ES-Artist (1979–85)
Thinbody double-cut archtop, winged-f peghead inlay
• 16-inch semi-hollow archtop body of laminated maple, 1¾-inch deep, no *f*-holes, tune-o-matic bridge, TP-6 tailpiece, laminated beveled-edge pickguard, multiple-bound top and back, gold-plated hardware, Cherry Sunburst, Ebony or Antique Fireburst finish.
• Single-bound ebony fingerboard, off-center dot inlay near bass edge of fingerboard, pearl logo.
• 2 humbucking pickups, active electronics, 3 knobs (bass, treble, volume), 3-way selector switch, 3 mini-toggle switches (bright, compression/expansion, active on/off).

ES-Studio: See ES-335.

ES ARTIST SIGNATURE MODELS

Larry Carlton ES-335 (2002–current): Chrome-plated hardware, small block inlays, slim neck profile, "Carltonburst" finish (yellow-to-red Sunburst).
Eric Clapton ES-335 (2005): Tune-o-matic bridge with white plastic saddles, small block inlays, long neck tenon, aged chrome and gold hardware, Cherry finish. Production: 250.
Herb Ellis Signature ES-165 (1991–2004)
Single-cut archtop, pointed horn, 1 humbucker
16-inch full-depth archtop, pointed cutaway, tune-o-matic bridge on rosewood base, T-shaped tailpiece with zigzag wires, multiply top binding, single-bound back, gold-plated hardware. Mahogany neck, bound rosewood fingerboard, double-parallelogram inlay, decal model name and logo on peghead (crown peghead inlay, pearl logo from 2002).
1 humbucking pickup, 2 knobs (1 floating mini-humbucking pickup, control knob in pickguard from 2002).
Herb Ellis Signature ES-165 Plus (2002–04): Curly top, removable f-hole inserts, 2 humbucking pickups mounted in top, 4 knobs, selector switch on upper bass bout.
Steve Howe Signature ES-175 (2001–current): Based on Howe's 1964, multiply top binding, pearl-inlaid ebony bridge base, zigzag tailpiece, nickel-plated hardware.
Paul Jackson Jr. ES-346: See ES-346
Alvin Lee "Big Red" ES-335 (2005–current): Based on Lee's 1959 with replaced fingerboard, small block inlays, 2 exposed-coil humbuckers and 1 Seymour Duncan uncovered single-coil in middle position, 3 volume knobs, 2 tone knobs, 1 switch, peace symbol and other Woodstock era graphics, Custom Authentic faded Cherry finish. Production: limited run of 50 with signed certificate, then unlimited production.
Lee Roy Parnell CS-336 (2004): Custom fat-profile neck, aged nickel hardware.
Andy Summers 1960 ES-335 (2001): Replica of Summers' personal guitar, 1960 specs, aged Cherry finish. Production: 50.

EXPLORER MODELS

Explorer (1958–59, 1975–79) / **Explorer I** (1981–82) / **Explorer 83** (1983) / **Explorer** (1984–89) / **Explorer Reissue** (1990) / **Explorer '76** (1991–2003) / **X-Plorer** (2003–current)
Angular solidbody, six-on-a-side tuners
• Korina (African limba wood) body (mahogany from 1975, some Korina 1976, alder 1982–84, mahogany from 1986), elongated upper treble bout and lower bass bout, tune-o-matic bridge, stop tailpiece, optional vibrato 1981–89, white pickguard (no pickguard 1984–89).
• Unbound rosewood fingerboard (ebony optional 1983–86, ebony 1987–88, rosewood 1989, ebony or rosewood from 1990), dot inlays, scimitar-shape peghead curves to treble side (a few early with forked peghead), pearl logo (decal 1981–89).
• 2 humbucking pickups, 3 knobs in straight line, selector switch on treble horn (knobs in triangular configuration, switch near knobs 1984–89, in straight line from 1990).
Production: 19 (1958); 3 (1959); 175 (1966–70).

1958 Korina Explorer (1993–current): Replica of 1958 version (5 with "split V" peghead shape), Korina body and neck, gold-plated hardware, Antique Natural finish.

Explorer 400/400+ (1985–86): 400-series electronics, 1 Dirty Fingers humbucking pickup and 2 single-coil pickups, master tone and master volume knob, 3 mini-switches for on/off pickup control, push/pull volume control for coil tap, Kahler Flyer vibrato, black chrome hardware, Alpine White, Ebony, Ferrari Red or Pewter finish.

Explorer Black Hardware (1985): Kahler vibrato standard, black hardware.

Explorer Centennial (Apr. 1994 guitar of the month): Serial number in raised numerals on tailpiece, numeral 1 of serial number formed by row of diamonds, letter i of logo dotted by inlaid diamond, gold medallion on back of peghead, gold-plated hardware, Antique Gold finish, limited run of no more than 101 serial numbered from 1894–1994, package includes 16 x 20 framed photograph and gold signet ring.

Explorer CM: See The Explorer.

Explorer Gothic (1998–2001) / **X-Plorer Gothic** (2001): No pickup covers, black pickguard, ebony fingerboard, moon-and-star inlay at 12th fret (no other inlay), white-outline headstock logo, black chrome hardware, flat black finish.

Explorer Heritage (1983): Reissue of 1958 version, Korina body, black knobs, 3-piece Korina neck (first 8 with 1-piece neck), pearloid keystone tuner buttons, serial number of 1 followed by a space and 4 digits, Antique Natural, Ebony or Ivory finish. Production: 100.

Explorer Korina (1982–84): Reissue of 1958 version, Korina body, Nashville wide-travel tune-o-matic bridge, gold knobs, metal tuner buttons, standard 8-digit serial number, Candy Apple Red, Ebony, Ivory, or Antique Natural finish.

Explorer Left Hand (1984–87): Left-handed.

Mahogany Explorer (2002–03): Green, copper, blue and silver satin metallic finishes. Production: 15 in each finish.

Mahogany Explorer Split Headstock (2003–04): Mahogany body and neck, V-shaped headstock.

X-plorer New Century (2006–current): Full-body mirror pickguard, rosewood fingerboard, mirror dot inlays, 2 exposed-coil humbuckers.

Explorer Satin Finish (2003–04): Mon-gloss finish.

Explorer Synthesizer (1985): Roland 700 synthesizer system, Alpine White or Ebony finish.

Explorer Voodoo (2002–04): Swamp ash body, Juju finish (black with red wood filler), ebony fingerboard, voodoo doll inlay at 5th fret (no other inlays), red logo, red/black pickup coils.

Explorer II (1979–83)
Angular multi-layer solidbody with beveled edges
• 5-layer walnut and maple body with walnut or maple top, beveled body edges, tune-o-matic bridge, TP-6 tailpiece, gold-plated hardware, Natural finish.
• 22 frets, 24¾-inch scale, unbound ebony

fingerboard, dot inlays, E/2 on truss-rod cover.
• 2 humbucking pickups with exposed coils, 3 knobs in straight line, knobs mounted into top, 3-way selector switch into pickguard on upper treble horn.

Explorer III (1984–85)
Angular solidbody, 3 pickups
• Alder body, tune-o-matic bridge, locking nut vibrato system optional, Alpine White or military-style camouflage finish.
• Maple neck, unbound rosewood fingerboard, dot inlays, metal tuners, decal logo.
• 3 soapbar HP-90 pickups, 2 knobs, 2 selector switches.

Explorer III Black Hardware (1985): Kahler vibrato standard, black hardware.

Explorer 90 (1988)
Angular solidbody, strings through body
• Angular mahogany solidbody, tune-o-matic bridge, lightning-bolt tailpiece with strings through body, Floyd Rose vibrato optional, black chrome hardware, Alpine White, Ebony or Luna Silver finish.
• 25½-inch scale, ebony fingerboard, split-diamond inlays, pearl logo.
• 1 humbucking pickup, 2 knobs.

Explorer 90 Double (1989–90): Single-coil neck pickup, humbucking bridge pickup, 2 knobs, push/pull volume knob for coil tap, selector switch between knobs.

Explorer Pro (2002–05, 2007–current)
Angular body, ⅞ of standard Explorer size, flame maple top
• Angular-design mahogany solidbody, ⅞ of standard Explorer size, flame maple top optional, tune-o-matic bridge, Antique binding, chrome-plated hardware.
• Mahogany neck, bound rosewood fingerboard, dot inlays, curved peghead with 6-on-a-side tuner configuration, pearl logo.
• 2 exposed-coil humbucking pickups, 3 knobs in line parallel to edge of guitar, selector switch on treble horn.

The Explorer/Explorer CM (1976, 1981–84)
Angular solidbody, curly maple top, fine-tune tailpiece
• Angular maple solidbody, bound curly maple top, tune-o-matic bridge, TP-6 fine-tune tailpiece, gold-plated hardware, Antique Sunburst, Vintage Cherry Sunburst or Antique Natural finish.
• Maple neck, unbound ebony fingerboard, dot inlays, some with E/2 on truss-rod cover, pearl logo.
• 2 exposed-coil Dirty Fingers humbucking pickups, 3 knobs in straight line, knobs mounted into top, 3-way selector switch on upper treble horn.

X-plorer Studio (2004)
Angular body, ⅞ of standard Explorer size
• Angular-design poplar solidbody, tune-o-matic bridge, no pickguard.
• Mahogany neck, unbound rosewood fingerboard, dot inlays, curved peghead with 6-on-a-side tuner configuration, pearl logo.
• 2 exposed-coil humbucking pickups, 3 knobs in line parallel to edge of guitar, selector switch on treble horn.

EXPLORER ARTIST SIGNATURE MODELS

Allen Collins Explorer (2003): Based on 1958 version, Signature model for Lynyrd Skynyrd band member, Korina body and neck, Maestro vibrato, additional strap button on neck heel, aged Natural finish, belt buckle wear on back. Production: 100.

FIREBIRD MODELS

Firebird: See Firebird V.

Firebird I, reverse-body (1963–65, 1991–92) / **1963 Firebird I** (2000–current)
Solidbody with treble horn larger than bass horn, 1 mini-humbucker
• Angular body, 9-piece mahogany/walnut neck-through-body with mahogany side wings, 3-ply white-black-white pickguard with beveled edge, wraparound bridge with raised integral saddles, no vibrato, (a few with Firebird III vibrato), nickel-plated hardware (gold-plated, 1991–92).
• Unbound rosewood fingerboard, dot inlays, 6 tuners all on treble side of peghead, beveled peghead edge, Kluson banjo-style tuners, logo on truss-rod cover.
• 1 mini-humbucking pickup with no polepieces, 2 knobs.
Production: 1,377 (1963–65, includes some non-reverse).

Firebird I, non-reverse (1965–69)
Solidbody with bass horn larger than treble horn, 1 P-90 pickup
• Bass horn larger than treble horn, wraparound bridge with raised integral saddles, white pickguard with red Firebird logo.
• Set neck, unbound rosewood fingerboard, dot inlays, non-beveled peghead. right-angle tuners all on bass side of peghead.
• 2 black soapbar P-90 pickups, wraparound bridge with raised integral saddles, white pickguard with red Firebird logo, short-arm vibrato with tubular lever and plastic tip.
Production: 1,590 (1966–69, also some in 1965).

Firebird II (1981–82)
Solidbody with treble horn longer than bass horn, 2 full-size humbuckers, TP-6 tailpiece
• Reverse body shape, maple body with figured maple top cap, tune-o-matic bridge, TP-6 fine-tune tailpiece, bound top, large backplate for electronics access, Antique Sunburst or Antique Fireburst finish.
• 3-piece maple neck, unbound rosewood fingerboard, dot inlays, pearl logo at tip of peghead.
• 2 full-size humbucking pickups, active electronics 4 black barrel knobs, selector switch. 2 mini-switches for standard/active and brightness control.

Firebird III, reverse-body (1963–65) / **1964 Firebird III** (2000–current)
Solidbody with treble horn larger than bass horn, 2 mini-humbuckers, dot inlays
• Treble horn larger than bass horn, 9-piece mahogany/walnut neck-through-body with mahogany side wings, 3-ply white-black-white pickguard with beveled edge, wraparound bridge with raised integral saddles, simple spring vibrato with flat arm.
• Single-bound rosewood fingerboard, dot inlays, tuners all on treble side of peghead (all on bass side, 1965), Kluson banjo-style tuners (some with right-angle tuners, 1965), logo on truss-rod cover.
• 2 mini-humbucking pickups with no polepieces, 3-way toggle switch.
Production: 2,546 (1963–65, includes some non-reverse).

Firebird III, non-reverse (1965–69)
Solidbody with bass horn longer than treble horn, 2 P-90 pickups
• Bass horn larger than treble horn, wraparound bridge with raised integral saddles, white pickguard with red Firebird logo, vibrato with tubular arm.
• Set neck, unbound rosewood fingerboard, dot inlays, non-beveled peghead, right-angle tuners all on bass side of peghead.
• 3 black soapbar P-90 pickups, black sliding selector switch.
Production: 1,535 (1966–69, also some produced in 1965).

Firebird V, reverse-body (1963–65, 1986–87) / **Firebird Reissue** (1990) / **Firebird V** (1991–current**)** / **1964 Firebird V** (Custom Shop, 2000–current)
Solidbody with treble horn larger than bass horn, 2 mini-humbuckers, trapezoid inlays
• Treble horn larger than bass horn, 9-piece mahogany/walnut neck-through-body (7-piece from 1990) with mahogany side wings (all mahogany body with solid finish colors from 2002), 3-ply white-black-white pickguard with beveled edge, tune-o-matic bridge, Deluxe vibrato with metal tailpiece cover engraved

with Gibson and leaf-and-lyre (Kahler vibrato or stopbar tailpiece optional, 1986–87; no vibrola from 1990).
• Single-bound rosewood fingerboard, trapezoid inlays, tuners all on treble side of peghead (all on bass side, 1965, 1991–current), Kluson banjo-style tuners (some with right-angle tuners, 1965), logo on truss-rod cover.
• 2 mini-humbucking pickups with no polepieces, 3-way toggle switch.
Production: 925 (1963–65, includes some non-reverse).

Firebird (1980): 1-piece neck-through-body, unbound rosewood fingerboard, dot inlays, Cherry, Ebony or Natural finish.
Firebird V Celebrity Series (1991–93): Reverse body, black finish, white pickguard, gold-plated hardware.
Firebird (V) (1972–73): *LE* limited edition medallion, logo embossed on pickup covers. Production: 366.

Firebird V, non-reverse (1965–69)
Solidbody with bass horn longer than treble horn, 2 mini-humbuckers
• Bass horn larger than treble horn, tune-o-matic bridge, white pickguard with red Firebird logo, Deluxe vibrato with tubular arm, metal tailpiece cover engraved with Gibson and leaf-and-lyre decoration), nickel-plated hardware.
• Set neck, unbound rosewood fingerboard, dot inlays, non-beveled peghead. right-angle tuners all on bass side of peghead.
• 2 mini-humbucking pickups with no polepieces, black sliding selector switch.
Production: 492 (1966–69, also some produced in 1965).

Firebird V 12-string (1966–67): Standard headstock with six tuners per side. Production: 272.

Firebird VII, reverse-body (1963–65, 1991–93, 2003–current) / **1965 Firebird VII** (Custom Shop 2000–current)
Solidbody with treble horn larger than bass horn, 3 mini-humbuckers, block inlays
• Treble horn larger than bass horn, 9-piece mahogany/walnut neck-through-body with mahogany side wings (all-mahogany body with red metallic finish, 2002–current), 3-ply white-black-white pickguard with beveled edge, tune-o-matic bridge, Deluxe vibrato (tubular lever arm with plastic end cap, metal tailpiece cover engraved with Gibson and leaf-and-lyre decoration), gold-plated hardware (chrome-plated 1991–93).
• Single-bound ebony fingerboard, block inlay beginning at 1st fret, tuners all on treble side of peghead (all on bass side, 1965), beveled peghead edge, large Kluson banjo-style tuners, logo on truss-rod cover.
• 3 mini-humbucking pickups with no

polepieces, 3-way toggle switch, pearl block inlay (aged inlay 1991–93).
Production: 303 (1963–65, includes some non-reverse).

Firebird VII Centennial (September 1994 guitar of the month): Vintage Sunburst finish, serial number in raised numerals on tailpiece, numeral *1* of serial number formed by row of diamonds, letter *i* of logo dotted by inlaid diamond, gold medallion on back of peghead, gold-plated hardware, limited run of no more than 101 serial numbered from 1894–1994, package includes 16 x 20 framed photograph and gold signet ring.

Firebird VII, non-reverse (1965–69)
Solidbody with bass horn longer than treble horn, 3 mini-humbuckers
• Bass horn larger than treble horn, tune-o-matic bridge, white pickguard with red Firebird logo Deluxe Vibrato with tubular arm, metal tailpiece cover engraved with Gibson and leaf-and-lyre decoration), gold-plated hardware.
• Set neck, unbound rosewood fingerboard, dot inlays non-beveled peghead. right-angle tuners all on bass side of peghead.
• 3 mini-humbucking pickups with no polepioeces, black sliding selector switch.
Production: 283 (1966–69, also some produced in 1965).

Firebird VII non-reverse (2003–04): 3 mini-humbucking or 3 P-90 pickups, gold-plated hardware, unbound rosewood fingerboard, dot inlays, Limed TV finish.

Firebird 76 (1976–78)
Solidbody with treble horn longer than bass horn, Firebird with stars on pickguard
• Reverse body, tune-o-matic bridge, red-and-blue Bicentennial Firebird figure (with stars) on pickguard near switch, gold-plated hardware, Sunburst, Natural mahogany, white or Ebony finish.
• Neck-through-body, unbound rosewood fingerboard, dot inlays, straight-through banjo tuners with metal buttons.
• 2 mini-humbucking pickups, 4 knobs, selector switch.
Production: 2,847.

Firebird Reissue: See Firebird V.

Firebird Studio (2004–current)
Solidbody with treble horn longer than bass horn, smaller than standard Firebird
• Mahogany body shorter than standard Firebird, tune-o-matic bridge, stopbar tailpiece, chrome or gold-plated hardware.
• Set neck, unbound rosewood fingerboard, dot inlays, reverse headstock, logo on truss-rod cover.
• 2 standard humbucking pickups, 4 knobs.

Non-reverse Firebird (2002–04)
Solidbody with bass horn longer than treble, humbuckers with polepieces, uniform finish
- Bass horn larger than treble horn, tune-o-matic bridge, Cardinal Red, Walnut or Pthalo Blue finish.
- Set neck, unbound rosewood fingerboard, dot inlay.
- 2 humbucking pickups with 2 rows of polepieces, 4 knobs.

Non-reverse Firebird Plus (2002)
Solidbody with bass horn longer than treble, humbuckers with polepieces, swirl finish
- Mahogany solidbody, bass horn longer than treble horn, Blue, red or green swirl finish, some with brushed aluminum pickguard.
- Unbound ebony fingerboard, dot inlays, peghead finish matches body.
- 2 humbucking pickups, 4 knobs, some with coil tap.
Production: 60 of each color.

FLYING V MODELS

Flying V (1958–59, 1965–69, 1971–79, 1984–89 /
Flying V I (1981–82) / **Flying V 83** (1983) /
Flying V Reissue (1990) / **Flying V '67**
(1991–2003) / **X-Factor V** (2003–current)
V-shaped solidbody
- Korina (African limba wood) V-shaped solidbody (mahogany 1965–79, alder 1981–89, mahogany from 1990), some *Limited Edition Reissue* medallion on top 1971–74, strings anchor through body in V-shaped anchor plate (stopbar or vibrato from 1965), white pickguard (a few early with black, no pickguard 1981–89), body shoulders square at neck, gold-plated hardware (chrome from 1965).
- Unbound rosewood fingerboard (ebony 1981–83, rosewood or ebony 1981–88), dot inlays, triangular peghead with rounded top, raised plastic peghead logo (logo on truss-rod cover from 1965–79, decal from 1981).
- 2 humbucking pickups (exposed-coil 1975–79), 3 knobs in straight line (triangular knob configuration from 1965.
Production: 81 (1958); 17 (1959); 2 (1965); 111 (1966); 15 (1969); 47 (1970); 350 (1971); 2 (1973); 1 (1974), 3,223 (1975–79).

1958 Korina Flying V (1991–current) / **1959 Korina Flying V** (1994–current): Replica of 1958 style, Korina body and neck, gold-plated hardware, Antique Natural finish.
Flying V '98 (1998): 2 ceramic-magnet humbucking pickups with exposed coils, 1958-style controls (3-in-line knob configuration, switch above knobs, jack in lower treble bout), Grover tuners with metal buttons, Natural or Naturalburst finish with gold-plated hardware

or Translucent Purple finish with chrome-plated hardware.
Flying V '98 Gothic (1998–2001): 2 '57 Classic humbucking pickups with no covers, Flying V '98 control configuration with 3-in-line knobs, black pickguard, ebony fingerboard, moon-and-star inlay at 12th fret, no other inlay, white outline of logo on peghead, black chrome hardware, satin Ebony finish.
Flying V 400/400+ (1985–86): 400-series electronics, 1 Dirty Fingers humbucking pickup and 2 single-coil pickups, master tone and master volume knob, 3 mini-switches for on/off pickup control, push/pull volume control for coil tap, Kahler Flyer vibrato, black chrome hardware, Alpine White, Ebony, Ferrari Red or Pewter finish.
Flying V Black Hardware (1985): Kahler vibrato standard, black hardware
Flying V Centennial (July 1994 guitar of the month): Serial number in raised numerals on tailpiece, numeral *1* of serial number formed by row of diamonds, letter *i* of logo dotted by inlaid diamond, gold medallion on back of peghead, gold-plated hardware, Antique Gold finish, limited run of no more than 101 serial numbered from 1894–1994, package includes 16 x 20 framed photograph and gold signet ring.
Flying V Standard Quilt Top (2004–06): Quilted maple top cap.
Flying V Custom (2002, 2004): Knobs in straight line, ebony fingerboard, pearl block inlays, Ebony (2002) or Classic White (2004) finish. Production: 40 (2002).
Flying V FF 8 (1981): Made for Frankfurt (Germany) trade show, same specs as Flying V I.
Flying V Heritage (1981–82): Reissue of 1958 version, 3-piece Korina neck, Antique Natural, Ebony, Candy Apple Red, or white finish, serial number of letter followed by 3 digits (example: A 123).
Flying V Korina (1983): Same as Flying V Heritage except for black barrel knobs, 8-digit serial number
Flying V Left Hand (1984–87): Left-handed, Ebony or red finish.
Mahogany Flying V (2002–04): Mahogany neck and body, green, copper, blue and silver satin metallic finishes. Poduction: 15 in each finish.
Flying V Mirror Pickguard (2002): Mirror pickguard, Cherry, Ebony or Classic White finish.
Flying V Primavera (1994): Primavera wood (light mahogany), gold-plated hardware with Antique Natural finish, chrome-plated hardware with translucent and metallic finishes.
Flying V Voodoo (2002): Swamp ash body, Juju finish (black with red wood filler), ebony fingerboard, voodoo doll inlay at 5th fret (no other inlays), red logo, red/black pickup coils.
Flying V XPL (1984–86) Kahler vibrato or combination bridge/tailpiece with individual string adjustments (tune-o-matic optional from

1985), maple neck, unbound ebony fingerboard, Explorer-style peghead, 6-on-a-side tuner arrangement.
Flying V XPL Black Hardware (1985): Black hardware, Kahler vibrola standard, Ebony, Alpine White, or red finish.
X-Factor V Faded (2003–current): Rosewood fb, 2 exposed-coil humbuckers, three knobs in triangular configuration, worn Cherry finish.
X-Factor V New Century (2006–current): Mirror dot inlays, full body mirror pickguard.

Flying V II (1979–82)
V-shaped layered body, boomerang pickups
- 5-layer maple/walnut body with walnut or maple top, beveled top and back body edges, tune-o-matic bridge, gold-plated hardware, Natural finish.
- Unbound ebony fingerboard, dot inlays.
- 2 boomerang-shaped pickups.

Flying V 90 (1988)
V-shaped solidbody, split-diamond inlays
- Floyd Rose vibrato optional, black chrome hardware, Alpine White, Ebony or Nuclear Yellow finish.
- 25½-inch scale, unbound ebony fingerboard, split-diamond inlays, pearl logo.
- 1 humbucking pickup.

Flying V 90 Double (1989–90) 1 single-coil and 1 double-coil pickup, 2 knobs, push/pull volume knob for coil tap, tune-o-matic bridge, Floyd Rose vibrato optional, pearl logo, Alpine White, Ebony or Luna Silver finish.

Flying V CMT / The V (1981–85)
V-shaped solidbody, curly maple top
- Maple body (earliest with mahogany body), curly maple top, no pickguard, bound top, vibrato optional, gold-plated hardware, Antique Sunburst, Antique Natural or Vintage Cherry Sunburst finish.
- Maple neck, ebony fingerboard, dot inlays, pearl logo.
- 2 Dirty Fingers humbucking pickups with exposed creme coils, 3 knobs in curving line, selector switch between upper knobs.

FLYING V ARTIST SIGNATURE MODELS

Jimi Hendrix '69 Flying V Custom (1991–1993): Based on 1969 model, mahogany body, 490R and 490T humbucking pickups, signature on pickguard, mahogany neck, split-diamond inlays, gold-plated hardware, first run of 400 numbered on truss-rod cover, Hall of Fame series logo on back of peghead, Ebony finish. Production: 25 promotional instruments for RCA Records.
Jimi Hendrix Psychedelic Flying V (2006): Based on 1967 version hand-painted by Hendrix,

Maestro vibrato, chrome-plated hardware, witch hat knobs. Production: 150.

Judas Priest Flying V (2005–current): 1960s styling, tune-o-matic bridge with plastic saddles, 2 exposed-coil 57 Classic humbuckers, 3 knobs in triangular configuration, Custom Authentic Candy Apple Red finish, certificate signed by K.K. Downing and Glenn Tipton. Production: 30 (sold as a set with Judas Priest SG).

Lenny Kravitz 1967 Flying V (2001–04): Mirror pickguard, black finish with sparkles, maestro vibrato. Production: 125.

Lonnie Mack Flying V (1993–94): Mahogany body, 1958-style control arrangement, Bigsby vibrato with anchor bar between lower bouts.

LES PAUL MODELS

Les Paul Acoustic (2001–02) / **Les Paul Acoustic Plaintop** (2003–05)
Single-cut solidbody, carved top, undersaddle pickup
• Single-cutaway solidbody, carved top of figured maple (plain top from 2003), no binding, strings through body.
• Unbound rosewood fingerboard, trapezoic inlays, Les Paul silkscreen on peghead, pearl logo.
• Piezo pickup under bridge, controls on rim.

Les Paul Active: See L.P. Artist

Les Paul Anniversary (1992–93)
Single-cut solidbody, carved top, 40th Anniversary at 12th fret
• Single-cutaway solidbody, carved top, gold-plated hardware, black finish.
• *40th Anniversary* engraved in 12th fret inlay.
• 2 P-100 stacked coil humbucking pickups with cream soapbar covers.
Production: No more than 300.

Les Paul Artisan (1976–1981)
Single-cut solidbody, carved top, hearts-and-flowers (banjo-style) inlays
• Carved maple top, tune-o-matic bridge (larger rectangular bridge from 1980), TP-6 tailpiece, Walnut, Tobacco Sunburst, or Ebony finish.
• Single-bound ebony fingerboard, multiple-bound peghead, hearts-and-flowers inlay on fingerboard and peghead, pearl logo in thin pre-war style script, gold-plated hardware.
• 2 humbucking pickups (3 pickups optional, 1976–78; 3 pickups standard from 1979).
Production: 2,220 (1976–79).

Les Paul Artist: See L.P. Artist

Les Paul Bantam Elite (1995) / **Les Paul Florentine Standard** (1995–1997)

Single-cut solidbody, carved top, f-holes or diamond holes
• Carved maple top, *f*-holes with Vintage Sunburst, Wine Red or black finish, diamond-shaped soundholes with sparkle finishes (sparkle finishes named Les Paul Elite Diamond Sparkle from 1995).
• Ebony fingerboard, pearl block inlays, 5-piece split-diamond peghead inlay, gold-plated hardware.
• 2 '57 Classic humbucking pickups.

Les Paul Bantam Elite Plus (1995) / **Les Paul Florentine Standard Plus** (1995–1998): Figured maple top, gold-plated hardware, Heritage Cherry Sunburst, Antique Natural or Emberglow finish standard, early examples also in purple, Emerald Green, Faded Blue, Midnight Blue, Rosa Red and Translucent Black finish.

Les Paul Elite Diamond Sparkle (1995–97): Diamond-shaped soundholes, sparkle (metalflake) gold, red or silver finish standard, early with Ice Blue, Brunswick Blue, black, copper or Lavender Sparkle finish.

Les Paul Baritone: See Les Paul Studio Baritone.

Les Paul BFG (2007–current)
Single-cut solidbody, carved top, P-90 and zebra-coil pickups
• Single-cutaway solidbody, carved top, no top figuration, no binding, distressed black or gunmetal hardware, transparent finishes.
• P-90 neck pickup, zebra-coil, humbucker bridge pickup, 2 volume knobs, 1 tone control, "kill switch" toggle, selector switch on upper bass bout, no tips on switches.
• Unbound rosewood fingerboard, no inlays, no truss-rod cover, distressed black chorme or gunmetal hardware.

Les Paul Black Beauty: See Les Paul Custom.

Les Paul Catalina (1996–97)
Single-cut solidbody, carved top, Custom Shop inlay on peghead
• Single-cutaway solidbody, carved maple top, tune-o-matic bridge, nickel-plated hardware, Pearl Black, Canary Yellow or Riverside Red finish.
• Ebony fingerboard with compound radius, pearl trapezoid inlays, pearl Custom Shop logo inlay on peghead.
• 2 humbucking pickups, 4 knobs, selector switch on upper bass bout.

Les Paul Class 5 (2001–current)
Single-cut solidbody, carved top, figured top, lightweight body
• Single-cutaway solidbody, carved maple top (figured top 2003–04, quilt top 2003–current),

weight-relieved mahogany back.
• Bound rosewood fingerboard, '60s slim-taper neck profile, pearloid trapezoid inlays, Les Paul silkscreen on peghead, long neck tenon.
• 2 humbucking pickups, 4 knobs, selector switch on upper bass bout.

Les Paul Classic (1990–current)
Single-cut solidbody, carved top, no pickup covers, inked serial number
• Single-cutaway solidbody, carved maple top, uniform-depth binding inside cutaway, *1960* on pickguard (some without pickguard), nickel-plated hardware.
• Low-profile neck, *Les Paul Model* on peghead *Classic* on truss-rod cover (*Les Paul Classic* silkscreen from 1993), 1960 style serial number with 1st digit corresponding to last digit of year.
• 2 exposed-coil humbucking pickups, 4 knobs, selector switch on upper bass bout.

Les Paul Classic Antique (2007–current): Flamed top, exposed-coil '57 Classic humbucking pickups, rosewood fingerboard, Antiqued binding crown peghead inlay (no Les Paul silkscreen), nickel-plated hardware.

Les Paul Classic Birdseye (1993): Birdseye maple top.

Les Paul Classic Celebrity Series: Black finish, white pickguard, gold-plated hardware: July 1991.

Les Paul Classic Centennial (Feb. 1994 guitar of the month): Goldtop finish, serial number in raised numerals on tailpiece, numeral *1* of serial number formed by row of diamonds, letter *i* of logo dotted by inlaid diamond, gold medallion on back of peghead, gold-plated hardware, limited run of no more than 101 serial numbered from 1894–1994, package includes 16 x 20 framed photograph and gold signet ring.

Les Paul Classic Custom (2007–current): Exposed-coil '57 Classic humbucking pickups with gold polepieces, ebony fingerboard, multiply binding, crown peghead inlay (no Les Paul silkscreen), gold-plated hardware, Antique Ebony finish.

Les Paul Classic Mahogany Top (2000): Mahogany top cap, long neck tenon, 2 exposed-coil zebra-coil humbuckers.

Les Paul Classic Plus (1991–96, 1999–current): Figured maple top.

Les Paul Classic Premium Plus (1993–97): Highly figured maple top (flame runs all the way to the edge).

Les Paul Classic M-III electronics (1991–93): 1 humbucking and 2 single-coil pickups.

Les Paul CMT (1986–mid 1989)
Single-cut solidbody, carved top, curly top, metal jackplate, made primarily for Sam Ash stores
• Single-cutaway solidbody, carved curly maple top, deeper binding inside cutaway than other top binding.

- Bound rosewood fingerboard, trapezoid inlays, Les Paul signature and MODEL silkscreened on peghead, stamped 8-digit serial number.
- 2 humbucking pickups, 4 knobs, selector switch on upper bass bout, metal jack plate.

Les Paul Custom (late 1953–63, 1968–current) *Single-cut solidbody, carved top, pearl block inlays, 5-piece diamond peghead inlay*
- Single-cutaway solidbody (SG-shape double-cutaway with pointed horns, 1961–63), carved mahogany top, mahogany back (1-piece mahogany 1961–63) (4-piece "pancake" body 1969–76), tune-o-matic bridge, stop tailpiece, optional Bigsby (listed as a separate catalog model, some with pearl-inlaid ebony tailblock 1962), multiple-bound top and back, gold-plated hardware.
- Single-bound ebony fingerboard, pearl block inlay (*20th Anniversary* at 15th fret, 1974), *Les Paul Custom* on truss-rod cover, 5-piece split-diamond peghead inlay, pearl logo, closed-back Kluson tuners (Grover Rotomatics from 1959), plastic tulip-shaped tuner buttons.
- Alnico V neck pickup (rectangular poles), black soapbar P-90 bridge pickup (most with 3 humbuckers 1957–60, 3 pickups 1961–63, 2 pickups from 1969).

Production: 1,912 (1954–60); 1,075 (1961–63, may include some SGs); 5,398 (1968–70); 50,605 (all variations 1971–79).

Les Paul '57 Black Beauty 3-Pickup Centennial (Nov. 1994 guitar of the month): 3 pickups, Ebony finish, serial number in raised numerals on tailpiece, numeral *1* of serial number formed by row of diamonds, letter *i* of logo dotted by inlaid diamond, gold medallion on back of peghead, gold-plated hardware, limited run of no more than 101 serial numbered from 1894–1994, package includes 16 x 20 framed photograph and gold signet ring.
Les Paul Black Beauty '82 (1982–83): Multiply cream binding, unbound ebony fingerboard, trapezoid inlays, speed tuners, black finish, 4-digit serial number (some with additional standard 8-digit serial number).
Les Paul Custom/3 pickups (1971–73, 1976, 1978): 3 pickups.
Les Paul Custom 20th Anniversary (1974): All Les Paul Customs in 1974 have *Twentieth Anniversary* engraved in block letters on the 15th-fret inlay, black or white finish.
Les Paul Custom 25th Anniversary (1977): *25th Anniversary* engraved in script on tailpiece, *Les Paul* signature on pickguard, chrome-plated hardware, silver metallic finish.
Les Paul Custom 35th Anniversary (1989): 3 humbucking pickups, *35th Anniversary* etched on middle peghead inlay, 1959-style inked-on serial number.
Les Paul Custom '54 (1972): Reissue of 1954 Les Paul Custom, Alnico V neck pickup, P-90

bridge pickup, standard 6-digit serial number with *LE* prefix.
Les Paul '68 Custom Figured Top (2000–05): Flame maple top.
Les Paul Custom/400 (1991–92): Custom Shop model, Super 400-style slashed-block fingerboard inlay, Ebony or Antique White finish.
Les Paul Custom Black Beauty '54 Reissue (1991–current): Alnico V and P-90 pickups, Bigsby vibrato optional, Ebony finish.
Les Paul Custom Black Beauty '57 Reissue (1991–current): 2 or 3 humbucking pickups, Bigsby vibrato optional, Ebony finish.
Les Paul Custom/maple fingerboard (1975–81): Maple fingerboard, Ebony or Natural finish.
Les Paul Custom/nickel-plated parts (1976, 1979–86, 1996): Nickel-plated hardware (chrome 1985–86), 2 humbucking pickups (3 pickups 1996).
Les Paul Custom Plus (1991–97): Figured maple top, Honeyburst, Dark Wine, Heritage Cherry Sunburst or Vintage Sunburst finish.
Les Paul Custom Showcase Edition (Mar. 1988 guitar of the month): EMG pickups, Ruby finish. Production: 200 for U.S., 50 for overseas.
Les Paul Mahogany Custom (1997): 1-piece mahogany body with carved top, 3 '57 Classic humbucking pickups, gold plated hardware, faded Cherry finish.
Les Paul Super Custom (1984): Prototypes for Steve Perry model, earliest made in Kalamazoo factory, then in Nashville, 1 humbucking pickup with cover, 1 exposed-coil humbucking pickup, curly maple top, back and sides covered with curly maple veneer, multiple-bound top, 3-piece maple neck, single-bound fingerboard, Super 400-style slashed-block inlays, *LE* on truss-rod cover, Cherry Sunburst finish all over.
10th Anniversary '68 Les Paul Custom (2003): Diamond White Sparkle finish, white pickguard, ebony fingerboard, pearl block inlays, *10th Anniversary* at 12th fret, gold-plated hardware Production: 30.

Les Paul Custom Lite (1987–89) *Thin single-cut solidbody, carved top, block inlays, 3 knobs*
- 1 ³⁄₈-inch deep (5/8-inch thinner than Les Paul Custom), contoured back, Floyd Rose vibrato or tune-o-matic bridge and stopbar tailpiece, chrome- or gold-plated hardware (black chrome 1989).
- Ebony fingerboard, block inlay.
- 2 PAF humbucking pickups (SW-5 sidewinder pickup in neck position, L-8 humbucking pickup in bridge position, black pickup covers with no visible poles, 1989), 2 volume knobs, master tone knob, coil-tap switch, pickup selector switch on upper bass bout.

Les Paul Custom Lite Showcase Edition

(Aug. 1988 guitar of the month): EMG pickups, active electronics, gold-top finish. Production: 200 for U.S., 50 for overseas.

Les Paul DC Pro (1997–98, 2006–current) *Double-cut solidbody, carved top, trapezoid inlays, crown peghead inlay*
- Double-cutaway body shape like 1959 Les Paul Jr., rounded horns, carved highly figured maple top, weight-relieved mahogany back, tune-o-matic or wraparound bridge, nickel-plated hardware.
- 24³⁄₄-inch or 25¹⁄₂-inch scale, unbound rosewood fingerboard, aged trapezoid inlays, tapered peghead for straight string-pull (standard peghead shape for 2006), crown peghead inlay (no Les Paul silkscreen).
- 2 humbucking pickups or 2 P-90 white soapbar pickups (P-90s with wraparound bridge only, humbuckers only from 2006), 2 knobs, 1 switch.

Les Paul DC Studio (1997–98) *Double-cut solidbody, carved top, dot inlays, 2 knobs*
- Double-cutaway body shape like 1959 Les Paul Jr., rounded horns, carved maple top, wraparound bridge (tune-o-matic 1998), unbound top and back, chrome-plated hardware, Ebony, Heritage Cherry Sunburst, Emerald Green or Ruby finish.
- 24³⁄₄-inch scale, unbound rosewood fingerboard, dot inlays, standard peghead shape.
- 2 humbucking pickups, 2 knobs.

Les Paul DC Standard (Les Paul Standard-DC) (1998) *Double-cut solidbody, carved top, trapezoid inlays, no ornamental peghead inlay*
- Double-cutaway body shape like 1959 Les Paul Jr., rounded horns, carved flame maple top, tune-o-matic bridge, unbound top, unbound back, chrome- or gold-plated hardware, translucent finish colors: Amber Serrano, Blue Diamond, Black Pepper, Red Hot Tamale or Green Jalapeno; limited edition finish colors: Tangerineburst or Lemonburst.
- Bound rosewood fingerboard, trapezoid inlays, standard peghead shape, pearl logo, no Les Paul designation on peghead or truss-rod cover.
- 2 humbucking pickups, 2 knobs, switch near bridge, 24³⁄₄-inch scale.

Les Paul Standard Doublecut Plus (2001–current): Figured top, chambered body, 2 knobs, gold-plated hardware, "Standard" on truss-rod cover, Les Paul signature silkscreen on peghead, transparent finishes.
Les Paul Standard Doublecut w/ P-90s (2003–05): P-90 pickups.

Les Paul Deluxe (1969–85, 1992)
Single-cut solidbody, carved top, mini-humbuckers
- Carved maple top, 2-piece mahogany back with maple center laminate (1 piece mahogany from 1977) maple layer in middle, carved maple top cap).
- Bound rosewood fingerboard, trapezoid inlays, *Deluxe* on truss-rod cover, *Les Paul* signature and *MODEL* silkscreened on peghead.
- 2 mini-humbucking pickups (some with soapbar pickups).
Production: 2,587 (1970), 35,520 (1971–79 all variations).

Les Paul Deluxe BB (1975–77): Blue sparkle top finish.
Les Paul Deluxe Hall of Fame Edition (1991): All gold finish.
Les Paul Deluxe RR (1975): Red sparkle top finish.
30th Anniversary Les Paul Deluxe (2000): Ebony, Wine Red or Bullion Gold finish.

Les Paul Diamond (2003–05)
Single-cut solidbody, relief-carved top with diamond pattern
- Single-cutaway solidbody, mahogany back, maple top cap carved with relief diamond pattern, gold-plated hardware, 2-tone finish.
- Bound rosewood fingerboard, trapezoid inlays.
- 2 humbucking pickups, 4 knobs, selector switch on upper bass bout.

Les Paul Double-Cutaway (various models): also see Les Paul DC, Les Paul Faded Doublecut.

Les Paul Double-Cutaway XPL (1984–86):
Double-cut solidbody, carved top, 6-on-a-side tuners
- Symmetrical double-cutaway, carved top, Gibson/Kahler Supertone vibrato or tune-o-matic bridge, bound top, 24¾-inch scale, chrome-plated hardware.
- Bound ebony fingerboard, 22 frets, dot inlays, 6-on-a-side tuner configuration, peghead points to treble side, decal logo.
- 2 humbucking pickups, 4 knobs, selector switch above knobs.

Les Paul Double-Cutaway XPL/400 (1984):
400-series electronics, 1 Dirty Fingers humbucking pickup and 2 single-coil pickups, master tone and master volume knob, 3 mini-switches for on/off pickup control, push/pull volume control for coil tap, rosewood or ebony fingerboard, cream binding.

Les Paul Elegant (1996–current)
Single-cut solidbody, carved top, abalone fingerboard and peghead inlay

- Highly flamed maple top, nickel-plated hardware, Heritage Darkburst or Firemist finish.
- Ebony fingerboard with compound radius, abalone trapezoid inlays, abalone Custom Shop peghead inlay.
- 2 humbucking pickups, 4 knobs, selector switch on upper bass bout.
Les Paul Elegant Quilt (1997): Quilted maple top.
Les Paul Elegant Double Quilt (1997): Quilted maple top, figured mahogany back.
Les Paul Elegant Super Double Quilt (1997): Highly quilted maple top, highly figured mahogany back, Antique Natural or Butterscotch finish.

Les Paul Elite: See Les Paul Bantam Elite.

Les Paul Faded Doublecut (2003–current)
Double-cut solidbody, flat top, faded finish
- Double-cutaway solid mahogany body, flat top, rounded horns (like 1959 Les Paul Special), tune-o-matic bridge, chrome-plated hardware, worn Cherry, worn yellow or satin Ebony finish.
- Unbound rosewood fingerboard, dot inlays, Les Paul silkscreen on peghead, decal logo.
- 2 soapbar P-90 pickups, 4 knobs, 1 switch.

Les Paul Flame (2003–05)
Single-cut solidbody, relief-carved top with flame pattern
- Single-cutaway solidbody, mahogany back, maple top cap carved with relief flame pattern, gold-plated hardware, 2-tone finish.
- Bound rosewood fingerboard, trapezoid inlays.
- 2 humbucking pickups, 4 knobs, selector switch on upper bass bout.

Les Paul Flametop: See Les Paul Reissue.

Les Paul Florentine: See Les Paul Bantam Elite.

Les Paul Gothic: See Les Paul Studio Gothic.

Les Paul GT (2006)
Single-cut solidbody, carved top, monochrome finish with flames
- Single-cutaway solidbody, carved maple top, mahogany back, bound top, tune-o-matic bridge, extended strap buttons, chrome-plated hardware, monochrome flame finishes.
- Bound ebony fingerboard, mirror trapezoid inlays, model name on truss-rod cover, Les Paul signature silkscreen on peghead, locking tuners, pearl logo.
- 490R chrome and 498T Smoky Coil humbucking pickups, 4 push/pull knobs, high-pass tone filter, coil taps on both pickups.

Les Paul Goddess (2006–current)
Single-cut solidbody, carved top, 2 pickups, 2 knobs
- Single-cutaway solidbody, carved maple top, mahogany back, wraparound bridge, bound top, chrome-plated hardware.
- Bound ebony fingerboard, trapezoid inlays, model name on truss-rod cover, Les Paul signature silkscreen on peghead, decal logo.
- 2 humbucking pickups with clear bobbins, 1 volume knob, 1 tone knob, selector switch on upper bass bout.

Les Paul Heritage 80 (1980–82)
Single-cut solidbody, carved top, Heritage 80 on truss-rod cover
- 2-piece highly flamed maple top, binding inside cutaway same depth as rest of top binding, nickel-plated hardware.
- 3-piece neck, *Heritage 80* on truss-rod cover, earliest with 4-digit serial number (0001, 0002, etc.), small peghead.
- 2 humbucking pickups, 4 knobs, selector switch on upper bass bout.

Les Paul Heritage 80 Elite (1980–82): 1-piece neck, ebony fingerboard, *Heritage 80 Elite* on truss-rod cover, chrome-plated hardware.
Les Paul Heritage 80 Award: 1-piece mahogany neck, ebony fingerboard, pearl trapezoid inlays, gold-plated hardware, oval pearl medallion on back of peghead with limited edition number: 1981.

Les Paul Jumbo (1969–71)
Single-cut flat-top acoustic, rounded horn, 2 oblong pickups
- Single-cutaway dreadnought size flat-top, rosewood back and sides (catalogued with maple 1971).
- Rosewood fingerboard, dot inlays, decal logo.
- Two oblong low-impedance pickups, 4 knobs.
Production: 139

Les Paul Junior (1954–63, 1986–92) (2001–02)
Single-cut solidbody, 1 P-90 pickup, Les Paul Junior on headstock
- Solid mahogany body with flat top (double-cutaway with rounded horns 1958–60, thinner SG-style with pointed horns 1961–63, single-cutaway 1986–92), stud-mounted bridge/tailpiece, tortoiseshell plastic pickguard (black laminated from 1961), Maestro vibrato optional from 1962, nickel-plated hardware (chrome 1986–92).
- Unbound rosewood fingerboard, 16 frets clear of body (22 frets clear from 1958), dot inlays, plastic tuner buttons (metal (1986–92), yellow silkscreen logo and model name on peghead, decal logo.
- 1 black P-90 pickup with "dog-ear" cover (stacked-coil P-100 1990–92), 2 knobs.
Production: 19,035 (1954–60), 6,864 (1961–63, may include some SGs).

1957 Les Paul Jr. Double Cutaway
(1998–99): Nickel-plated hardware.
1957 Les Paul Jr. Single Cutaway
(1998–current): Nickel-plated hardware,
Vintage Original Spec aging treatment
optional from 2006.
1958 Les Paul Jr. Double Cutaway
(2000–current): Nickel plated hardware,
Vintage Original Spec aging treatment
optional from 2006.
Les Paul Junior ¾-scale (1956–61): Shorter
neck, 22¾-inch scale, 14 frets clear of body
(15 clear from 1959). Production: 787.
Les Paul Junior II (1989): Single cutaway,
tune-o-matic bridge, 2 black soapbar P-100
pickups, *Les Paul Special* on peghead.
Les Paul Jr. DC SP: See Les Paul Special
Double Cutaway.
Les Paul Jr. Double Cutaway (1987–92,
1995): Double cutaway with rounded horns,
P-90 pickup with black "dog-ear" cover (200
with P-100 stacked-coil humbucker, 1990–92),
tune-o-matic bridge, metal tuner buttons
(plastic from 1989), chrome-plated hardware
(nickel 1990–92).
Les Paul Jr. Double Cutaway Special:
See Les Paul Specials.
Les Paul Junior Lite (1999–2002): Double
cutaway, contoured back, tune-o-matic
brdige, unbound rosewood fingerboard, mini-
trapezoid (½-scale) inlay, *Les Paul Special*
silkscreen on peghead, 2 P-100 stacked
humbucking pickups, 4 knobs, selector switch
near bridge.
Les Paul Jr. Pro: See Junior Pro.
Les Paul Junior Special: See Les Paul
Special.
Les Paul Junior TV: See Les Paul TV.

Les Paul K-II (1980)
*Double-cut solidbody, carved top, K-II on
truss-rod cover*
• Double cutaway with rounded horns, carved
maple top.
• K-II on truss-rod cover.
• 2 humbucking pickups.

Les Paul Kalamazoo (1979)
*Single cut solidbody, carved top, KM on truss-
rod cover*
• Single-cutaway solidbody, carved 2-piece
maple top, large rectangular tune-o-matic
bridge, stop tailpiece, examples from first
run with *Custom Made* plate nailed onto top
below tailpiece, Antique Sunburst, Natural
or Cherry Sunburst finish.
• Bound rosewood fingerboard, pearl
trapezoid inlays, *Les Paul KM* on truss-rod
cover.
• 2 exposed-coil humbucking pickups with
cream-colored coils, 4 speed knobs, selector
switch on upper bass bout.
Production: 1,500.

Les Paul Korina (1997)
*Single-cut solidbody, carved top, Korina back and
neck (looks like light mahogany)*
• Single-cutaway solidbody, carved figured
maple top, Korina (African limba wood) back,
nickel-plated hardware.
• Korina neck.
• 2 humbucking pickups, 4 knobs.

Les Paul Mahogany (1993)
Single-cut solidbody, carved mahogany top
• Single-cutaway mahogany solidbody, carved
top (no maple top).
• Bound rosewood fingerboard, trapezoid inlays.
• 2 P-90 pickups, 4 knobs, selector switch on
upper bass bout.

Les Paul Melody Maker (2007–current)
Single-cut solidbody, narrow headstock, 1 P-90
• Single cutaway solid mahogany body, tune-o-
matic bridge (earliest with wraparound).
• Unbound rosewood fingerboard, dot inlays,
narrow headstock, decal logo, chrome-plated
hardware.
• 1 black "dog-ear" P-90 pickup with non-
adjustable polepieces, 2 knobs.

Les Paul Menace (2006–current)
*Single-cut solidbody, carved top, fist on
fingerboard*
• Single-cutaway solidbody, carved maple top
with "tribal" routs, mahogany back, tune-o-
matic bridge, black hardware, flat black finish.
• Unbound ebony fingerboard, brass fist inlay at
5th fret (no other inlays), brass frets, custom
multi-color logo.
• 2 exposed-coil Smoky Coil humbucking
pickups with brass stud poles, 4 knobs,
selector switch on upper bass bout.

Les Paul Model: See Les Paul Standard.

Les Paul New Century: See Les Paul
Special.

Les Paul North Star (1978)
Single-cut solidbody, carved top, star on peghead
• Carved maple top, mahogany back, multiple-
bound top.
• Single-bound fingerboard, trapezoid inlays,
star peghead inlay, *North Star* on truss-rod
cover.
• 2 humbucking pickups, 4 knobs, selector
switch on upper bass bout.

Les Paul Personal (1969–70)
*Single-cut solidbody, carved top, oblong pickups,
large block inlays*
• 14-inch wide, single cutaway solidbody, carved
top, 3-piece body of mahogany with center
maple laminate, contoured back (no contour
1970), tune-o-matic bridge, Gibson Bigsby
vibrato optional, gold-plated hardware, Walnut
finish.

• Low frets, block inlay (earliest with dot
inlay), 5-piece split-diamond peghead inlay.
• 2 oblong low-impedance pickups mounted
at a slant, *Gibson* embossed on pickup
covers, microphone input jack on side of
upper bass bout, mic volume control knob
and 1 switch on upper bass bout, guitar
input jack on side of lower treble bout,
4 knobs and 2 slide switches on lower
treble bout, tune-o-matic bridge.
Production: 370.

Les Paul Pro-Deluxe (1978–81)
*Single-cut solidbody, carved top, ebony
fingerboard, 2 P-90s*
• Carved maple top, tune-o-matic bridge,
cream binding, chrome-plated hardware,
gold-top, Ebony, Tobacco Sunburst or
Cherry Sunburst finish.
• Ebony fingerboard, trapezoid inlays,
Schaller tuners.
• 2 soapbar P-90 pickups, 4 knobs, selector
switch on upper bass bout.
Production: 1,416.

Les Paul Pro Showcase Edition (Dec.
1988 guitar of the month): Goldtop finish.
Production: 200 for U.S., 50 for overseas.

Les Paul Professional (1969–70)
*Single-cut solidbody, carved top, oblong
pickups, trapezoid inlays*
• 14-inch wide, single cutaway solidbody,
carved top, 3-piece body of mahogany with
center maple laminate, contoured back (no
contour 1970), tune-o-matic bridge, Gibson
Bigsby tailpiece optional, , chrome-plated
hardware, Walnut finish.
• Rosewood fingerboard, trapezoid inlay.
• 2 oblong low-impedance pickups mounted
at a slant, *Gibson* embossed on pickup
covers, pickup selector switch on upper
bass bout, 4 knobs, slide switch for in/out
phase, 3-position slide switch for tone,
3-prong jack.
Production: 901.

Les Paul Recording (1971–79)
*Single-cut solidbody, carved top, oblong
pickups, small block inlays*
• 13½-inch wide, single cutaway solidbody,
carved top, tune-o-matic bridge.
• Bound rosewood fingerboard, small block
inlays, 5-piece split-diamond peghead
inlay.
• 2 oblong low-impedance pickups mounted
at a slant with embossed *Gibson*, 4 knobs
(volume, treble, bass, "decade" tone
control) and pickup selector on control
plate, high/low impedance selector switch
(transformer built into guitar), 3-way tone
control and 2-way phase control on control
plate, jack on top into control plate.
Production: 5,380.

Les Paul Reissue (1983–1991) / **Les Paul '59 Flametop Reissue** (1991–current) / **Les Paul '60 Flametop Reissue** (1991–current)
Copy of 1958–60 Les Paul Standard, single-cut solidbody, carved top, trapezoid inlays, inked serial number
• Highly flamed maple top (plain top, quilt top or killer top from 1999), binding inside cutaway same depth as other top binding, nickel-plated hardware, Cherry Sunburst finish, Custom Authentic aging treatment optional from 2001, Vintage Original Spec aging treatment optional from 2006.
• Standard-production neck (optional fat '59 or slim '60 neck profile 1991–current), inked-on 1950s-style serial number with 1st digit corresponding to last digit of year (earliest with 9 as 1st digit, standard 8-digit serial number in control cavity; R9 or R0 in control cavity from 1993), no model name on truss-rod cover.
• 2 humbucking pickups, 4 knobs, selector switch on upper bass bout.

'52 Les Paul Goldtop Aged (2002): Aged finish and hardware. Production: 50.
'54 Les Paul Goldtop Reissue (1996–current): Soapbar P-90 pickups, wraparound bridge, gold-top finish, Vintage Original Spec aging treatment optional from 2006.
'54 Les Paul Oxblood (1997–2003): '57 Classic humbuckers with exposed black coils, wraparound bridge, Oxblood finish.
'56 Les Paul Goldtop Reissue (1991–current): Reissue, soapbar P-90 pickups, Custom Authentic aging treatment optional from 2001, Vintage Original Spec aging treatment optional from 2006.
'57 LP Goldtop (1993–current): Custom Authentic aging treatment optional from 2003, Vintage Original Spec aging treatment optional from 2006.
'57 LP Goldtop Darkback Reissue (2000–current): Dark-stained back, Vintage Original Spec aging treatment optional from 2006.
'57 Les Paul Goldtop Mary Ford (1997–current): '57 Reissue with ES-295 style gold leaves stenciled on pickguard, custom armrest on lower bass bout, 2 humbucking pickups, gold-top finish.
'58 Les Paul Figured Top (1996–99, 2001–03): Less top figuration than Flametop Reissue but more than '58 Plaintop, Custom Authentic aging treatment optional from 2001.
'58 Les Paul Plaintop (1994–99, 2003–current): Plain maple top, Custom Authentic aging treatment optional from 2003, Vintage Original Spec aging treatment optional from 2006.
Guitar Trader Reissue (1982–c1985): Special order by Guitar Trader, a Gibson dealer in Redbank, New Jersey, serial number begins with 9, except for a few beginning with 0 (with thinner 1960-style neck). Production: under 50.

Leo's Reissue (1982–c.1985): Special order by Leo's Music, a Gibson dealer in Oakland, California, made in Nashville, inked-on serial number starts with letter *L* followed by a space
Les Paul Reissue Goldtop (1983–91): Gold top finish, humbucking pickups (stacked-coil P-100s with soapbar covers from 1990).
Strings and Things Reissue (1975–78): Special order by Strings and Things, Gibson dealer in Memphis, Tennessee, curly top, uniform-depth binding in cutaway. Production: 28.
Jimmy Wallace Reissue (1978–97): *Jimmy Wallace* on truss-rod cover, special order by musician/dealer Jimmy Wallace of Sunnyvale, Texas.

Les Paul Session: See L.P. Session.

Les Paul/SG '61 Reissue: See SG Reissue.

Les Paul/SG: See SG Custom, SG Special, SG Standard.

Les Paul Signature (1973–77)
Thinbody double-cut archtop, asymmetrical body, oblong pickups
• 16-inch wide, thin body, rounded bass-side horn, more pointed treble-side cutaway, large rectangular tune-o-matic bridge, Sunburst or gold finish.
• Bound rosewood fingerboard, trapezoid inlay.
• 2 oblong low-impedance humbucking pickups with white covers (ectangular pickups with embossed *Gibson* from 1974, high/low impedance humbuckers from 1976), 4 knobs (volume, treble tone, midrange tone, in/out phase switch), 3-way selector on upper bass bout, 2 jacks (high impedence on top, low-impedance on rim).
Production: 1,453.

Les Paul Silver Streak (1982)
Single-cut solidbody, carved top, silver finish
• Single-cutaway solidbody, carved top, tune-o-matic bridge, all silver finish.
• Dot inlays Custom Shop decal on back of peghead, inked LE serial number and "reg." limited run number.
• 2 humbucking pickups, 4 knobs, selector switch on upper bass bout.
Production: 1,000.

Les Paul SM (1980)
Single-cut solidbody, carved top, dot inlays, silver Sunburst finish
• Contoured back, multiple-bound top, Silverburst finish.
• Bound fingerboard, dot inlays, *SM* on truss-rod cover.
• 2 humbucking pickups, 4 knobs, coil tap switch.

Les Paul Smartwood Exotic (1998–2002)
Thin single-cut solidbody, carved top, green leaf on truss-rod cover, dot inlays
• Thin single cutaway (like The Paul II) with body of exotic wood certified by the Rainforest Alliance, mahogany back, top cap options include curupay, taperyva guasu, cancharana, peroba, banara or ambay guasu, gold-plated hardware, SL (Sans Lacquer) matte polyurethane finish specified.
• Curupay fingerboard, dot inlays, green leaf on truss-rod cover.
• 2 humbucking pickups, 2 knobs, 1 switch.

Les Paul Smartwood (Standard) (1996–99)
Single-cut solidbody, carved top, bound top, green leaf on truss-rod cover
• Les Paul Standard with wood certified by the Rainforest Alliance, gold-plated hardware, Natural finish.
• Chechen fingerboard, pearl trapezoid inlays, green leaf on truss-rod cover.
• 2 humbucking pickups, 4 knobs, selector switch on upper bass bout.

Les Paul Smartwood Studio (2003–current)
Single-cut solidbody, carved top, green leaf on truss-rod cover
• Single-cutaway solidbody of certified muira piranga wood, gold-plated hardware, Natural finish.
• Unbound muira piranga fingerboard, dot inlays, green leaf on truss-rod cover.
• 2 humbucking pickups, 4 knobs, selector switch on upper bass bout.

Les Paul Special (1955–59) (1989–97)
Single- or double-cut solidbody, flat top, 2 P-90s
• Single cutaway mahogany solidbody (double cutaway with rounded horns 1959, single cutaway 1989–97), flat top, nickel-plated hardware, Limed Mahogany finish (a few very early with Natural finish).
• Bound rosewood fingerboard, dot inlays, pearl peghead logo, yellow silkscreen model name, pearl logo.
• 2 black soapbar P-90 pickups (P-100 stacked-coil humbuckers 1989–97), 4 knobs, toggle switch on upper bass bout.
Production: 5,949 (1954–59, also see SG Special 1959–60).

Also see Les Paul Junior listing for Specials with such model names as "Junior LIte" or "Junior II"
Les Paul Jr. Double Cutaway Special (1988): Double cutaway with rounded horns, tune-o-matic bridge, selector switch on treble side near bridge, chrome-plated hardware, metal tuner buttons, *Les Paul Model* on peghead, metal tuner buttons.
Les Paul Jr. Special (1999–2001): Single cutaway, contoured back on bass side, tune-o-matic bridge, unbound rosewood fingerboard,

mini-trapezoid inlay (½-scale), 2 P-100 stacked-coil humbucking pickups, selector switch on upper bass bout.

Les Paul Junior Special Plus (2001–05): Flat curly maple top cap, two humbucking pickups, gold-plated hardware, decal logo.

1960 Les Paul Special Single Cutaway (1998–current): 2 black soapbar P-100 pickups, Vintage Original Spec aging treatment optional from 2006.

1960 Les Paul Special Double Cutaway (1998–current): 2 black soapbar P-90 pickups, Vintage Original Spec aging treatment optional from 2006.

Les Paul Special ¾-scale (1959–63): 22¾-inch scale, 15 frets clear of body. Production: 51 (1954–60).

Les Paul Special 400 (1985): 400-series electronics, 1 Dirty Fingers humbucking pickup and 2 single-coil pickups, master tone and master volume knob, 3 mini-switches for on/off pickup control, push/pull volume control for coil tap, vibrato, early with rosewood fingerboard, later with ebony.

Les Paul Special Double CMT (1979): Double-cutaway, curly maple top. Production: 133.

Les Paul Special Double Cutaway (1976, 1978–85, 1993–94): Double cutaway, tune-o-matic bridge (wraparound 1993–94), selector switch on treble side near bridge, chrome-plated hardware (nickel-plated 1993–94) metal tuner buttons, *Les Paul Model* on peghead.

Les Paul Special Double Cut Centennial (Jan. 1994 guitar of the month): Serial number in raised numerals on tailpiece, numeral *1* of serial number formed by row of diamonds, letter *i* of logo dotted by inlaid diamond, gold medallion on back of peghead, gold-plated hardware, Heritage Cherry finish, limited run of no more than 101 serial numbered from 1894–1994, package includes 16 x 20 framed photograph and gold signet ring.

Les Paul Special New Century (2006–current): Full-body mirror pickguard, 2 exposed-coil humbucking pickups, unbound ebony fingerboard, mirror dot inlays, mirror headstock, Ebony finish.

Les Paul Special Single Cutaway Centennial (1994): Serial number in raised numerals on tailpiece, numeral *1* of serial number formed by row of diamonds, letter *i* of logo dotted by inlaid diamond, gold medallion on back of peghead, gold-plated hardware, gold or TV Yellow finish. Production: less than 10 prototypes only used for promotions.

Les Paul Special SL (Sans Lacquer) (1998): Single cutaway, 2 black soapbar P-100 pickups, urethane finish specified, many with lacquer.

Les Paul Spotlight Special (1983–84)
Single-cut solidbody, carved top with dark center piece
• 3-piece carved top with curly maple outer

pieces and walnut center, multiple cream-brown-cream top binding, gold-plated hardware, Antique Natural finish.
• Bound rosewood fingerboard, trapezoid inlays, walnut peghead veneer, oval pearloid tuner buttons, serial number of 83 followed by a space and 4-digit ranking.
• 2 PAF humbucking pickups, 4 knobs, selector switch on upper bass bout.
Production: at least 211.

Les Paul Standard (1958–63, 1968–69, 1972–current) / **Les Paul Model** (1952–57)
Single-cut solidbody, carved top, trapezoid inlays, 2 humbuckers
• Single-cutaway solidbody (SG-shape double-cutaway with pointed horns, 1961–63), carved maple top, mahogany back (1-piece mahogany 1961–63, 2-piece mahogany with maple laminate 1972–77), trapeze bridge/tailpiece combination with strings looping under bridge (wraparound 1954, tune-o-matic from 1955, side-pull vibrato 1961–63, some with pearl-inlaid ebony tailblock 1962), bound top (unbound 1961–63) nickel-plated hardware, gold-top finish (some with gold back and sides; Cherry Sunburst top from 1958–60; Cherry 1961–63, gold-top 1968–69; various finishes 1972–current).
• Single-bound rosewood fingerboard (earliest unbound), optional fat '50s or slim '60s neck from 2002, trapezoid inlays, pearl logo, *Les Paul* signature and MODEL silkscreened on peghead (crown inlay, Les Paul on truss-rod cover, 1961–63).
• 2 soapbar P-90 pickups with cream-colored cover (humbuckers 1958–63, soapbar P-90s 1968–69, humbuckers 1972–current).
Production: 9,557 (1954–60); 4,556 (1961–63, may include some SGs); 3,975 (1968–69); 10,078 (1971–79).

Les Paul Custom Shop Standard (1997–98): 1 zebra-coil pickup, 1 black-coil pickup, no pickup covers, Grover tuners, faded Cherry Sunburst finish, inked-on serial number.

Les Paul Standard '58 (1971–73): Similar to 1954 Les Paul Model, 2 soapbar pickups with *Gibson* embossed on covers, wraparound bridge/tailpiece, 1-piece neck with no volute, gold-top finish. Production: 1,077.

Les Paul Standard 82 (1980–82): Made in Kalamazoo plant, flamed maple top, uniform-depth binding in cutaway, 1-piece neck, *Standard 82* on truss-rod cover, nickel-plated hardware.

Les Paul Standard 83 (1983): Highly figured maple top, PAF-reissue humbucking pickups, tune-o-matic bridge, 1-piece mahogany neck, rosewood fingerboard, pearl trapezoid inlays, nickel-plated hardware, Antique Natural, Vintage Cherry Sunburst or Vintage Sunburst finish.

Les Paul Standard Birdseye (1993–96): Birdseye maple top.

Les Paul Standard Centennial (Oct. 1994 guitar of the month): Vintage Sunburst finish, limited serial number in raised numerals on tailpiece, numeral *1* of serial number formed by row of diamonds, letter *i* of logo dotted by inlaid diamond, gold medallion on back of peghead, gold-plated hardware, run of no more than 101 serial numbered from 1894–1994, package includes 16 x 20 framed photograph and gold signet ring.

Les Paul Standard-DC, Standard Double-Cut, Standard Double-Cut Plus: See Les Paul DC Standard.

Les Paul Standard Faded (2005–current): Exposed-coil pickups, nickel-plated hardware, fat '50s or slim '60s neck, handrubbed Sunburst finishes.

Les Paul Standard Limited Edition (2007): White binding, nickel-plated hardware, ebony fingerboard, crown peghead inlay (no Les Paul silkscreen), Manhattan Midnight, Pacific Reef Blue, Santa Fe Sunrise, Black Cherry w/ cream binding.

Les Paul Standard P-100 (1989): P-100 stacked humbucking pickups with soapbar covers, gold-top finish.

Les Paul Standard Plus (1995–97): Figured maple top, Honeyburst, Heritage Cherry Sunburst or Vintage Sunburst finish.

Les Paul Standard Premium Plus (2002–current): Highly flamed top.

Les Paul Standard Raw Power (2000–2001): Chrome-plated hardware, satin Natural finish.

Les Paul Standard Showcase Edition (June 1988): EMG pickups, Silverburst finish. Production: 200 for U.S., 50 for overseas.

Les Paul Standard Sparkle Top (2000): Frost, Sterling or Crimson Sparkle finish.

Les Paul Standard Special (1983): 2 PAF humbucking pickups, cream binding, bound ebony fingerboard, pearl trapezoid inlays, metal keystone tuner buttons, gold-plated hardware, Cardinal Red finish.

Les Paul Standard Lite (1999–current)
Single-cut solidbody, carved top, ¾-scale trapezoid inlays
• Double-cutaway body shape like 1959 Les Paul Jr., rounded horns, no binding, gold-plated hardware, Translucent Amber, Translucent Red or Translucent Blue finish.
• Rosewood fingerboard, medium (¾-scale) trapezoid inlays, no Les Paul designation on peghead or truss-rod cover.
• 2 humbucking pickups with covers.

Les Paul Standard reissues: See Les Paul Reissue

Les Paul Studio (1983–current)
Single-cut solidbody, carved top, no binding
• Single cutaway, mahogany back, carved

maple top, tune-o-matic bridge, black pickguard, no binding anywhere, chrome- or gold-plated hardware.
• Maple neck (mahogany from 1990), rosewood or ebony fingerboard, dot inlay (trapezoid from 1990, ¾-scale 1999–2000, full-size from 2001, no inlays with platinum finish), pearloid keystone tuner buttons, *Studio* on truss-rod cover, *Les Paul Model* decal on peghead, decal logo, plastic keystone tuner buttons.
• 2 PAF humbucking pickups with covers, 4 knobs, selector switch on upper bass bout.

Les Paul Smartwood Studio: See Les Paul Smartwood.
Les Paul Swamp Ash Studio (2003–current): Swamp ash body, no binding, rosewood fingerboard, dot inlays, Natural finish.
Les Paul Studio Baritone (2004–05): 28-inch scale, unbound fingerboard,dot inlays, Sunrise Orange, Pewter Metallic or black finish.
Les Paul Studio Custom (1984–85): Multiple-bound top, bound rosewood fingerboard, gold-plated hardware.
Les Paul Studio Gem (1996–97): 2 P-90 cream soapbar pickups, rosewood fingerboard, trapezoid inlays, *Studio* on truss-rod cover, pearl logo, gold-plated hardware, Ruby Red, Emerald Green, Topaz Yellow, Sapphire Blue or Amethyst Purple finish.
Les Paul Studio Gothic (2000–01): 2 exposed-coil humbuckers, satin Ebony finish, ebony fingerboard, moon-and-star inlay at 12th fret (no other inlay), black hardware.
Les Paul Studio Premium Plus (2006–current): Figured maple top, gold-plated hardware, cream truss-rod cover, transparent finishes.
Les Paul Studio Standard (1984–87): Cream binding on top, cream-bound rosewood fingerboard.
Les Paul Studio Synthesizer (1985): Roland 700 synthesizer system.

Les Paul Studio Lite (1987–98)
Thin single-cut solidbody, carved top, pearl logo
• 1⅜-inch deep solidbody, carved top, contoured back, tune-o-matic bridge, stop tailpiece (Floyd Rose vibrato optional 1989), chrome plated hardware (gold or black with various finishes).
• Unbound ebony fingerboard, dot inlay (trapezoid from 1991), *Les Paul Model* peghead decal, pearl logo, plain truss-rod cover.
• 2 humbucker pickups (black covers 1989, exposed coils 1991), 2 knobs, coil-tap switch.

Les Paul Studio Lite/lightly figured maple top (1991): limited run, 2-piece or 3-piece top of figured maple, 2 humbucking pickups with exposed coils, trapezoid inlays, Translucent Red or Translucent Amber finish.
Les Paul Studio Lite/M-III electronics

(1991–94): 2 humbucking pickups and 1 single coil pickup, 2 knobs, 1 slide switch, 1 mini-switch.

Les Paul Supreme (2003–current)
Single-cut solidbody, carved top, all curly maple, globe on peghead
• Single-cutaway solidbody, carved top, body covered in curly maple veneer, no back coverplates, tune-o-matic bridge, 7-ply top binding, 3-ply back binding gold-plated hardware.
• Bound ebony fingerboard, pearl split block inlays, metal truss-rod cover, peghead inlay of "Supreme" banner around globe.
• 2 humbucking pickups, 4 knobs, selector switch on upper bass bout.

Les Paul Tie-Dye (1996)
Single-cut solidbody, tie-dye top
• Top hand-finished by artist George St. Pierre in simulated tie-dyed pattern.
• Bound rosewood fingerboard, trapezoid inlays.
• 2 humbucking pickups, 4 knobs.
Production: 103.

Les Paul TV (1954–59)
Single- or double-cut solidbody, Limed Mahogany finish, 1 P-90
• Solid mahogany body with flat top (double-cutaway with rounded horns from 1958), stud-mounted bridge/tailpiece, tortoiseshell plastic pickguard, nickel-plated hardware, Limed Mahogany finish (early with Natural finish).
• Unbound rosewood fingerboard, yellow silkscreen logo and model name on peghead, decal logo.
• 1 black P-90 pickup with "dog-ear" cover.
Production: 2,270.

Les Paul Ultima (1996–current)
Single-cut solidbody, carved top, elaborate fingerboard inlay
• Highly flamed maple top, abalone top border, trapeze tailpiece.
• Optional fingerboard inlay patterns of flame, tree of life or harp (from an early Gibson harp guitar fingerboard inlay), pearl tuner buttons, gold plated hardware, Heritage Cherry Sunburst finish.
• 2 humbucking pickups, 4 knobs, selector switch on upper bass bout.

Les Paul Vixen (2006–current)
Thin single-cut solidbody, carved top, small diamond inlays
• Thin single-cutaway mahogany solidbody with scarfed back, wraparound bridge, chrome-plated hardware, opaque finish colors.
• 2 humbucking pickups, 2 knobs, selector switch on upper bass bout.
• Unbound rosewood fingerboard, small

diamond inlays, Les Paul signature silkscreen on peghead, decal logo.

Les Paul Voodoo (2002–04)
Single-cut solidbody, carved top, voodoo doll on fingerboard
• Single-cutaway swamp ash solidbody, carved top, Juju finish (black with red wood filler), black hardware.
• Ebony fingerboard, voodoo doll inlay at 5th fret (no other inlays), red logo.
• 2 humbucking pickups with red/black coils.

Les Paul XPL (1984)
Thin single-cut solidbody, carved top, 6-on-a-side tuners
• Single-cutaway solidbody, mahogany back, carved maple top.
• Explorer peghead, 6-on-a-side tuner configuration.
• 2 humbucking pickups.

Les Paul XR: See L.P. XR.

Les Paul 25th Anniversary (1978–79)
Single-cut solidbody, carved top, 25/50 on peghead (25th anniversary of model, 50th anniversary of Les Paul's career)
• Single-cutaway solidbody, carved maple top, mahogany back, tune-o-matic bridge, TP-6 tailpiece, gold-plated hardware, Cherry Sunburst, black, Wine Red or Natural finish.
• Bound fingerboard and peghead, slashed-block inlays, brass nut, metal keystone tuner buttons, *25/50* inlaid on peghead, regular serial number and limited edition number on back of peghead.
• 2 humbucking pickups, 4 knobs, coil-tap switch.
Production: At least 1,842 (highest serial number); shipping totals show 3,411.

Les Paul 30th Anniversary (1982–83)
Single-cut solidbody, carved top, 30th Anniversary at 19th fret
• Single-cutaway solidbody, carved maple top, mahogany back, tune-o-matic bridge with spring retainer, uniform-depth binding in cutaway, all-gold finish.
• 3-piece mahogany neck, 1-piece neck optional, pearl trapezoid inlays, *30th Anniversary* engraved on inlay at 19th fret, nickel-plated hardware, serial number with A-, B- or C-prefix followed by 3 digits.
• 2 PAF humbucking pickups, 4 knobs, selector switch on upper treble bout.

Les Paul 55 (1974–80)
Single-cut solidbody, Les Paul Special features, 2 P-90 pickups, "Les Paul Model" on silkscreen
• Single cutaway, slab mahogany body, tune-o-matic bridge (earliest with wraparound bridge/tailpiece).

• Mahogany neck, bound rosewood fingerboard, dot inlays, plastic keystone tuner buttons, *Les Paul Model* on peghead, pearl logo.
• 2 black soapbar P-90 pickups, 4 knobs. Production: 2,775 (1974–79).

L.P. Artist (Les Paul Artist, Les Paul Active) (1979–81)
Single-cut solidbody, carved top, LP *on peghead*
• Single cutaway, carved maple top, tune-o-matic bridge, TP-6 fine-tune tailpiece, multiple-bound top, gold-plated hardware.
• Bound ebony fingerboard, large block inlays, brass nut, triple-bound peghead, script *LP* peghead inlay.
• 2 humbucking pickups (3 pickups optional), active electronics, 3 knobs (volume, treble, bass), 3 mini switches (expansion, compression, brightness).
Production: 230 (1979).

L.P. Session (L.P. XR-III): No information unavailable.

L.P. XR-1 (1981–82)
Single-cut solidbody, 2 exposed-coil humbuckers, coil tap
• Single cutaway, flat top, unbound top, Tobacco Sunburst, Cherry Sunburst or Goldburst finish.
• 3-piece maple neck, unbound rosewood fingerboard, dot inlay.
• 2 exposed-coil Dirty Fingers humbucking pickups, coil-tap switch.

L.P. XR-II (1981–82)
Single-cut solidbody, carved top, 2 covered humbuckers, coil tap
• Flat or carved top of figured maple, laminated mahogany body, Nashville tune-o-matic bridge, bound top, chrome-plated hardware, honey Sunburst or Vintage Cherry Sunburst finish.
• 3-piece maple or 2-piece mahogany neck, unbound rosewood fingerboard, dot inlays, pearl logo, metal tuner buttons
• 2 super humbucking pickups (some with metal-covered mini-humbuckers with no polepieces and *Gibson* embossed on pickup covers), coil-tap switch

L.P. XR-III (1982): specs unavailable.

Old Hickory Les Paul (1998)
Single-cut solidbody, carved top, Andrew Jackson on peghead
• Tulip poplar body from 274-year-old tree on the grounds of The Hermitage (Andrew Jackson's residence in Nashville) felled by a tornado on April 16, 1998, image of The Hermitage on pickguard, multiply binding.
• Hickory fingerboard, *Old Hickory* pearl fingerboard inlay, Andrew Jackson's image on peghead inlay (same image as on a $20 bill).
• 2 humbucking pickups, 4 knobs.
Production: Under 200.

The Les Paul (1976–79)
Single-cut solidbody, carved flamed maple top, wood knobs and pickups covers
• Carved maple top, maple back, tune-o-matic bridge (larger rectangular bridge from 1978), stopbar tailpiece (TP-6 fine tune from 1978) rosewood pickguard, rosewood control plates on back, rosewood outer binding, green- and red-stained wood inner bindings, gold-plated hardware, Natural or Rosewood finish.
• Maple neck, 3-piece ebony-rosewood-ebony fingerboard, abalone block inlays, 5-piece split-diamond peghead inlay, pearl tuner buttons, pearl plate on back of peghead ith limited edition number.
• 2 super humbucking pickups, 5-sided rosewood pickup covers, rosewood knobs and switch tip.
Production: 73.

The Paul II (1996–97) / **The Paul II SL** (Sans Lacquer) (1998):
Thin single-cut solidbody, The Paul II *on truss-rod cover*
• 3-piece thin mahogany body (not sandwich), carved top, no binding, tune-o-matic bridge, Ebony or Wine Red finish (SL urethane finish specified but not on all examples 1998).
• Unbound rosewood fingerboard, dot inlays, model name on truss-rod cover, decal logo.
• 2 exposed-coil humbucking pickups, 4 knobs, selector switch on upper bass bout.

The Paul (Standard) (1978–81) / **Firebrand Les Paul** (1981)
Thin single-cut solidbody, walnut body
• Thin single-cutaway solidbody, walnut body, tune-o-matic bridge.
• Walnut neck, unbound ebony fingerboard, dot inlays, decal logo (routed logo with no inlay or hot-branded logo, 1981).
• 2 exposed-coil humbucking pickups, selector switch near control knobs, no pickguard.

The Paul Deluxe (1980–85)
Thin single-cut solidbody, dot inlays, exposed-coil pickups
• Thin single-cutaway solidbody, mahogany body, beveled edges around lower treble bout, no pickguard.
• Unbound ebony fingerboard, dot inlays, some with *Firebrand* on truss-rod cover but not a Firebrand (branded logo) model.
• 2 exposed-coil humbucking pickups, selector switch below tailpiece.

LES PAUL ARTIST SIGNATURE MODELS

(2 humbuckers and 4 knobs unless otherwise noted)
Duane Allman (2003): Based on 1959 Les Paul Standard, highly flamed top, Grover Rotomatic tuners, *Duane* spelled out in fretwire on back of guitar.
Billy Jo Armstrong Les Paul Junior (2006–current): 1950s specs, single-cutaway, rosewood fingerboard (Ebony with Classic White finish), 1 stacked double-coil H-90 pickup, wraparound tailpiece, Ebony or Classic White finish.
Dickey Betts '57 Redtop Les Paul (2002–03): 1957 Les Paul Standard specs, 2 humbuckers, red top finish. Production: 55.
Dickey Betts Ultra Aged 1957 Les Paul Gold Top (2001–2003): Scarfed back, concho-style jackplate and switch washer. Production: 114.
Peter Frampton Les Paul (2000–current): 3 exposed-coil pickups wired so that middle pickup is always on, Les Paul custom trim, weight-relieved body, maple top, Antiqued binding, signature at 12th fret, Ebony finish.
Ace Frehley Les Paul (1997–2001): 3 DiMarzio pickups, multiple-bound body, lightning bolt inlay, signature at 12th fret, bound peghead with Ace graphic, Heritage Cherry Sunburst finish.
Warren Haynes '58 Les Paul (2006): Based on 1958 Les Paul Standard.
Bob Marley Les Paul Special (2002–03): Based on c1972 model (never catalogued), single cutaway, aluminum pickguard and elliptical switch washer, 2 soapbar P-90 pickups, selector switch on upper bass bout, small block inlays, wide binding on peghead, aged Cherry finish appears stripped. Production: 200.
Gary Moore Les Paul (2000–01): Flamed maple top, no binding, 2 exposed-coil humbucking pickups with reverse-wound zebra-coil in neck position, unbound fingerboard, pearl trapzezoid inlay, Lemonburst finish.
Jimmy Page Les Paul, 1st version (1995–99): Based on Page's 1959 Standard, push/pull knobs to control phasing and coil tapping, signature on pickguard, .050-inch fret height, Grover tuners with kidney-bean buttons (after approx. 500 shipped, frets lowered to .038-inch, locking nut added to bridge height-adjustment, Kluson tuners with keystone buttons), gold-plated hardware.
Jimmy Page Les Paul, 2nd version (2004–current): Covered humbucker in neck position, exposed-coil in bridge, Pageburst finish. Production: 25 signed, 150 with Tom Murphy aging, unlimited with Custom Authentic finish.
Joe Perry Les Paul (1996–2000): Curly maple

top, no binding, pearloid pickguard and truss-rod cover, unbound rosewood fingerboard, trapezoid inlays, specially wound bridge pickup, push/pull tone control to activate mid-boost, master tone control, Translucent Blackburst stain finish.

Joe Perry Boneyard Les Paul (2003–current): Flamed top, weight-relieved body, aged nickel-plated hardware, optional Bigsby vibrato, Boneyard (hot sauce) logo on peghead, signature on truss-rod cover, Custom Authentic Green Tiger finish.

Gary Rossington Les Paul (2002): Replica of Rossington's '59 Les Paul Standard, aged nickel-plated hardware, 2 screws in headstock, Schaller tuners (with holes from original Klusons), aged Sunburst finish, large wear spot on back. Production: 250.

Neal Schon Les Paul (2005–current): Carved mahogany top, multiply binding on top, Floyd Rose vibrato, chrome-plated hardware, sculpted neck heel, pearl diamond inlays, bound ebony fingerboard, DiMarzio FastTrack/Fernandes Sustainer neck pickup, Gibson BurstBucker Pro bridge pickup, 4 knobs with push/pull for mid-cut, 3-way switch, 2 mini toggle switches for Sustainer on/off and octave effect, Green Gold, Alpine White or Ebony finish.

Slash Les Paul (1997): Slash image carved into top, Cranberry finish. Production: 50.

Slash Les Paul Signature (2004–current): Plain maple top, aged nickel-plated hardware, 2 Seymour Duncan Alnico Pro II humbucking pickups, Fishman Powerbridge pickup, 3 volume controls, 1 master tone, 3-way switch, 3-way mini-toggle for bridge pickup, Custom Authentic Dark Tobaccoburst finish.

John Sykes Les Paul Custom (2007): Based on 1978 Les Paul Custom, exposed-coil Dirty Fingers humbucking pickup in bridge position, exposed-coil '57 Classic humbucker in neck position, 4 knobs with bridge-pickup otne control disabled, chrome pickup mounting rings, mirror pickguard, brass nut, chrome-plated hardware, Ebony finish, available aged or non-aged.

Pete Townshend Les Paul Deluxe #9: Numeral 9 decal on front below bridge, 3-piece maple top, mahogany/poplar /mahogany sandwich back, Heritage Cherry Sunburst finish, chrome-plated hardware, Nashville wide-travel tune-o-matic, 3-piece maple neck with volute, 2 mini-humbuckers and 1 DiMarzio Dual Sound humbucker. 3 volume, 1 master tone, 3-way selector, 2 mini toggles (one taps DiMarzio, other puts it out of phase). Production: 75.

Pete Townshend Deluxe: Numeral 1 decal on front, Wine Red finish.

Pete Townshend Deluxe Goldtop: Numeral 3 decal on front, gold-top finish.

Zakk Wylde Bullseye Les Paul

(2000–current): Painted bullseye (Mylar applique optional 2002) EMG humbucking pickups with black covers, ebony fingerboard, pearl block inlays, 5-piece split-diamond peghead inlay, gold-plated tuners.

Zakk Wylde Camo Bullseye Les Paul (2004–current): Camouflage bullseye, maple fingerboard.

Zakk Wylde Rough Top Les Paul (2000–02): Unfinished roughed-up top.

Zakk Wylde Custom (Bottle Cap) (1999, 2002): Bottle caps on top of guitar.

SG MODELS

SG Artist (1981) / **SG-R1** (1980)
Double-cut solidbody, pointed horns, 2 switches, active electronics
- Thicker body than standard SG, no pickguard.
- Unbound ebony fingerboard, dot inlays, crown peghead inlay.
- 2 humbucking pickups, active solid-state electronics, 4 knobs (2 numbered 0-5-0), 3-way toggle, 2-way toggle.

SG Classic (1999–2001)
Double-cut solidbody, pointed horns, 2 pickups, Classic on truss-rod cover
- Double-cutaway mahogany solidbody, pointed horns, tune-o-matic bridge, large pickguard.
- Bound rosewood fingerboard, dot inlays.
- 2 P-90 pickups, 4 knobs.

SG Custom (1963–79) / **SG '62 Custom** (1986) / **SG Les Paul Custom** (1987–90) / **Les Paul/SG Custom Reissue** (1997–2005) / **SG Custom** (2006–current)
Double-cut solidbody, pointed horns, pearl block inlays.
- Double-cutaway mahogany solidbody with pointed horns, vibrato with lyre and logo on coverplate (Bigsby optional 1972–79, stopbar 1986–2001, Maestro optional from 2002), small pickguard does not surround pickups (larger pickguard 1966–71, wing-shaped 1972, small pickguard from 1972), Vintage Original Spec aging treatment optional from 2006.
- Ebony fingerboard, pearl block inlays, 5-piece split-diamond peghead inlay.
- 3 humbucking pickups, 4 knobs, 1 switch (controls on semi-circular plate 1972). Production: 1,566 (1964–70, also see Les Paul Custom 1961–63); 3,705 (1971–79).

Les Paul SG '67 Custom (1992–1993): Large 4-point pickguard, Wine Red or Classic White finish

SG Custom Showcase Edition (October 1988): EMG pickups, Ferrari Red finish. Production: 200 for U.S., 50 for overseas.

10th Anniversary SG Custom (2003–04): Diamond White Sparkle finish, white

pickguard, ebony fingerboard, pearl block inlays, *10th Anniversary* at 12th fret, gold-plated hardware: Production 40.

30th Anniversary SG Custom (1991): Engraved *30th Anniversary* engraved on peghead inlay, TV Yellow finish (darker than traditional TV Yellow). Production: No more than 300.

1967 SG Custom (1991): Large 4-point pickguard, Wine Red finish.

SG Deluxe (1971–72, 1981–84, 1998–2000)
Double-cut solidbody, pointed horns, semi-curcular control plate or 3 Firebird mini-humbuckers
- Solid mahogany double-cutaway body, pointed horns, non-beveled cutaways, triangular Les Paul Standard-style pickguard flush with top (large SG-style pickup from 1981), tune-o-matic bridge (large rectangular base 1981–84), Gibson Bigsby vibrato (no vibrato 1998, Maestro Bigsby-style from 1999), Natural, Cherry or Walnut finish (Ebony, Ice Blue or Hellfire Red 1998–2000).
- Bound rosewood fingerboard (unbound ebony from 1998), small block inlay (some with dots 1971–84, all with dots 1998–2000), decal logo.
- 2 humbucking pickups (3 Firebird-style mini-humbucking pickups with no polepieces from 1988)), 4 knobs (2 knobs, 6-way rotary switch 1998–2000), semi-circular control plate (no control plate from 1998). Production: 7,615.

SG Elegant Quilt Top (2004–06)
Double-cut solidbody, pointed horns, quilted maple top
- Mahogany double-cutaway with pointed horns, quilted maple top, gold-plated hardware.
- Bound rosewood fingerboard, abalone trapezoid block inlays.
- 2 humbucking pickups, 4 knobs, selector switch.

SG Elite (1987–89)
Double-cut solidbody, pointed horns, block inlays, locking nut
- Solid mahogany double-cutaway body, pointed horns, tune-o-matic bridge, TP-6 fine-tune tailpiece, gold-plated hardware, Pearl White or Metallic Sunset finish.
- Bound ebony fingerboard, block inlays, locking nut, crown peghead inlay.
- 2 Spotlight humbucking pickups, coil-tap switch.

SG Exclusive (1979)
Double-cut solidbody, pointed horns, block inlays, rotary coil-tap control
- Solid mahogany double-cutaway body, pointed horns, white pickguard, Ebony finish.
- Bound rosewood fingerboard, block inlays, pearl logo, crown peghead inlay.

- 2 humbucking pickups with or without covers, coil tap controlled by rotary knob (in standard volume knob position).
Production: 478.

SG Goddess (2006–current)
Double-cut solidbody, pointed horns, red logo
- Double-cutaway solid mahogany body, pointed horns, chrome-plated hardware.
- Bound ebony fingerboard, trapezoid inlays, Goddess on truss-rod cover, no peghead ornament, red logo.
- 2 exposed-coil humbucking pickups with transparent bobbins, 1 volume, 1 tone, 3-way switch.

SG Gothic: See SG Special Gothic.

SG GT (2006–current)
Double-cut solidbody, pointed horns, white center section
- Double-cutaway solid mahogany body, pointed horns, tune-o-matic bridge, massive chrome tailpiece, opaque finishes with white center section, chrome-plated hardware.
- Bound ebony fingerboard, mirror trapezoid inlays, GT on truss-rod cover, no peghead ornament.
- 2 humbucking pickups, 4 knurled knobs, 1 switch, locking cable jack, push/pull for coil tap, high pass tone filter.

SG Junior (1963–70, 1991–93)
Double-cut solidbody, pointed horns, 1 P-90. Also see Les Paul Junior 1961–63.
- Double-cutaway solid mahogany body, pointed horns, Maestro vibrato optional (standard 1965–70), Cherry finish.
- Unbound rosewood fingerboard, dot inlays, decal logo.
- 1 "dog-ear" P-90 pickup (soapbar 1966–70), 2 knobs.
Production: 12,133 (1964–70, also see Les Paul Junior 1961–63).

SG-100 Junior: See SG-100.

SG Les Paul (Les Paul with SG body): See Les Paul Custom, Les Paul Junior, Les Paul Standard, Les Paul/SG.

SG Menace (2006–current)
Double-cut solidbody, pointed horns, brass knuckles on fingerboard
- Double-cutaway solid mahogany body, pointed horns, tune-o-matic bridge, tribal body routings, black hardware, flat black finish.
- Unbound ebony fingerboard, brass knuckles inlay at 5th fret, no other inlay, special headstock logo, gold-tinted frets.
- 2 "smoky coil" humbucking pickups with brass studs, 4 knobs, 1 switch.

SG Pro (1971, 1973–74)
Double-cut solidbody, pointed horns, 2 P-90s, semi-circular control plate
- Double-cutaway solid mahogany body, pointed horns, wing-shaped pickguard (Les Paul Standard-style) mounted on top, tune-o-matic bridge with rectangular base, Gibson Bigsby vibrato, Cherry, Walnut or Natural Mahogany finish.
- Single-bound rosewood fingerboard, dot inlays, pearl logo.
- 2 black soapbar P-90 pickups with mounting rings, semi-circular control plate.
Production: 2,995.

SG R-1: See SG Artist
SG Reissue (1986–87) / **SG '62 Reissue** (1988–90) / **Les Paul SG '61 Reissue** (1993–97) / **SG '61 Reissue** (1998–current) (also see Les Paul/SG Standard Reissue)
Double-cut solidbody, pointed horns, trapezoid inlays
- Double-cutaway solid mahogany body, pointed horns, tune-o-matic bridge, small pickguard, nickel-plated hardware, Heritage Cherry finish.
- Bound rosewood fingerboard, trapezoid inlays, crown peghead inlay, plastic keystone tuner buttons.
- 2 humbucking pickups, 4 knobs, selector switch near pickguard, jack in top.

SG Select (2007–current)
Double-cut solidbody, pointed horns, trapezoid inlays, flame maple top
- Double-cutaway solid mahogany body, pointed horns, flame maple top and back, gold-plated hardware.
- 3-piece flame maple neck, bound rosewood fingerboard with Antique binding, trapezoid inlays, metal truss-rod cover, crown peghead inlay, metal tuner buttons, pearl logo.
- 2 humbucking pickups, 4 knobs, 1 switch.

SG Special (1959–70, 1972–78, 1985–current) / **Gibson Special** (1985), also see Special I, Special II
Double-cut solidbody, pointed horns, dots or small block inlays, 2 pickups
- Solid mahogany double-cutaway body, rounded horns (SG-style pointed horns from 1961), pickguard does not surround pickups (larger pickguard surrounds pickups 1966–70, no pickguard 1986–90, larger pickguard from 1991), wraparound bridge (Maestro vibrato optional 1962–64, vibrato standard 1965–70, rectangular-base tune-o-matic 1972, regular tune-o-matic from 1973, Kahler Flyer vibrato optional 1985, Floyd Rose vibrato optional 1986).
- Bound rosewood fingerboard (unbound from 1985, ebony from 1986, rosewood from 1996), dot inlay (small blocks 1973–85, dots from

1986), SG on truss-rod cover from 1996, pearl logo (decal from 1985).
- 2 black soapbar P-90 pickups (black-covered mini-humbuckers 1972–78, 1 or 2 exposed-coil humbuckers 1985, 2 humbuckers from 1986), 4 knobs (3 knobs 1985–95, 4 from 1996), 1 switch.
Production: 22,295 (1960–70), 9,363 (1971–79).

Generation Swine SG Special (mid 1997): Promotional guitars for Motley Crue's *Generation Swine* CD and tour, Ebony finish, red pickguard with "Generation Swine" logo. Production: 5 given away at Guitar Center stores, 1 given away nationally.
Les Paul/SG Special Reissue (2001–03) / SG Special (Custom Shop version 2004–current): Reissue of early 1960s version, wraparound bridge, small pickguard, 2 soapbar P-90s, nickel-plated hardware, Maestro vibrato optional 2001–05, Vintage Original Spec aging treatment optional from 2006.
SG Special ¾-scale (1959–61): 22-inch scale, no model name on peghead, Cherry finish.
SG Special Faded (2002–current): worn Cherry or worn brown finish, 2 exposed-coil humbuckers, unbound rosewood fingerboard, decal logo, worn Cherry or worn brown finish.
SG Special Faded 3 Pickup (2007–current): 3 humbuckers, 2 knobs, 1 rotary selector switch, plain truss-rod cover, worn Ebony or worn white finish.
SG Special Gothic (1999–2000 / SG Gothic (2001–02): 2 exposed-coil humbuckers, satin Ebony finish, ebony fingerboard, moon-and-star inlay at 12th fret (no other inlay), black hardware.
SG Special New Century (2006–current): 2 exposed-coil humbuckers, full-body mirror pickguard, ebony fingerboard, mirror dot inlays, Ebony finish.
SG Special Reissue (2004–current): Small pickguard, 2 soapbar P-90 pickups.

SG Standard (1963–70 1972–80 1983–86 1988–current) (also see SG Reissue, The SG)
Double-cut solidbody, pointed horns, trapezoid inlays.
- Double-cutaway solid mahogany body, pointed horns (walnut 1981), pickguard does not surround pickups (larger pickguard surrounds pickups 1966–86, small pickguard 1988–90, large pickguard from 1991), tune-o-matic bridge (rectangular bridge base (1972–73), Maestro vibrato (up-and-down pull) with lyre and logo on coverplate (no vibrato 1972–75, Bigsby optional 1976–80).
- Mahogany neck (walnut 1981), bound rosewood fingerboard (unbound 1972–81), trapezoid inlay (small blocks 1972–80, dots 1981, small blocks 1983–86, trapezoids from 1988), crown peghead inlay, pearl logo, no *Les Paul* on truss-rod cover.
- 2 humbucking pickups with metal covers (black plastic covers 1973–80, no covers 1981),

4 knobs, selector switch by pickguard (near knobs 1980–86; near edge of body from 1988), jack into top (into side 1980–89; into top from 1991).
Production: 16,677 (1964–70, also see Les Paul Standard 1961–63); 17,394 (1971–79).

Les Paul/SG Standard Reissue (2001–03) / SG Standard (Custom shop version 2004–current): reissue of early 1960s version, does not say *Les Paul* anywhere, small pickguard, nickel-plated hardware, optional Maestro vibrato, aged hardware optional 2001–05, Vintage Original Spec or Custom Authentic aging treatment optional from 2006.
SG '62 Showcase Edition (April. 1988 guitar of the month): EMG pickups, blue finish. Production: 200 for U.S., 50 for overseas.
SG/Les Paul with Deluxe Lyre Vibrato (2000–2002): Vibrato with lyre and logo on coverplate.
SG Standard Celebrity Series (August 1991): Black finish, white knobs, white pickguard, gold-plated hardware.
SG Standard Korina (1993–94): Korina (African limba wood) body, 3-piece sandwich body with rosewood center laminate, gold-plated hardware, Antique Natural finish. Production: 500.

SG Studio (1978)
Double-cut solidbody, pointed horns, bound fingerboard, dot inlays, 2 humbuckers
• Solid mahogany double-cutaway body, pointed horns, no pickguard, some with satin finish.
• Bound rosewood fingerboard, dot inlays.
• 2 humbucking pickups, 3 knobs, 1 toggle switch.
Production: 931.

SG Supreme (1999–2004 2007–current) / **SG Supreme '57 Humbucker** (2005–2006)
Double-cut solidbody, pointed horns, curly maple top, split-diamond inlays
• Double cutaway with pointed horns, mahogany back, flamed maple top cap, gold-plated hardware, Fireburst (3-tone Sunburst shaded from bottom of body to horns) finish.
• Bound ebony fingerboard, split-diamond inlay, bound peghead , 5-piece split-diamond (SG Custom style) peghead inlay.
• 2 P-90A soapbar pickups with black covers ('57 Classic humbuckers from 2005), 4 knobs.

SG TV (1960–67)
Double-cut solidbody, pointed horns, yellow finish, 1 P-90 pickup
• Solid mahogany double-cutaway body, pointed horns, Maestro vibrato optional (standard 1965–70), TV Yellow finish.
• Unbound rosewood fingerboard, dot inlay.
• 1 "dog-ear" P-90 pickup (soapbar 1966–67). Production: 3,480.

SG Voodoo (2002–04)
Double-cut solidbody, pointed horns, voodoo doll on fingerboard
• Single-cutaway swamp ash solidbody, carved top, Juju finish (black with red wood filler), black hardware.
• Ebony fingerboard, voodoo doll inlay at 5th fret (no other inlays), red logo.
• 2 humbucking pickups with red/black coils.

SG-X: See All American I.

SG-Z (1998)
Double-cut solidbody, pointed horns, Z-shaped tailpiece
• Double cutaway with pointed horns, tune-o-matic bridge, Z-shaped tailpiece with strings through body, small pickguard.
• Bound rosewood fingerboard, split-diamond inlay, 3-piece reverse-Z pearl peghead inlay, black chrome hardware, platinum or verdigris finish.
• 1 stacked-coil and 1 standard humbucking pickup, 2 knobs, selector switch between knobs.

SG I (1972–73)
Double-cut solidbody, pointed horns, black mini-humbuckers
• Double cutaway with pointed horns, beveled edges, mahogany body, triangular wing-shaped pickguard, wraparound bridge/tailpiece, Cherry or Walnut finish.
• Dot inlays standard Gibson peghead shape.
• Black plastic-covered mini-humbucking pickup with no poles, 2 knobs, semi-circular control plate.
Production: 2,331.

SG I with Junior pickup (1972): P-90 pickup. Production: 61.
SG II (1972): 2 pickups, 2 knobs, 2 slide switches, Cherry or Walnut finish. Production: 2,927.
SG III with humbuckers (1975): Humbucking pickups. Production: 61.
SG III (1972–73): 2 pickups, 2 slide switches, tune-o-matic bridge, Cherry Sunburst finish. Production: 953.

SG-3 (2007–current)
Double-cut solidbody, pointed horns, 3 humbuckers
• Double-cutaway solid mahogany body, pointed horns, small pickguard does not surround pickups, gold-plated hardware.
• Bound rosewood fingerboard with Antiqued binding, trapezoid inlays, crown peghead inlay, plastic keystone tuner buttons plastic.
• 3 humbucking pickups, 2 knobs, 6-position rotary selector switch with pointer knob.

SG '61 Reissue, SG '62 Reissue: See SG Standard.

SG '62 Showcase Edition: See SG Standard.
SG 90 Single (1988–90)
Double-cut solidbody, pointed horns, strings through body
• Pearloid pickguard, strings mounted through body, Floyd Rose vibrato optional, Alpine White, Metallic Turquoise, or Heritage Cherry finish.
• Unbound ebony fingerboard, 25½-inch scale, 2-piece split-diamond inlay, crown peghead inlay, pearl logo.
• 1 humbucking pickup with black cover.

SG 90 Double (1988–90): 1 oblong single-coil pickup mounted diagonally in neck position, 1 black-covered humbucking pickup in bridge position, 2 knobs, push/pull for coil tap, selector switch between knobs.

SG-100 (1971)
Double-cut solidbody, pointed horns, oblong pickup, oblong control plate
• Double cutaway with pointed horns, solid poplar body (some mahogany), metal bridge cover with engraved *Gibson*, some with triangular Les Paul-type pickguard, some with large SG-type pickguard, Cherry or Walnut.
• Unbound rosewood fingerboard, dot inlays, standard Gibson peghead shape.
• Oblong Melody Maker type pickup, large pickup mounting plate, oblong control plate.
Production: 1,229.

SG-100 Junior (1972): P-90 pickup. Production: 272.
SG-200 (1971): 2 pickups, 2 slide switches, Cherry, Walnut or black finish. Production: 2,980.
SG-250 (1971): 2 pickups, 2 slide switches, Cherry Sunburst finish. Production: 527.

SG 400 (1985–86)
Double-cut solidbody, pointed horns, 3 pickups, 3 mini-switches
• Solid mahogany double-cutaway body, pointed horns, vibrato, black hardware.
• Bound rosewood fingerboard, dot inlays.
• 400-series electronics, 1 Dirty Fingers humbucking pickup, 2 single-coil pickups, master tone and master volume knob, 3 mini-switches for on/off pickup control, push/pull volume control for coil tap.

The SG (1979–80) / **SG Standard** (1981)
Double-cut solidbody, pointed horns, walnut body, exposed-coil pickups
• Double-cutaway walnut solidbody, pointed horns, tune-o-matic bridge, small pickguard, chrome-plated hardware, Natural finish.
• 1 standard humbucking pickup, 1 Super humbucking "velvet brick" pickup, no pickup covers, 4 knobs.
• Walnut neck, ebony fingerboard, dot inlays, decal logo or routed logo with no inlay ("Firebrand" branded logo 1980, pearl logo 1981).

The SG / The SG Deluxe (1979–84)
Double-cut solidbody, pointed horns, exposed-coil pickups
• Solid mahogany double-cutaway body, pointed horns, tune-o-matic bridge, small pickguard.
• Walnut neck, ebony fingerboard, dot inlays, chrome-plated hardware.
• 1 standard humbucking pickup, 1 Super humbucking "velvet brick" pickup, no pickup covers, black mounting rings, 4 knobs.

SG ARTIST SIGNATURE MODELS

Elliot Easton Custom SG (2007–current): 2 humbucking pickups, Maestro vibrola with Tiki-man engraved on cover, small pickguard, chrome-plated hardware (Pelham Blue finish) or gold-plated (Classic White finish), left-hand or right-handed.
Tony Iommi Les Paul SG (1998, 2001–05): 2 custom-wound humbucking pickups with no polepieces, ebony fingerboard, iron cross inlays, chrome-plated hardware, left-handed or right-handed, Ebony finish.
Judas Priest SG (2005–current): Large chrome pickguard, 1 EMG and 2 Gibson 57 Classic exposed-coil humbuckers, custom stud-mounted bridge tailpiece, bound rosewood fingerboard, dot inlay Custom Authentic Ebony finish, certificate signed by K.K. Downing and Glenn Tipton. Production: 30 (sold as a set with Judas Priest Flying V).
Gary Rossington SG (2003): Early 1960s SG Standard specs, Maestro vibrola, aged and faded Cherry finish. Production: 250.
Angus Young Signature SG (2000–current): Based on SG Standard, large pickguard, 2 humbucking pickups (1 custom wound), Maestro vibrato with lyre and logo engraved in cover, "devil signature" ornament on peghead, nickel-plated hardware, aged Cherry finish.

OTHER MODELS

All American I (1995–97) / **SG-X** (1998–2000)
SG body, 1 humbucker
• Solid mahogany double-cutaway body, pointed horns, tune-o-matic bridge, chrome-plated hardware, Ebony finish.
• Unbound rosewood fingerboard, dot inlays, decal logo.
• 1 exposed-coil humbucking pickup 2 knobs, coil tap.

All American II (1995–97)
Double-cut solidbody, pointed horns (not as pointed as SG)
• Double cutaway with pointed horns (not SG-shape, similar to early 1960s Melody Maker), vibrato, Ebony or Deep Wine Red finish.

• Unbound rosewood fingerboard, dot inlays, II on truss-rod cover.
• 2 oblong single-coil pickups with non-adjustable polepieces, 2 knobs, 1 switch.

Alpha Series: See Q-100.

Black Beauty: See Les Paul Custom.

Black Knight Custom (1984)
Single-cut solidbody, bolt-on neck, 6-on-a-side tuners
• Single-cutaway solidbody, flat top with beveled edges, 4 knobs, 3-way selector switch near knobs, Kahler vibrato, black chrome-plated hardware, Ebony finish
• Bolt-on neck, rosewood fingerboard, dot inlays, 6-on-a-side tuner arrangement,
• 2 humbucking pickups

BluesHawk (1996–2003)
Single-cut solidbody, Varitone rotary control, diamond inlay
• Single cutaway, mahogany back, flat maple top, semi-hollow poplar body, f-holes, Maestro Bigsby-style optional 1998.
• 25½-inch scale, unbound rosewood fingerboard, diamond inlay, stacked-diamond peghead inlay, pearl logo, gold-plated hardware, Ebony or Cherry finish.
• 2 special Blues 90 pickups with cream soapbar covers and non-adjustable poles, 2 knobs (with push/pull to disable Varitone), slide switch, 6-position Vari-tone control, combination bridge/tailpiece with individual string adjustments, strings through body, single-bound top.

Byrdland (1955–current)
Thinbody archtop, short-scale version of L-5CES, pearl block inlays. Billy Byrd/Hank Garland model
• 17-inch wide, rounded cutaway (a few double-cutaway, 1958–62, pointed cutaway 1960–69), 2¼-inch deep, carved spruce top, carved maple back, triple-loop tubular tailpiece, tortoiseshell celluloid pickguard (a few early with pearloid), 7-ply top binding, triple-bound back, 7-ply pickguard binding, single-bound f-holes, gold-plated hardware, Sunburst or Natural finish.
• 2 Alnico V pickups (humbuckers from late 1957, a few with 1 humbucker and 1 Charlie Christian).
• Ebony fingerboard with pointed end, 5-ply fingerboard binding, 23½-inch scale, pearl block inlays, flowerpot peghead inlay, 7-ply peghead binding.
Production: 2,670 (1955–79).

Byrdland Florentine (1998–current): Pointed cutaway.

CF-100E (1951–58)
Single-cut acoustic flat-top, pointed horn

• 14⅛-inch wide single-cutaway flat-top, pointed horn, spruce top, mahogany back and sides.
• Bound rosewood fingerboard, pearloid trapezoid inlays, crown peghead inlay, pearl logo (earliest with no peghead inlay and decal logo).
• 1 single-coil pickup with adjustable polepieces mounted at end of fingerboard, 2 knobs.
Production: 1,257.

Challenger I (1983–84)
Single-cut solidbody, bolt-on neck, standard peghead
• Single-cutaway solidbody, flat top, pickguard surrounds pickup(s), combination bridge/tailpiece with individual string adjustments, chrome-plated hardware, silver finish standard.
• Bolt-on maple neck, unbound rosewood fingerboard, dot inlays, standard peghead shape, decal logo.
• 1 humbucking pickup with black cover and no visible poles, 2 knobs.

Challenger II (1983–84): 2 pickups, 3 knobs

Citation (1969–70, 1975, 1979–83, 1993–current)
Single-cut archtop, fleur de lis on pickguard
• 17-inch wide, full-depth body, rounded cutaway, solid spruce top, solid maple back and sides, wood pickguard with fleur-de-lis inlay, control knob(s) on pickguard, fancy tailpiece, multiple-bound top and back, gold-plated hardware, varnish (non-lacquer) finish in Sunburst or Natural.
• Bound ebony fingerboard with pointed-end, 25½-inch scale, cloud inlay, multiple-bound peghead, fleur-de-lis inlays on front and back of peghead and on bridge.
• 1 or 2 floating mini-humbucking pickups (some without visible polepieces), 5-ply maple neck.

Corvette: See Custom models.

Corvus I (1982–84)
Solidbody shaped like battle ax, six-on-a-side tuners, bolt-on neck
• Solidbody with cutout along entire bass side of body, cutout on upper treble side, deep V-shaped cutout from bottom end almost to bridge, chrome-plated hardware, silver finish.
• Bolt-on maple neck, 24¾-inch scale, unbound rosewood fingerboard, dot inlays, 6-on-a-side tuners, decal logo.
• 1 humbucking pickup with black cover and no visible poles, pickup dipped in epoxy, 2 knobs, combination bridge/tailpiece with individual string adjustments.
Corvus II (1982–84): 2 pickups, 3 knobs.
Corvus II (1982–84): 3 high-output single-coil pickups, 2 knobs, 5-way switch.

Crest (1969–71)
Thinbody double-cut archtop, Brazilian rosewood body
• 16-inch hollow thinbody archtop body of laminated Brazilian rosewood, double rounded cutaways, flat back (some arched), multiple-bound rosewood pickguard, adjustable rosewood bridge, multiple-bound top, triple-bound back, single-bound f-holes, backstripe marquetry, gold-plated (Crest Gold) or silver-plated (Crest Silver) hardware.
• Neck-body joint at 17th fret, fingerboard raised off of top, block inlays, multiple-bound peghead, 5-piece split-diamond peghead inlay.
• 2 floating mini-humbucking pickups.
Production: 162

Crest Special (1961–63, 1969)
Thinbody single-cut archtop, crest on peghead
• Thin hollowbody, carved spruce top, pointed cutaway, crest-shaped insert in trapeze tailpiece, gold-plated hardware, some labeled *L-5CT Spec.*
• Ebony fingerboard, slashed-block (Super 400 style) inlay, crest peghead inlay with 3 crescent moons and castle.
• 2 humbucking pickups, Varitone control.

CS-336, CS-346: See ES-336, ES-346

CS-356 (2003–current)
Thinbody double-cut archtop, rounded horns, smaller body than ES-335, block inlays
• 13¾-inch double-cutaway semi-hollowbody, routed mahogany back with solid center area, arched (routed) figured maple top, f-holes, rounded double cutaways, body lines similar to ES-335, back beveled on bass side, tune-o-matic bridge, optional Bigsby vibrato, bound top and back, gold-plated hardware.
• Bound rosewood fingerboard, pearl block inlays, decal logo, 5-piece split-diamond peghead inlay, sealed-back tuners, gold-plated hardware.
• 2 '57 Classic humbucking pickups, 4 knobs.

10th Anniversary CS-356 (2003–2004): Diamond White Sparkle finish, white pickguard, ebony fingerboard, pearl block inlays, *10th Anniversary* at 12th fret, gold-plated hardware. Production: 20.

Doubleneck: any combination of necks was available by custom order from 1958–69. For regular production models see EDS-1275, EMS-1235, EBS-1250.

EBSF-1250 (1962–68)
Bass neck and 6-string neck
• SG-style solid mahogany body pointed horns, beveled edges.
• 4-string bass neck and 6-string guitar neck, rosewood fingerboards, double-paralellogram inlays.

• 2 humbucking pickups for each neck, 4 knobs on lower treble bout, 1 switch between tailpieces, 1 switch on upper treble bout, fuzz-tone on bass.
Production: 22.

EDS-1275 Double 12 (1958–68, 1974–current)
6-string neck and 12-string neck
• Hollowbody with maple back and sides and carved spruce top, double cutaway with pointed horns, (SG-style solidbody with pointed horns from c.1962), no soundholes, tune-o-matic bridges, triple-bound top and back (unbound with change to SG shape), nickel-plated hardware (gold on Alpine White finish from 1988).
• 12-string and 6-string necks, 24¾-inch scales, bound rosewood fingerboards, double-parallelogram inlay, pearl logo (decal from 1977).
• 2 humbucking pickups for each neck, 2 knobs for each neck, 1 switch on treble side, 1 switch on bass side, 1 switch between bridges (with change to SG body: 4 knobs on lower treble bout, 1 switch between tailpieces, 1 switch on upper treble bout).
Production: 110 (1958–68); 1,145 (1974–79).

EDS-1275 Centennial (May 1994 guitar of the month): Ebony finish, serial number in raised numerals on tailpiece, numeral *1* of serial number formed by row of diamonds, letter *i* of logo dotted by inlaid diamond, gold medallion on back of peghead, gold-plated hardware, limited run of no more than 101 serial numbered from 1894–1994, package includes 16 x 20-inch framed photograph and gold signet ring.

Jimmy Page Double Neck (2007): see Other Artist Signature models.

EDS custom: Any combination of guitar, bass, mandolin or banjo necks was available by custom order.

EMS-1235 Double Mandolin (1958–60)
Short 6-string guitar neck and standard 6-string guitar neck
• Double pointed cutaways, hollow maple body with carved spruce top, no soundholes (SG-style solidbody with pointed cutaways from c1962), tune-o-matic bridge for standard neck, height-adjustable bridge for short neck.
• Standard guitar neck and short 6-string neck with 15½-inch scale, bound rosewood fingerboards, double-parallelogram inlay, no peghead ornament.
• 1 humbucking pickup for short neck, 2 humbucking pickups for standard neck, 4 knobs on lower treble bout, 1 switch between tailpieces, 1 switch on upper treble bout.
Production: 61.

EMS custom: Any combination of guitar, bass, mandolin or banjo necks was available by custom order.

EXP 425 (1985–86)
Angular solidbody, humbucker and 2 single-coils
• Angular olid mahogany body, no pickguard, black hardware, Kahler vibrato.
• Ebony fingerboard, six-on-a-side tuner arrangement.
• 1 humbucking and 2 single-coil pickups, no pickup covers, 2 knobs, 3 mini-toggle switches.

Firebrand: See The SG, The Paul, 335-S.

Futura (1982–84)
Solidbody shaped like battle axe, six-on-a-side tuners, set neck
• Neck-through-body, cutout along entire bass side of body, cutout on upper treble side, deep cutout from bottom end almost to bridge, Gibson/Kahler Supertone vibrato optional, large tailpiece with individually adjustable saddles, gold-plated hardware, Ebony, Ultra Violet or Pearl White finish.
• Rosewood fingerboard, dot inlays, 6-on-a-side tuners.
• 2 humbucking pickups with no visible poles, 2 knobs.

Futura Reissue (1996) / **Mahogany Futura** (2002–04)
Angular body, V-shaped peghead (reissue of Explorer prototype)
• Mahogany body, body shape similar to Explorer but with sharper angles and narrower treble horn
• Unbound rosewood fingerboard, dot inlays, V-shaped peghead.
• 2 humbucking pickups, 3 knobs.
Production: 100 (1996); 15 in each of four metallic colors (2002–2004).

GGC-700 (1981–82)
Single-cut solidbody, flat top, oversized black pickguard
• Single-cutaway solidbody, flat top, beveled edge on bass side, tune-o-matic bridge, large black pickguard covers three-quarters of body, chrome-plated hardware.
• Unbound rosewood fingerboard, dot inlays, decal logo *The Gibson Guitar Company*, metal keystone tuner buttons.
• 2 humbucking pickups with exposed zebra coils, 4 black barrel knobs, selector switch near bridge, coil tap switch, jack into top.

GK-55 (1979–80)
Les Paul shape, bolt-on neck, TP-6 tailpiece
• Single cutaway mahogany solidbody, flat top, rectangular tune-o-matic bridge,

TP-6 tailpiece or stop tailpiece, no pickguard, Tobacco Sunburst finish.
- Bolt-on neck, unbound rosewood fingerboard, dot inlays, model name on truss-rod cover, decal logo.
- 2 Dirty Fingers pickups with exposed coils, 4 knobs.

Production: 1,000.

Guitar Trader Reissue: See Les Paul Standard Reissue.

KZ-II (1980–81)
Double-cut solidbody, rounded horns (different from Les Pauls), 2 humbuckers
- Double-cutaway solidbody, with Melody Maker style rounded horns, made in Kalamazoo factory, tune-o-matic bridge, chrome-plated hardware, Walnut stain with satin non-gloss finish.
- Dot inlays metal tuner buttons, standard Gibson peghead size, *KZ-II* on truss-rod cover.
- 2 humbucking pickups.

Invader (1983–88, prototypes from 1980)
Single-cut solidbody, bolt-on neck, stopbar tailpiece
- Single-cutaway mahogany solidbody, beveled bass-side edge, tune-o-matic bridge, stop tailpiece, chrome-plated hardware.
- Bolt-on maple neck, ebony fingerboard, dot inlays, standard Gibson peghead shape, decal logo.
- 2 ceramic magnet humbucking pickups with exposed zebra coils, 4 knobs, 3-way selector switch.

Invader variations (designed to use up bodies, model names unknown) (1988–89):
- 1 narrow pickup, 2 knobs, Kahler vibrato, set maple neck, ebony fingerboard, dot inlays, crown peghead inlay, black chrome hardware.
- 2 humbucking pickups with black plastic covers and no visible polepieces, 2 knobs, 1 switch, Kahler Flyer vibrato, pearloid pickguard covers most of treble side of body, jack into pickguard, set neck, unbound ebony fingerboard, dot inlays, Explorer-style peghead with 6-on-a-side tuner arrangement, black chrome hardware.

Graceland (1995–96)
Thinbody acoustic guitar shape, ELVIS on fingerboard
- Acoustic J-200 body shape, thin body, poplar back, spruce top, multiply top binding, tune-o-matic bridge, pickguard with modern-art design from Elvis Presley's custom J-200 acoustic, gold-plated hardware.
- Maple neck, bound ebony fingerboard, *ELVIS* and 2 stars inlaid on fingerboard.
- 2 black soapbar pickups.

J-160E (1954–78, 1990–96) / **J-160 Standard** (2002) / **J-160 VS Standard** (2002, 2005–current)
Dreadnought-size flat-top, pickup at end of fingerboard
- 16-inch wide acoustic flat-top, round-shouldered dreadnought shape (square-shouldered 1969–78), spruce top, mahogany back and sides, 2 large saddle-height adjustment screws nuts (small nuts from 1959).
- Bound rosewood fingerboard, trapezoid inlays, crown peghead inlay, pearl logo.
- 1 single-coil pickup with adjustable polepieces mounted at end of fingerboard, 2 knobs.

Production: 6,988 (1954–79).

J-160E Montana Special (1995): No specifications available.
J-160E Yamano Reissue (1996): Made for Japan distribution only.

J-190EC Super Fusion (2001–04)
Acoustic flat-top, rounded cutaway, 3 knobs
- 16-inch wide acoustic flat top, rounded cutaway, moustache bridge.
- Bound ebony fingerboard, slashed-block inlays, 5-piece slashed-diamond peghead inlay, pearl logo.
- 1 single-coil pickup mounted at end of bridge, 1 under-saddle pickup, 3 knobs, selector switch on upper bass bout.

Junior Pro (1988)
Single-cut solidbody, flat top, humbucker with black cover, no Les Paul designation
- Single cutaway mahogany body, (beveled waist on treble side, small pickguard extends from treble-side waist to end of fingerboard, Steingerber KB-X locking-nut vibrato, black chrome hardware.
- Ebony fingerboard, dot inlays, decal logo.
- Slim-coil humbucking pickup with black cover and no visible polepieces, 2 knobs.

Kalamazoo Award (1978–84)
Single-cut archtop, flying bird inlay on peghead
- 17-inch wide, full-depth body, carved spruce top, maple back and side, adjustable ebony bridge with pearl inlays, wood pickguard with abalone inlay, knobs mounted on pickguard, multiple-bound top and back, bound f-holes, gold-plated hardware, Sunburst or Natural varnish (non-lacquer) finish.
- Bound ebony fingerboard, abalone block inlays, multiple-bound peghead, flying bird peghead inlay.
- 1 floating mini-humbucking pickup (some without visible polepieces).

Kalamazoo Award 100th Anniversary (1991): 2 made for Japan.

L-4CES (1958, 1969, 1986–2003) / **L-4CES**

Mahogany (2004–06)
Single-cut archtop, pointed horn, spruce top
- 16¼-inch archtop, solid spruce top, maple back and sides (mahogany from 1986, solid carved mahogany back from 2004), triple-bound top, single-bound back (triple-bound from 1986).
- Bound rosewood fingerboard, double-parallelogram inlay, crown peghead inlay.
- Charlie Christian pickup (2 humbuckers from 1986), 2 knobs (4 knobs on lower treble bout, switch on upper bass bout from 1986).

Production: 9 (1969).

10th Anniversary L-4 Thinline (2003): Diamond White Sparkle finish, white pickguard, ebony fingerboard, pearl block inlays, *10th Anniversary* at 12th fret, gold-plated hardware.

Production: 30

L-5CES (1951–current)
Single-cut archtop, block inlay
- 17-inch wide, rounded cutaway (pointed cutaway 1960–69), solid carved spruce top, carved maple back (laminated 1-piece back 1960–69), maple sides, single-bound f-holes, multiple-bound top and back.
- Ebony fingerboard with pointed end, block inlays, multiple-bound fingerboard and peghead, flowerpot peghead inlay.
- 2 P-90 pickups (Alnico V from 1954, humbuckers from late 1957), 4 knobs, selector switch.

Production: 2,963 (1951–79).

L-5CES Centennial (Dec. 1994 guitar of the month): Ebony finish, serial number in raised numerals on tailpiece, numeral *1* of serial number formed by row of diamonds, letter *i* of logo dotted by inlaid diamond, gold medallion on back of peghead, gold-plated hardware, limited run of no more than 101 serial numbered from 1894–1994, packaged with 16 x 20 framed photograph and gold signet ring.

L-5 CEST (1954–62, 1983): thinline body, rounded cutaway, 2 humbuckers (1 floating humbucker in 1983).

L-5 Custom: See Super V

L-5S (1973–84)
Single-cut solidbody, flowerpot peghead inlay
- 13½-inch wide, single cutaway, carved maple top, contoured back, large rectangular tune-o-matic bridge, large L-5 style plate tailpiece with silver center insert (stopbar from 1975, TP-6 from 1978), no pickguard, 7-ply top binding and 3-ply back binding with black line on side, maple control cavity cover, gold-plated hardware, Natural, Cherry Sunburst or Vintage Sunburst finish.
- 5-piece maple/mahogany neck, 24¾-inch scale, 17 frets clear of body, bound ebony fingerboard with pointed end, abalone block inlays, 5-ply fingerboard binding with black line on side, 22 frets, 5-ply peghead binding, flowerpot peghead inlay.

- 2 large oblong low-impedance pickups with metal covers and embossed logo (humbuckers from 1974), 4 knobs.

Production: 1,813 (1973–79).

L-5 Signature (2001–05)
Single-cut archtop, rounded horn, scaled-down L-5
- 15½-inch single-cutaway archtop, 2⅝-inch deep, rounded cutaway, tune-o-matic bridge, multiply top binding, single-bound back, gold-plated hardware.
- 25½-inch scale, bound ebony fingerboard, pearl block inlays, flowerpot peghead inlay.
- 2 humbucking pickups.

L-5 Studio (1996–current)
Single-cut archtop, black binding, dot inlays
- 17-inch wide maple body, rounded cutaway, solid carved spruce top, tune-o-matic bridge, trapeze tailpiece, "ice cube marble" pattern celluloid pickguard, black binding on top and back, Translucent Blue or Translucent Red finish.
- Unbound ebony fingerboard, dot inlays, pearl logo.
- 2 humbucking pickups, 4 knobs, switch on cutaway bout.

L-6S/L6-S Custom: (1973–75 L-6S; 1975–79 L-6S Custom)
Single-cut solidbody, narrow peghead
- 13½-inch wide, 1⅛-inch deep, single cutaway, maple body, large rectangular tune-o-matic bridge, stop tailpiece.
- Unbound maple fingerboard with Natural finish, unbound ebony fingerboard with Tobacco Sunburst finish, small block inlay (dots from 1975), 24 frets, 18 frets clear of body, 24¾-inch scale, narrow peghead with similar shape to snakehead L-5 of late 1920s.
- 2 5-sided humbucking pickups with no polepieces (rectangular from 1975), 3 knobs (volume, midrange and tone), 6-position rotary tone selector switch for parallel and phase selection, chrome-plated hardware, Natural or Cherry finish.

Production: 12,460.

L-6S Deluxe (1975–80)
Single-cut solidbody, strings through body, 5-sided pickups
- 13½-inch wide, 1⅛-inch deep, single cutaway, maple body, beveled top around bass side, large rectangular tune-o-matic bridge, strings anchor through body, string holes on
a line diagonal to strings.
- 2 5-sided humbucking pickups with black covers, 3 screws in pickup mounting rings, 2 knobs, 3-way pickup selector switch.
- Unbound rosewood fingerboard, small block inlay (dots from 1978), metal tuner buttons.

Production: 3,483 (1975–79).

Landmark (1996–97)
Single-cut solidbody, flat top, strings through body, Firebird mini-humbuckers
- Single cutaway, mahogany back, flat maple top, low profile bridge, strings through body, bound top, combination bridge/tailpiece with individual string adjustments.
- 25½-inch scale, unbound rosewood fingerboard, dot inlays, pearl logo, gold-plated hardware, Glacier Blue, Sequoia Red, Mojaveburst, Navajo Turquoise or Everglades Green finish.
- 2 Firebird mini-humbucking pickups, 2 knobs, 3-way slide switch with coil-tap capability.

Le Grand: See Johnny Smith Artist Signature model.

Leo's Reissue: See Les Paul Standard Reissue.

Little Lucille: See B.B. King Artist Signature model.

The Log (2003)
Replica of Les Paul's Log, 4 x 4-inch centerpiece
- Solid 4 x 4-inch center block, detachable wings from full-depth archtop, homemade vibrato.
- Rosewood fingerboard with varied-pattern inlay (originally from a Larson Bros. guitar), 7-piece star-shaped peghead inlay (from 1930s Gibson L-12 acoustic), Epiphone tuners.
- 2 pickups with brown oblong covers.

Production: 3.

Lucille, Lucille Standard: See B.B. King Artist Signature model.

M-III Standard (1991–95)
Solidbody, swooping double cutaway with extended bass horn
- Double-cutaway poplar solidbody, extended bass horn, Floyd Rose vibrato.
- 25½-inch scale, 24 frets, maple neck and fingerboard, black arrowhead inlay flush with bass side, peghead points to bass side, 6-on-a-side tuner arrangement with tuners all on treble side, logo reads upside down to player.
- 2 ceramic magnet humbucking pickups with no covers in neck and bridge positions, NSX single-coil pickup with slug polepiecesin middle position, 2-way toggle switch and 5-way slide switch for 10 pickup combinations.

M-III (1996–97): Mahogany body, 3 humbucking pickups, Ebony or Wine Red finish.
M-III Deluxe (1991–92): Laminated body of maple/walnut/poplar, same electronics as M-III Standard, Floyd Rose vibrato, maple neck and fingerboard, arrowhead inlay flush with bass side, Antique Natural finish.
M-III-H (Standard) (1991–92): 2 humbucking pickups, no pickguard, Translucent Red or Translucent Amber finish.
M-III-H Deluxe (1991): 5-ply body with walnut top, curly maple back and poplar core, 2 humbucking pickups, 6-way switch, no pickguard, satin (non-gloss) neck finish, Antique Natural finish.
M-III Standard (1991–95): No pickguard, Translucent Red or Translucent Amber finish.
M-III Stealth (1991): Black limba wood body (similar to walnut), Floyd Rose vibrato, black chrome hardware, satin neck finish.
M-IV S Standard (1993–95): Steinberger vibrato, black chrome hardware, Ebony finish.
M-IV S Deluxe (1993–95): Steinberger vibrato, Natural finish.

Mach II: See U-2.

Map-shape (1983)
Body shaped like United States
- Mahogany body shaped like United States, combination bridge/tailpiece with individual string adjustments, Natural Mahogany finish standard, 9 made with American flag finish.
- 3-piece maple neck, ebony fingerboard, dot inlays crown peghead inlay, pearl logo, metal tuner buttons.
- 2 humbucking pickups, 4 knobs, 1 switch.

Production: Promotional model for dealers only.

Marauder (1975–81)
Single-cut solidbody, humbucker and blade pickups
- 12¾-inch wide, Les Paul-shape single cutaway, maple or mahogany body, large pickguard covers entire upper body and extends around lower treble bout.
- Bolt-on maple neck, unbound rosewood fingerboard (maple from 1978), dot inlays, triangular peghead with rounded top, decal logo.
- Humbucking pickup in neck position, blade pickup in bridge position, pickups set in clear epoxy, 2 knobs, rotary tone selector switch between knobs (some with switch on cutaway bout, 1978).

Production: 7,029 (1975–79).

Marauder Custom (1976–77): 3-way selector switch on cutaway bout, bound fingerboard, block inlays, Tobacco Sunburst finish.
Production: 83.

Melody Maker / MM (1959–70, 1986–92) (also see Les Paul Melody Maker)
Thin single- or double-cut solidbody, oblong pickup
- Single rounded cutaway (symmetrical double cutaway with rounded horns, 1961–62; horns slightly more open, 1963–64; SG shape with pointed horns, 1965–70; single cutaway 1986–92, body 1⅜-inch deep, wraparound

bridge/tailpiece, pickguard surrounds pickups, vibrato optional from 1962.
• Unbound rosewood fingerboard, dot inlays, narrow (2¼-inch) peghead (standard width 1970, narrow 1986–92), decal logo.
• ⅞-inch-wide oblong pickup (⅝-inch-inch from 1960) with black plastic cover and no visible poles, 2 knobs.
Production: 23,006 (1959–70).

MM ¾-scale (1959–70): 22¾-inch scale, 12 frets clear of body. Production: 3,356.

MM-D/Melody Maker Double 1st version (1960–70, 1976): 2 pickups, 4 knobs standard peghead size. Production: 19,456 (1960–70).
Melody Maker Double 2nd version (1977–83): Rounded horns, horns point away from neck,
2 pickups, tune-o-matic bridge (earliest with stud-mounted wraparound bridge/tailpiece), 4 knobs, earliest with bolt-on neck, narrow peghead, metal tuner buttons, Cherry or Sunburst finish. Production: 1,085 (1977–79).
MM-III (1967–71): 3 pickups. Production: 352.
MM-12 (1967–71): 12-string, 2 pickups, no vibrato. Production: 210.

Midnight Special (1974–79)
Thin single-cut solidbody, 2 humbuckers with no polepieces
• Solid maple body, single-cutaway, non-beveled top around bass side, large rectangular tune-o-matic bridge, strings anchor through body on a diagonal line, chrome-plated hardware.
• Bolt-on maple neck, maple fingerboard, decal logo, metal tuner buttons.
• 2 humbucking pickups with metal covers and no polepieces, 2 knobs, 2-way tone switch, jack into top.
Production: 2,077.

MM: See Melody Maker.

Moderne Heritage (1982–83)
Asymmetrical solidbody with V at bottom, wide flared headstock
• Korina solidbody with scooped treble side, tune-o-matic bridge.
• Unbound rosewood fingerboard, dot inlays, string guides on peghead, serial number of letter followed by 3 digits.
• 2 humbucking pickups, 3 barrel knobs, gold-plated hardware.

MV-2, MV-II, MV-10, MV-X: See Victory

Nighthawk Custom (1993–98)
Single-cut solidbody, strings through body, trapezoid inlay
• single cutaway, mahogany back, flat maple top, low profile bridge, strings through body, optional Floyd Rose vibrato (1994), gold-plated hardware, Antique Natural, Fireburst or Translucent Amber finish.
• 25½-inch scale, ebony fingerboard, trapezoid inlay.
• 1 Firebird mini-humbucking pickup in neck position, 1 NSX single-coil pickup in middle position, 1 slant-mounted humbucking pickup, master volume, push/pull master tone, 5-way switch, optional 2-pickup version with no single-coil and no push/pull tone control.
Nighthawk Special (1993–98): Rosewood fingerboard, dot inlays, gold-plated hardware, Ebony, Heritage Cherry or Vintage Sunburst finish.
Nighthawk Standard (1993–98): Rosewood fingerboard, double-parallelogram inlay, gold-plated hardware, optional 2-pickup version with no single-coil and no push/pull tone control, optional Floyd Rose vibrato (1994), Fireburst, Translucent Amber or Vintage Sunburst finish.

Pioneer Cutaway (2004–current)
Thin acoustic solidbody, cutaway dreadnought shape
• 16-inch dreadnought cutaway (acoustic style) shape, thin body, routed mahogany back, spruce top, "upper belly" bridge with bridge pins, black pickguard.
• Bound rosewood fingerboard, dot inlay.
• Piezo under-saddle pickup, controls on rim.

Q-100 (Alpha Series) (1985)
Double-cut asymmetrical solidbody, bolt-on neck
• Double-cutaway body shape similar to Victory MV, tune-o-matic bridge, optional Kahler Flyer vibrato, chrome-plated hardware without Kahler, black chrome hardware with Kahler, Ebony or Panther Pink finish.
• Bolt-on neck, ebony fingerboard, dot inlays, 6-on-a-side tuner arrangement.
• 1 Dirty Fingers humbucking pickup.

Q-200 (1985): 1 HP-90 single-coil pickup in neck position, 1 Dirty Fingers humbucking pickup in bridge position, coil tap, Kahler Flyer vibrato, Ebony, Alpine White, Ferrari Red or Panther Pink finish.
Q-300/Q-3000 (1985): 3 HP-90 single-coil pickups, 2 knobs, selector switch, "mid" switch, Kahler Flyer vibrato, Ebony or red finish.
Q-4000 (1985) / **400** (1986): 1 humbucking pickup, 1 Dirty Fingers humbucking pickup and 2 single-coil pickups, master tone and master volume knob, 3 mini-switches for on/off pickup control, push/pull volume control for coil tap, Kahler Flyer vibrato, earliest with neck-through-body, Ebony, Ferrari Red or Panther Pink finish.

Ranger (2004–current)
Thin acoustic solidbody, small L-00 shape
• 14¾-inch acoustic body style (like prewar L-00), thin body, routed mahogany back, spruce top, "upper belly" bridge with bridge pins, satin Natural or Saddle Brown finish.
• Unbound rosewood fingerboard, dot inlay.
• Piezo under-saddle pickup, controls on rim.

RD: See RD Artist.

RD Custom (1977–78) / **77 Custom** (1979)
Solidbody with longer treble horn, maple fingerboard
• Double cutaway, 14⅝-inch wide, upper treble horn longer than upper bass horn, lower bass horn larger than lower treble horn, tune-o-matic bridge, chrome-plated hardware, large backplate, Natural or Walnut finish.
• 25½-inch scale, maple fingerboard, dot inlays, model name on truss-rod cover, decal logo.
• 2 humbucking pickups, active electronics, 4 knobs (standard Gibson controls), 3-way pickup selector switch, 2-way mini switch for mode selection (neutral or bright).
Production: 1,498 (1977–79).

RD Standard (1977–1978)
Solidbody with longer treble horn, dot inlays, 2 humbuckers
• Double cutaway, 14⅝-inch wide, upper treble horn longer than upper bass horn, lower bass horn larger than lower treble horn, tune-o-matic bridge, chrome-plated hardware, Natural, Tobacco Sunburst or Walnut finish.
• 25½-inch scale, rosewood fingerboard, dot inlays, model name on truss-rod cover, decal logo.
• 2 humbucking pickups, 4 knobs, 1 selector switch.

RD Artist/79 (1979–80) / **RD** (1981)
Solidbody with longer treble horn, winged-f on peghead
• Double cutaway, 14⅝-inch wide, upper treble horn longer than upper bass horn, lower bass horn larger than lower treble horn, tune-o-matic bridge, TP-6 tailpiece, large backplate, gold-plated hardware.
• 3-piece mahogany neck, 24¾-inch scale, bound ebony fingerboard (some unbound), block inlays, multiple-bound peghead, winged-f peghead inlay, pearl logo.
• 2 humbucking pickups, active electronics, 4 knobs (standard Gibson controls), 3-way pickup selector switch, 3-way switch for mode selection (neutral, bright, front pickup expansion with back pickup compression).
Production: 2,340 (1977–79).

RD Artist/77 (1980): 25½-inch scale.
RD Artist CMT (1981): Maple body, bound curly maple top, gold speed knobs, TP-6 fine-tune tailpiece, maple neck, 24¾-inch scale, bound ebony fingerboard, block inlays, chrome-plated hardware, Antique Cherry Sunburst or Antique Sunburst finish. Production: 100.

S-1 (1976–79)
Thin single-cut solidbody, 3 pickups
• 12¾-inch wide, Les Paul-shape single cutaway, rectangular tune-o-matic bridge, stop tailpiece, large pickguard covers entire upper bodyuy and extends around lower treble bout.
• Bolt-on neck, maple fingerboard (some early with rosewood), dot inlays, triangular peghead with rounded top.
• 3 single-coil pickups with center bar, pickups set in clear epoxy (black pickup covers from 1978), 2-way toggle on cutaway bout (selects bridge pickup alone), 4-position rotary switch for pickup selection, 2 knobs (volume, tone).
Production: 3,089.

Sonex-180 (1980) / **Sonex-180 Deluxe** (1981–83)
Single-cut solidbody, bolt on neck, exposed-coil pickups
• Les Paul body size and shape, beveled edge on bass side, Multi-Phonic body (wood core, resin outer layer), tune-o-matic bridge, pickguard covers three-quarters of body, chrome-plated hardware.
• Bolt-on 3-piece maple neck, rosewood fingerboard, dot inlays, metal tuners, decal logo.
• 2 exposed-coil Velvet Brick humbucking pickups, 3-way selector switch.

Sonex-180 Deluxe Left Hand (1982): Left-handed.
Sonex-180 Custom (1980–82): Coil-tap switch, ebony fingerboard.
Sonex Artist 1981–84: Active electronics, 2 standard humbuckers, 3 mini-switches (bright, compression, expansion), TP-6 tailpiece, no pickguard, *Artist* on truss-rod cover.

Special I (1983–85)
Double-cut solidbody, pointed horns, 1 humbucker
• Solid mahogany double-cutaway body, pointed horns, combination bridge/tailpiece with individual string adjustments.
• Unbound rosewood fingerboard, dot inlays, *Special* on truss-rod cover.
• 1 exposed-coil humbucking pickup, 2 knobs, jack into top.

Special II (1983–85): 2 exposed-coil humbucking pickups.

Spiderman: See Custom models, Web Slinger One.

Spirit I: (1982–87)
Double-cut solidbody, rounded horns, carved top, 1 humbucker
• Combination bridge/tailpiece with individual

string adjustments, tortoiseshell celluloid pickguard, chrome-plated hardware, silver finish standard,.
• 3-piece maple neck, 24¾-inch scale, unbound rosewood fingerboard, 22 frets, dot inlays, plastic keystone tuner buttons, decal logo.
• 1 exposed-coil humbucking pickup with creme coils, 2 barrel knobs.

Spirit I XPL (1985–86): 1 pickup with creme coils, Kahler Flyer vibrato, bound top, bound fingerboard, Explorer-style peghead with 6-on-a-side tuner arrangement.
Spirit II (1982–87): Curly maple top optional (1983), 2 pickups, 3 knobs, selector switch below knobs, no pickguard, bound top.
Spirit II XPL (1985–86): 2 pickups, 3 knobs, selector switch below knobs, bound top, bound fingerboard, Explorer-style peghead with 6-on-a-side tuner arrangement.

SR-71 (1987–89)
Double-cut solidbody, Strat-like shape, set neck, designed by Wayne Charvel
• Body shape similar to Fender Stratocaster, Ebony, Nuclear Yellow or Alpine White finish.
• Glued-in maple neck, 25½-inch scale, 6-on-a-side tuner arrangement, point on treble side of peghead, prewar script logo, Custom Shop model, 250 made, limited edition number on truss-rod cover.
• 1 humbucking and 2 single-coil pickups, Floyd Rose locking nut vibrato system.
Production: 250.

Strings and Things Reissue: See Les Paul Reissue.

Super V CES (1978–92) / **L-5CES Custom** (1973–77)
Single-cut archtop, 2 pickups, 6-finger tailpiece
• 17-inch wide maple body, rounded cutaway, solid carved spruce topsingle-bound *f*-holes, multiple-bound top and back, TP-6 6-finger tailpiece.
• Ebony fingerboard, split-block inlays, 5-piece split-diamond headstock inlay, multiple-bound headstock.
• 2 humbucking pickups, 4 knobs.
Production: 17 (1973–77), 124 (1978–79).

Super V/BJB (1978–83): 1 floating pickup.
Production: 43 (1979).

Super 300CES (1954)
Single-cut archtop, 18-inch wide, double-parallelogram inlays
• 18-inch wide maple body, carved spruce top, triple-bound top and back, tailpiece with 3 cutouts, laminated beveled-edge pickguard.
• Single-bound fingerboard with square end, double-parallelogram inlay, single-bound headstock, crown headstock inlay.
• 1 or 2 P-90 pickup.

Super 400CES (1951–current)
Single-cut archtop, large flat tailpiece, split-block inlays
• 18-inch wide maple body, rounded cutaway (pointed cutaway 1960–69), solid carved spruce top, carved maple back (laminated 1-piece back 1960–69), maple sides, multiple-bound top, back and *f*-holes.
• Ebony fingerboard with pointed end, split-lock inlay, multiple-bound fingerboard and peghead, 5-piece split-diamond peghead inlay.
• 2 P-90 pickups (Alnico V from 1954, humbuckers from late 1957), 4 knobs, selector switch.
Production: 1,476 (1951–79).

Super 400C 50th Anniversary (1984): BJB floating pickup, engraved heelcap, binding on back of peghead comes to point (similar to Citation binding but with no volute), *Super 400 1935 50th Anniversary 1984* engraved in abalone inlay on back of peghead, Kluson Sealfast tuners with pearl buttons.

Switchmaster: See ES-5 Switchmaster.

TF-7: See Tal Farlow Artist Signature model.

The Explorer: See Explorer models.

The Hawk (1996–97)
Single-cut solidbody, Hawk *on truss-rod cover*
• Nighthawk body shape, single cutaway mahogany solidbody (no top cap), no binding, Ebony or Wine Red finish.
• 25½-inch scale, unbound rosewood fingerboard, dot inlays, model name on truss-rod cover, American flag decal on back of peghead.
• 2 humbucking pickups, 2 knobs, 1 switch.

The Les Paul: See Les Paul models.

The SG: See SG models.

The V: See Flying V CMT.

Traveling Songwriter (2005–current)
Solidbody acoustic, circular control plate
• 16-inch wide thin solidbody, single rounded cutaway, spruce top, mahogany back, moustache bridge shape, bridge pins, bound top, tortoise pickguard with two points.
• Mahogany neck, unbound rosewood fingerboard with treble-side extension, dot inlays, gold-plated tuners.
• Under-saddle pickup, slider controls on circular plate on upper bass bout.

U-2/Mach II (1987–90)
Double-cut solidbody, Strat-like shape, raised plastic peghead logo
• Asymmetrical double-cutaway solidbody

similar to Fender Stratocaster, basswood body, contoured back.
- 25½-inch scale, unbound rosewood fingerboard, 24 frets, dot inlays, unbound peghead, 6-on-a-side tuner arrangement, large raised plastic logo.
- 2 single-coil pickups and 1 HPAF humbucking pickup, 2 Spotlight humbucking pickups optional, Floyd Rose vibrato, 2 knobs, 3 mini-switches, bound top, maple neck, black chrome hardware,.

U-2 Showcase Edition (Nov. 1988 guitar of the month): EMG pickups. Production: 200 for U.S., 50 for overseas.

US-1: (1986–90)
Double-cut solidbody, Strat-like shape, split-diamond inlays
- Double cutaway solidbody similar to Fender Stratocaster, maple top, mahogany back, Chromyte (balsa) core, tune-o-matic bridge or Kahler locking nut vibrato system, bound top and back, gold-plated hardware with tune-o-matic bridge, black chrome hardware with Kahler vibrato.
- Maple neck, 25½-inch scale, bound ebony fingerboard, split-diamond inlays, bound peghead, 6-on-a-side tuner arrangement, large raised plastic logo (pearl from 1987), mini-Grover tuners.
- 3 humbucking pickups (2 with stacked-coil design) with no visible poles, 3 mini-switches for on/off pickup control, 2 knobs (push/pull volume control for coil tap).

V-Factor X: See Flying V.

Vegas High Roller (2006–current)
Thin double-cut archtop, asymmetrical body, block inlays
- Asymmetrical semi-hollowbody with bass horn longer than treble, flat AAA maple top, f-holes, mahogany back, 3-ply top binding, gold-plated hardware, tune-o-matic bridge.
- Bound ebony fingerboard, block inlays, six-on-a-side tuner configuration, Gibson logo on truss-rod cover.
- 2 humbucking pickups, 1 volume, 1 tone, selector on upper bass bout.

Vegas Standard (2006–current): Diamond-shaped soundholes, single-ply top binding, chrome-plated hardware, split-diamond fingerboard inlays.

Victory MV-2 or **MV-II** (1981–84)
Double-cut solidbody, extended pointed horns, peghead points to bass side
- Maple body, 13-inch wide, asymmetrical double cutaway with extended horns, horns come to a point, wide-travel "Nashville" tune-o-matic bridge, chrome-plated hardware, Candy Apple Red or Antique Fireburst finish.

- 3-piece bolt-on maple neck, bound rosewood fingerboard, dot inlay positioned near bass edge of fingerboard, 6-on-a-side tuner arrangement, peghead points to bass side, decal logo and *Victory* decal near nut.
- Velvet Brick zebra-coil neck pickup, special design black-coil humbucking bridge pickup, 2 knobs, coil-tap switch, 3-position slide switch.

Victory MV-10 or MV-X (1981–84): 2 zebra-coil humbucking pickups and 1 stacked-coil humucking pickup (middle position), 2 knobs, master coil-tap switch, 5-position slide switch, bound ebony fingerboard, Antique Cherry Sunburst, Candy Apple Red or Twilight Blue finish.

Jimmy Wallace Reissue: See Les Paul Standard Reissue.

WRC (1987–89)
Double-cut solidbody, Strat-like shape, 3 mini switches, designed by Wayne Charvel
- Alder body similar to Fender Stratocaster, beveled lower bass bout, Floyd Rose or Kahler vibrato, Ebony, Honeyburst or Ferrari Red finish.
- Bolt-on maple neck, 25½-inch scale, ebony fingerboard, dot inlays, 6-on-a-side tuner arrangement, point on treble side of peghead, *WRC* or *WC* on truss-rod cover, prewar script logo (earliest with Charvel decal on peghead).
- 1 humbucking pickup and 2 stacked-coil humbucking pickups with black covers and no polepieces, 3 on/off mini-switches, push/pull volume control for coil tap.

WRC Showcase Edition (Sept. 1988 guitar of the month): 3 EMG pickups (1 humbucking, 2 single-coil), 3 knobs, 4 toggle switches, Kahler vibrato, Sperzel tuners. Production: 200 for U.S., 50 for overseas.

X-Factor V: See Flying V Reissue.

X-plorer: See Explorer Reissue.

XPL Custom (1985–86)
Angular solidbody, cutout in lower treble horn
- Solidbody somewhat similar to Explorer but with sharply pointed horns, cutout at lower treble horn, bound curly maple top, locking nut vibrato system, bound top, Cherry Sunburst or Alpine White finish.
- Dot inlays 6-on-a-side tuner configuration.
- 2 Dirty Fingers exposed-coil humbucking pickups, 2 knobs, 1 switch.

XPL Standard (1985)
Solidbody with shape similar to small Firebird, 2 exposed-coil humbuckers

- Solidbody, "sculptured" edges, small Firebird shape, tune-o-matic bridge or Kahler Flyer vibrato, chrome-plated or black chrome hardware, Ebony, Kerry Green or Alpine White finish.
- 6-on-a-side tuner configuration.
- 2 Dirty Fingers exposed-coil humbucking pickups.

77 Custom: See RD Custom.
335-S Deluxe (1980–82) *Thin double-cut solidbody, rounded horns (ES-335 shape)*
- Solid mahogany body, double rounded cutaways (like ES-335 but smaller), tune-o-matic bridge, TP-6 tailpiece, triangular wing-shaped pickguard.
- Bound ebony fingerboard, dot inlays, brass nut.
- 2 Dirty Fingers exposed-coil humbucking pickups, coil-tap switch.

335-S Custom (1980): Unbound rosewood fingerboard, branded headstock logo (some routed for inlay but no inlay).
335-S Standard (1980): No coil tap, branded headstock logo (some routed for inlay but no inlay).

1275: See EDS-1275.

OTHER ARTIST SIGNATURE MODELS

Johnny A. Signature (2003–current)
Double-cut archtop, pointed horns, gamba soundholes
- Thin hollowbody with double pointed cutaways, carved maple top, solid mahogany back and rims, gamba soundholes, tune-o-matic bridge, stopbar or Bigsby vibrato, bound top and back, gold-plated hardware.
- Mahogany neck, 25½-inch scale, bound ebony fingerboard, custom 3-piece pearl inlay, signature on truss-rod cover, bound peghead, custom pearl peghead inlay, pearl logo.
- 2 humbucking pickups, 4 knobs, selector switch near knobs.

Tom DeLonge Signature (2003–current)
Thinbody double-cut archtop, rounded horns, 1 pickup, racing stripe
- ES-335 style semi-hollowbody, tune-o-matic bridge, bound top and back, brown finish with cream racing stripes.
- Bound rosewood fingerboard, dot inlays, Natural finish peghead.
- 1 exposed-coil Dirty Fingers humbucking pickup, 1 volume knob.

Duane Eddy Signature (2005–current)
Single-cut archtop, moustache inlays
16-inch single-cutaway hollowbody of

laminated maple, 3-inch deep, f-holes, tune-o-matic bridge, Bigsby vibrato, bound top and back, nickel-plated hardware, Rockabilly Brown finish.

Maple/walnut neck, bond ebony fingerboard, pearl moustache inlay, pearl logo.

2 custom single-coil pickups Baggs transducer pickup under bridge, 4 knobs.

Tal Farlow Signature (1962–67, 1993–current)
Single-cut archtop, simulated scroll in cutaway bout
• Full-depth archtop of laminated maple, deep rounded cutaway, binding material inlaid in cutaway to simulate scroll, 4-point single-bound pickguard, tune-o-matic bridge, trapeze tailpiece with raised diamond, model name on wood tailpiece insert, triple-bound top, Viceroy Brown finish (Wine Red added 1993).
• 25½-inch scale, bound fingerboard, fingerboard inlay like inverted J-200 crest inlay, bound peghead, double-crown peghead inlay.
• 2 humbucking pickups, toggle switch just below pickguard.
Production: 215 (1962–67).

TF-7 (1991): No specs available, possibly 7-string.

Barney Kessel Custom (1961–73)
Double-cut archtop, pointed horns, bowtie inlay
• 17-inch wide, full-depth body, laminated spruce top (some with laminated maple 1961–64, standard from 1965), double pointed cutaways, gold-plated hardware, Cherry Sunburst finish.
• Maple neck, bound rosewood fingerboard, 25½-inch scale, bowtie inlay, bound peghead, musical note peghead inlay.
• 2 humbucking pickups, tune-o-matic bridge, trapeze tailpiece with raised diamond, model name on wood tailpiece insert, laminated beveled-edge pickguard, triple-bound top and back.
Production: 740.

Barney Kessel Regular (1961–73): Mahogany neck, double-parallelogram inlay, crown peghead inlay, nickel-plated hardware. Production: 1,117.

B.B. King Standard (1980) / **Lucille Standard** (1981–85)
Thinbody double-cut archtop, no f-holes, dot inlays, Lucille on peghead
• Thin double-cutaway semi-hollowbody of laminated maple, no f-holes, Nashville tune-o-matic bridge, TP-6 tailpiece, laminated beveled-edge pickguard, multiple-bound top and back, chrome-plated hardware, Ebony or Cherry finish.

• Single-bound rosewood fingerboard, dot inlays, *Lucille* peghead inlay.
• 2 PAF humbucking pickups, stereo electronics with 2 jacks.

B.B. King Custom (1980) / **Lucille** (1981–85) / **B.B. King Lucille** (1986–current)
Thinbody double-cut archtop, no f-holes, block inlays, Lucille on peghead
• Thin double-cutaway semi-hollowbody of laminated maple, no f-holes, TP-6 tailpiece, multiple-bound top and back, single-bound pickguard, tune-o-matic bridge, gold-plated hardware, Ebony or Cherry finish.
• Bound ebony fingerboard, large block inlays, *Lucille* peghead inlay.
• 2 PAF humbucking pickups, Vari-tone rotary tone selector switch, stereo wiring with 2 jacks.

B.B. King "Little Lucille" (1999–current)
Single-cut solidbody, pointed horn, Little Lucille on top
• Semi-hollow poplar body, flat top, f-holes, TP-6 fine-tune tailpiece, gold-plated truss-rod cover engraved with *B.B. King*, black finish, *Little Lucille* on upper bass bout next to fingerboard, black finish.
• 25½-inch scale, unbound rosewood fingerboard, diamond inlay, stacked-diamond peghead inlay, pearl logo.
• 2 special design Blues 90 pickups with cream soapbar covers and non-adjustable poles, 2 knobs (with push/pull to disable Varitone), slide switch, 6-position Vari-tone control.

John Lennon J-160E Bed In (1998): Based on Lennon's stripped 1963, with line drawing of Lennon and Yoko Ono on top. Production: 47 sets (sold with Fab Vour Magical Tour and Bed In models).
John Lennon J-160E Fab Four (1998): Based on 1963 version, Sunburst finish. Production: 47 sets (sold with Magical Tour and Bed In models).
John Lennon J-160E Magical Tour (1998): Based on Lennon's custom-painted 1963, with purple, blue and red swirl-pattern finish. Production: 47 sets (sold with Fab Four and Bed In models).
John Lennon J-160E Peace (2002): Natural finish. Production: 750.

Trini Lopez Signature Deluxe (1964–71)
Double-cut archtop, pointed horns, diamond soundholes
• 16-inch laminated maple hollowbody, double pointed cutaways, tune-o-matic bridge, trapeze tailpiece with raised diamond, model name on wood tailpiece insert, bound pickguard, triple-bound top and back, Cherry Sunburst finish.
• Bound fingerboard and peghead, slashed-diamond inlay, 6-on-a-side tuner arrangement, no peghead ornament.

• 2 humbucking pickups, 4 knobs, 3-way pickup selector on treble cutaway bout, standby switch on bass cutaway bout.
Production: 302 (1964–70).

Trini Lopez Signature Standard (1964–71)
Thin double-cut archtop, rounded horns, diamond soundholes
• 16-inch wide semi-hollowbody of laminated maple, double rounded cutaways, tune-o-matic bridge, trapeze tailpiece with raised diamond, model name on wood tailpiece insert, laminated beveled-edge pickguard, single-bound top and back, Cherry finish (some with Sparkling Burgundy finish, Pelham Blue).
• Bound fingerboard, slashed-diamond inlay, 6-on-a-side tuners, no peghead ornament, decal logo.
• 2 humbucking pickups, 4 knobs, selector switch.
Production: 1,966 (1964–70).

Pat Martino Custom / Pat Martino Signature (1999–2006)
Thinbody single-cut archtop, no fingerboard inlay, curly top
• 16-inch thin semi-hollowbody, single pointed cutaway, carved flamed maple top, routed mahogany back, f-holes, tune-o-matic bridge, stopbar tailpiece, Caramel or Heritage Cherry Sunburst finish.
• Mahogany neck, bound ebony fingerboard, no inlay, narrow peghead with straight string-pull, pearl logo.
• 2 humbucking pickups, 4 knobs, selector switch on upper bass bout.

Pat Martino Standard (1999–2000): Plain maple top, Ebony or Vintage Red finish.

Wes Montgomery Signature (1993–current)
Single-cut archtop, 1 humbucker
• 17-inch single-cutaway archtop, maple back and sides, carved spruce top, gold-plated hardware, Vintage Sunburst or Wine Red finish.
• Bound ebony fingerboard, pearl block inlays.
• 1 humbucking pickup in neck position.

Wes Montgomery Heart (1997): Reissue of one of Wes Montgomery's personal L-5s, heart-shaped pearl inlay with engraved *Wes Montgomery* in cutaway bout, special leather case, certificate. Production: 25.

Jimmy Page EDS-1275 Double Neck (2007): Mahogany solidbody, pointed horns, 2 exposed-coil humbucking pickups on 6-string neck, VOS (Vintage Original Spec) finish treatment. Production 25 aged to match Page's original and signed by Page, 250 additional.

Lee Ritenour L-5 Signature (2003–current)
Single-cut archtop, rounded horn, scaled-down L-5
As L-5 Signature with floating pickup, TP-6 fine-tune tailpiece.

Howard Roberts Custom (1970, 1974–80)
Single-cut archtop, oval soundhole
• 16-inch wide, full-depth body, pointed cutaway, laminated maple top, oval hole, height-adjustable ebony bridge, multiple-bound pickguard, multiple-bound top and back, chrome-plated hardware (some labeled Howard Roberts Artist, 1974–76).
• Bound ebony fingerboard (rosewood from 1974), slotted-block inlays, multiple-bound peghead, vine-pattern peghead inlay.
• 1 floating humbucking pickup.
Production: 1,152.

Howard Roberts Artist (1976–80): Ebony fingerboard, gold-plated hardware. Production: 129.

Howard Roberts Artist Double Pickup (1979–80): 2 pickups, bridge pickup mounted into top with mounting ring.

Howard Roberts DE (1970): 2 pickups. Production: 2.

Howard Roberts Standard Electric (1970): Bound rosewood fingerboard, slotted-block inlays, vertical oval peghead inlay, 1 floating mini-humbucking pickup. Production: 3.

Howard Roberts Fusion (1979–1990) /
Howard Roberts Fusion II (1988–90) /
Howard Roberts Fusion III (1991–current)
Thin single-cut archtop, pointed horn, wider cutaway than other models
• 14⅛-inch wide, semi-hollowbody, 2⁵⁄₁₆-inch deep, cutaway shape similar to Les Paul solidbody models, tune-o-matic bridge, TP-6 tailpiece (6-finger from 1990), triple-bound top, bound back, , chrome-plated hardware (gold-plated from 1991).
• Dot inlays crown peghead inlay, Sunburst, Fireburst, or Ebony finish.
• 2 humbucking pickups, 4 knobs.

Johnny Smith (1961–88) / **Chet Atkins (JS) Double** (1989–91) / **Le Grand** (1993–current)
Single-cut archtop, floating pickup, split-block inlays
• 17-inch wide, 3⅛-inch deep (not as deep as L-5), single rounded cutaway, X-braced carved spruce top, maple back and sides, adjustable ebony bridge, L-5 style tailpiece with model name on center insert (TP-6 6-finger from 1979), multiple-bound top and back, gold-plated hardware, Sunburst or Natural finish.
• 25-inch scale, multiple-bound ebony fingerboard with square end, split-block inlays, multiple-bound peghead, 5-piece split-diamond peghead inlay.

• 1 floating mini-humbucking pickup (some with experimental pickups 1989–91), knobs on pickguard.
Production: 963 (1962–79).

Johnny Smith Double (1963–89): 2 floating mini-humbucking pickups. Production: 625 (1962–79).

CUSTOM MODELS

Product or personality themes

Les Paul '60 Corvette (1995–97): Based on Les Paul Standard, top scooped out top to simulate side scoops on 1960 Chevrolet Corvette, *Corvette* stylized script inlay on fingerboard, crossed racing flags on peghead, Cascade Green, Tuxedo Black, Horizon Blue, Roman Red, Sateen Silver or Ermine White finish.

Les Paul '63 Corvette Sting Ray (1995–97): Based on SG, maple body and neck top carved to resemble back split-window of 1963 Chevrolet Corvette Stingray, 1 humbucking pickup with no polepieces ebony fingerboard, *Sting Ray* inlay, crossed racing flags on peghead, nickel-plated hardware, Riverside Red, silver or black finish.

Chevrolet SSR (2003): Based on CS-336, features from Chevrolet pickup/roadster model. Production: 25.

Copperhead SG (2003): Features from 1967 Chevrolet Copperhead pickup truck including snakeskin carving on top of guitar, *COPPERHEAD* inlay on fingerboard. Production: 25

Crazy Horse Les Paul (2003): Features from Parnelli-period Ford Bronco vehicle including tire tread, unbound fingerboard, trapezoid inlays. Production: 25.

Dale Earnhardt Les Paul (1999–2001): Based on single-cutaway Les Paul Special, top overlay with graphic by Sam Bass, hood pins, lug nut control knobs, Simpson racing harness strap, chrome-plated hardware, ebony fingerboard, signature inlay, Ebony finish. Production: 333.

Dale Earnhardt "The Intimidator" Les Paul (2000–01): Based on single-cutaway Les Paul Special, top overlay with graphic by Sam Bass, silver finish with black drawings and red trim, "The Intimidator" inlaid on fingerboard, 3 inlaid on peghead. Production: 333.

Dale Earnhardt Jr. Les Paul (2001): Based on single-cutaway Les Paul Special, graphics include #8 race car, signature and Bud logo, ebony fingerboard with inlaid signature, Earnhardt Red finish. Production: 333.

Hummer Les Paul (2003–04): Based on single-cutaway Les Paul Special, 2 humbucking pickups, features from Hummer

automobile, yellow finish. Production: 100.

Indian Chief Les Paul (2002): Features from Indian motorcycles. Production: 100.

Jim Beam Les Paul (2000–03): Features from Jim Beam whiskey.

Playboy 2001 Playmate of the Year (2001): Based on Les Paul Standard, Pinkburst finish. Production: 50.

Playboy Hottie SG (2003–04): Based on SG Standard, 2 humbucking pickups, image of sexy woman on body, *Playboy* bunny head logo on peghead, red finish.

Playboy CS-356 (2003–04): Alpine White finish, silver *Playboy* magazine bunny head logo on body.

Playboy Rabbit Head CS-356 (2003–04): Ebony/white finish. Production: 50.

Kiefer Sutherland KS-336 (2007–current): *Double-cutaway, smaller than ES-335, double slashed-block inlays*
• 13¾-inch double-cutaway semi-hollowbody, routed mahogany back with solid center area, carved maple top, "Kiefer Gold" aged gold top finish.
• Ebony fingerboard, double-slashed block inlays, bone nut, crown peghead ornament.
• 2 '57 Classic humbuckers, 4 knobs.

Web-Slinger One (1999): Spiderman graphic, mahogany body, single cutaway, ebony fingerboard, web-pattern inlay. Production: 75 signed by Stan Lee, 75 signed by John Romita Sr.

X-Men Wolverine Les Paul (2001): X-men graphic finish. Production: 50.

50th Anniversary Les Paul Corvette (2003): Based on double-cutaway Les Paul Special, scoop carved into top, 2 black soapbar P-90 pickups, 50th Anniversary logo on top, ebony fingerboard with Corvette script inlay, tune-o-matic bridge, strings anchor through body, chrome-plated hardware, pearl logo, Corvette 50th Anniversary Red finish.

index

Page numbers in **bold type** indicate an illustration, usually a guitar, musician, or catalog/ad etc. Page numbers in *italic type* indicate a listing in the Reference Section.